An Ordinary Guy, An Extraordinary Tale

An Ordinary Guy, An Extraordinary Tale

My Life and Times

John S. Klumpp

iUniverse, Inc.
Bloomington

AN ORDINARY GUY, AN EXTRAORDINARY TALE
MY LIFE AND TIMES

iUniverse books may be ordered through booksellers or by contacting:

iUniverse
1663 Liberty Drive
Bloomington, IN 47403
www.iuniverse.com
1-800-Authors (1-800-288-4677)

ISBN: 978-1-4620-5354-4 (sc)
ISBN: 978-1-4620-5355-1 (hc)
ISBN: 978-1-4620-5358-2 (ebk)

Printed in the United States of America

iUniverse rev. date: 09/16/2011

Contents

I hear babies cry
I watch them grow
They'll learn much more
than I'll ever know

and I say to myself
what a wonderful world

"What a Wonderful World"
by B. Thiele and G Weiss

To my grand-daughters.

Kelly and Eliza, may you never lose your sense of wonder
because it is a wonderful world.

Love, Pop

July, 2011

Foreword

Seven Years ago I celebrated, if that's the proper word, my sixty-fifth birthday. I teased, and probably aggravated Brenda, when I said, "Now I'm in my sixty-sixth year!" "You're only sixty-five," said she. No matter. That's when I began to realize that I was older than I really wanted to be, and perhaps it was time to try to do what other people did when threatened with the awareness of advancing years. I decided to write an autobiography of sorts. I say "of sorts" because I had hoped, if my talent allowed me, to incorporate my story into the history of the times that I have been fortunate enough to have witnessed.

Let's take, for example, the monumental event of Neil Armstrong and the landing of the first man on the moon in 1968. I was Mate at the time aboard the tug *Catherine McAllister* and we happened to be waiting for a fuel barge to unload at the Hess Oil Dock in Little Ferry, NJ, on the Hackensack River. It was evening and it was raining pretty hard. We had an old Greek engineer, John, who worked the boat with us. I listened to the radio and heard, "The Eagle has landed" followed by the famous line, "That's one small step for man, and one giant leap for mankind." The United States had successfully landed a spacecraft on the moon and a human walked its surface for the first time. I was excited and told John, "Wow that's it! They've landed on the moon!" I'll never forget his reply. Old John asked me, "Is he getting wet up there too?" So there it is, my half-baked idea to write not only about me, but also where I was, and to write about the thoughts and the experiences that have been woven into the events of my life. If anyone ever cares to read this they might get a glimpse then not only of me, but also history as I've lived it.

And perhaps I do have a lot to write about.

The Novice Years

The Early Years, Down By The Stoop, Growing Up In the Old Neighborhood, The Old Neighborhood, The Block, School Days, A Little History, Television Sets, Baseball Memories, Nineteen Fifties, Asthma, Changing America, Cardinal Hayes High School, Early Work, Time To Reminisce

THE NOVICE YEARS

The Early Years

I first became me on the evening of the Third of December in the year Nineteen Thirty-Nine. Adolf Hitler had just invaded Poland, so maybe I figured that it was my time to invade the world. I was born at St. Elizabeth's Hospital in the Inwood Section of Manhattan, NYC. My parents were of Irish and German extraction. I mention this only because almost 100% of my friends' parents were extractions from one place or another. The combination of German and Irish was common in those times. My mother's name was Gertrude Frances Kelly. (born November 17, 1913 in NYC and passed on April 2, 1992 in Sparta, NJ) Her parents were Irish immigrants. Nora Dillon married John Cornelius Kelly in 1908, shortly after arriving on these shores from

Kilrush, County Clare, Ireland. Of my grandmother I don't remember much; only that she used needles for her diabetes and wore her gray hair with in an old-fashioned bun in the back. She died when I was six years old. I called my grandfather "Pal" because that's what he called me. I remember him as the big Irish cop that he was, and the St. Paddy's Day parades that he would take me to. Oh! I was hot stuff sitting on his shoulders while he directed traffic on Fifth Avenue while the bagpipers droned by. He really was my Pal. He would take me for walks—usually to Finnerty's Bar and Grill on Fordham Road. He would prop me up at the bar and I would drink Ginger Ales with a cherry in it while he drank his Ballantine Ale.

I don't remember how young I was, but I really do remember this one event. I swallowed a quarter. I was lying on my back on the bed at my grandparents' house and flipping a quarter in the air and catching it in my mouth (kids do the darndest things). I caught it all right. But I swallowed it, too. My mother rushed me to the doctor's office and it was decided that we should wait to see if it passed or not. So, my mother had to rig some kind of a net to catch my poop and sift through it to find the elusive quarter. She left me with Pal one day and I had to go. I suppose that's when it passed, but Pal never checked. My mother yelled at him for not checking, but he knew just how to handle the situation. He presented me with a silver dollar and said that if I'd swallow this, the next time it will be easier to find!

My father represented the German side. His name was Carl William Klumpp (born October 7, 1912 in Bayonne, NJ. He passed on November 24, 1998 in Sparta, NJ. His mother, Pauline Weber, was from what was called a "Pennsylvania Dutch" family. Actually, the term is a misnomer because they were really German immigrants and the "Dutch" referred only to the German, or "Deutch" language they spoke. My grandfather was named Gotlob (the name means "God's love") Klumpp. He was born in a Black Forest village in Southwest Germany called Bairesbronn. I always felt the Klumpp name rather odd until I visited Bairesbronn. I met a million Klumpps and traced back a lot of my grandfather's roots—even to the house where he was born. He came from a large family, and during my visits I became close to the family of his brother Ernst. If anyone cares to look it up there are still family there in Bairesbronn. I keep in touch with my cousin Dr. Ernst Klumpp, and I am excited that his daughter Juliane will visit us in New Jersey this summer. Sorry to relate, you will find there is no royalty in my family tree. As far back as the 1700's all the Klumpps were shoemakers, and they all married farmer's daughters. I wonder sometimes if the occupation of making shoes and boots resulted in the onomatopoeic word signifying the sound of heavy boots "klumpping" over the floor. Other people claim a klumpp is an imp, or even a doltish person not smart enough to stay out of trouble. I guess it really makes no difference anyway, but it is a thought. I remember how Grandpa, who spoke English very well, could not say "AND." It came out "UND" every time!

How my father's parents met was always something of a family mystery that we were never to learn. Gotlob was about 12 years older than Pauline and we suspect it was an arraigned marriage that my grandmother never really accepted. I remember her saying something like "free at last!" when Gotlob died. There was kind of a sick family joke about Grandpa's passing. The house he lived in was built into a hill. You had to climb about a twenty step staircase to enter via the front door, but the rear of the house was level with the ground. When Grandpa passed away it was a lot easier for the undertaker to take him out the back way rather than negotiate the front steps. So out the back bedroom window he went! And we never saw him again. Anytime my mother (who was known to be fairly irreverent) was peeved at my father, she would say to him, "How'd you like to go out the window like your old man!" She didn't mean it of course, but it was a sick family line that we used often in good humor.

Looking back on it now, I realize that Nana Pauline was probably one of the first of the strong women who rejected the traditional role of housewife and who resented the limits of opportunities for women in those remnants of the Victorian era. The fact that she was the only girl growing up doing household chores for four brothers was probably a factor also. She lived longest of my grandparents. Nana was born in 1888 and passed away in 1977 shortly after my son Kevin was born. She never saw him. She had real long brown hair that she braided up, and she wore a corset that would probably seem like an instrument of torture to you liberated women of today (if you don't know what a corset is, then you have to look it up). She was a big woman. Not fat at all, but rather statuesque. Even well into her eighties she would walk long distances and kept in fairly good condition. I really don't think she died of anything in particular, just old age at eighty-eight I guess. And she loved to eat! At our wedding she exclaimed to anybody listening that she was really impressed with that "hunk of beef" that she was served. I remember one time my father took her to dinner when she was older and living in assisted living in Connecticut. He took Nana Pauline to a nice restaurant by the water on Long Island Sound and suggested some nice reasonable fish dinner to her. Her quote was, "It'll cost you more than that, Big Boy." She then proceeded to order the stuffed lobster and continued from there. The "Big Boy" quote is another expression that made it into our family vocabulary and it always brought a laugh. My family laughed often.

My grandfather was an old world German who came to this country and started a machine shop in New York. I believe he owned a building around 40th Street and 2nd Avenue for his shop in those days at the turn of the century. (Imagine what the property would be worth now?) He took my father into his shop as an apprentice when my father was about 12 years old. My father, "Moof" we called him in his later years when the grandchildren came, never had much formal schooling. I remember him telling me about his education at night school, or at various technical institutions where he learned his trade. He worked in machine shops all his life and became a tool and die maker. I asked him one time if he ever learned to speak German at home with his parents. His answer was interesting. He reminded me that when both he and I were small, when we could readily have absorbed the language, it wasn't popular to be German. My father was born in 1912 and I was born in 1939. Check your history and tell me what was going on in the world when my father and I were both 6 years old. My grandparents were almost stereotypical; the Irish were social, the Germans, more austere. My memories of them are good.

So that's how I came to be here. There will be much more about my parents as we proceed with this narrative, but first, what was the world like when baby John Stephen entered it? Let's take a look back at 1939.

Well, to begin with, gasoline, if you were lucky enough to afford an automobile, would cost you 12 cents a gallon. If you wanted a new car it would set you back $700. You could buy a new house for the average price of $3850, but it was still three times the average annual income of $1729 a year. I remember my father telling us he could live like a king if he could make $100 a week at the shop. He told me once that some houses in Yonkers could have been purchased for $5000 around the time when I was born. I asked him why he didn't buy one and he looked at me like I had three heads. "Who the hell had $5000 in those days?" But I guess it was all relative. Bread was 8 cents a loaf, and coffee was 40 cents a pound. We were never poor. I got a new suit at Easter "on credit", and new shoes when the leather soles on my old ones finally separated from the leather uppers and flapped when I walked. No big deal—all my friends' shoes flapped, just like mine did.

You could watch "Gone with the Wind" with Clark Gable, or "Wizard of Oz" with Judy Garland, or "Stagecoach" with John Wayne. These cinematic classics came out the same year that I did: 1939. Oh! And you wouldn't go broke talking your best girl to the show. Tickets to the movies cost you 25 cents a piece. Movie houses, theaters they were called, were places of elegance. Not those little soundproof rooms you squeeze into today at the Cinemaplex or whatever the hell they call it, but a real theater where you felt special. The Loew's Paradise—a theater in my neighborhood in the Bronx—featured fountains with goldfish. There were marble Greek statues that were inset into alcoves with recessed lighting along the walls, and a ceiling complete with twinkling stars and clouds overhead. There were uniformed ushers and white clad matrons, who made kids behave in the "Children's Section." You could buy orchestra tickets, or if you wanted to impress, then you could buy a Loge or a Balcony ticket and walk up the red carpeted marble staircases to your seat. The closest you might come to the theater standards of my youth would be to take a visit to Radio City Music Hall in Rockefeller Center, Manhattan.

Monumental international events occurred that year of 1939. Franklin D. Roosevelt presided over a nation on the brink of war. Adolph Hitler invaded Poland, and France and England declared war on Germany. The United States issued a statement of neutrality that year, but of course, that was not to last. There really isn't much I can remember about those war years; I was too young. I was spared the anguish of the adults as they survived the trauma of Pearl Harbor, the draft of its best young men to the war, and the Gold Star Flags mournfully displayed in tenement and farmhouse windows to indicate a loved one had been lost in battle. FDR died in office. Harry Truman succeeded him and the war finally ended a few weeks after the first atomic bombs were dropped on the Empire of Japan. I remember air raid wardens and the air raids in the Bronx. "Lights out up there on the second floor" these guardians of the night would yell from the streets. I remember Hunter College being converted for use by the Navy, and Navy Waves marching down University Avenue. They aren't called "Waves" anymore, but that was the female branch of the Navy during those years. I think I do remember the end of World War 2. I was 6 years old by then, and I remember our neighborhood parties, streamers of red, white, and blue, and we kids making paper helicopters and throwing them out of the windows to watch them whirl through the air and land on the revelers in the street. We did a lot of celebrating and socializing with our neighbors and friends in the street. Every apartment house had a main entrance with a stair or two leading to it. It was called "The Stoop." All the neighbors would gather outside to socialize "Down by the Stoop."

Down by the Stoop

You have to know that there were no television sets when I was a young kid. People went outside the home to socialize. The stoop was the spot. People like my parents who lived in apartment houses would take their folding chairs down to the street and while away the cool evenings schmoozing with neighbors while the kids played various street games until dark. Air conditioning was unheard of, and the streets of the city were where folks gathered to enjoy air cooler than that of the stuffy apartments upstairs. Sometimes Nick, the super in my building, would take out his accordion and play songs from his native Italy on the stoop. It was just like the song says, "Pretty Nellie Shannon, with a Dude as light as a cork, first picked up the waltz step on the sidewalks of New York."

Growing Up in the Old Neighborhood

We didn't have a lot of open space growing up in the city so we kids utilized the sidewalk for our neighborhood games. "Stoop Ball" was a big pastime. You could play with one or with two on a side. One kid would throw a pink rubber ball usually called a "Spaldeen" (because it was manufactured by the A. J. Spaulding Co.) against the stairs of the stoop and the defender would have to catch the rebound. If the Spaldeen bounced once before it was caught, it was a single, two bounces was a double and, of course, four bounces became a "Home Run." If the ball was caught on the fly it was an out. The best way to guarantee a Home Run was to throw the ball so that it hit exactly on the point of the cement stair. This would send the ball flying over everyone's head and guarantee four bounces before it was retrieved. Sometimes it wasn't retrieved. Sometimes an errant ball would roll down the sewer. It wasn't unusual for us to hear the cry from somewhere, "Get the BAWLLL!" When that cry was heard, all eyes, even the adults, would focus on stopping that pink rubber sphere from its apparent destiny with the storm drains that lined the city streets. It wasn't a problem, though. Every kid had a Spaldeen and we just used another. Another that is, until the gaping maw of the sewer gobbled our last ball. That was when we went "Sewer Hunting." (They really weren't "sewers." They were really storm drains for water run-off, but we didn't know the difference. So, they were "sewers".) We would hunt the sewers, looking down through the grates until we found a pink ball floating in the muck. Then, carefully, we would lower an empty coffee can on a string into the sewer and maneuver the can under the ball. The can had holes that we had punched into the bottom and it would sink. As we gently pulled the can up under the ball, the water would drain out, and we were in business again. You could always tell a sewer ball. It was pink on one hemisphere and stained black on the other. We used the Spaldeen for lots of games. We played stickball all day long in the streets using the manhole covers as bases when possible, or fenders of parked cars as bases when the manhole covers were inconvenient. A guy who was a "Three Sewer Hitter" could hit the ball three sewer covers on the fly. That took some doing. I never could. We had games like hide and seek to play when it got too dark for stickball. (Of course when we first began to notice girls we invented other games to play in the dark, but I'm talking about my childhood here.)

There were always a bunch of kids in the old neighborhood. There was an unwritten but very real social stratum in effect, too. There were the "Big Guys"—they were the ones who usually smoked already and had developed fluency with all the bad words. Then came the "Middle Guys," then the "Little Guys." The difference in classes roughly coincided with family members who were born about two or three years apart. The kids knew they had to wait their turn to become one of the Big Guys. The Big Guys got the basketball courts first, they got the playground for stickball games first, and that was the way it was. The little kids could watch and maybe retrieve balls and envy the Big

Guys athletic abilities. Sometimes we would be "choosed in" to fill a gap in a team and that would really make our day! But we all knew that one day we would be the Big Guys. Today generations are delineated arbitrarily by adult rules governing Little League or governing weight or whatever, but we kids just knew it instinctively—and the system worked. If you got out of line one of the Big Kids would make sure you didn't do it again!

Most of the games I played in the streets during those young years I remember only by name now. Red Light Green Light, Four Steps to Germany, Ring-a-Leevio, and May I? are all just names from the past. You will never again see kids pitching pennies against a wall, or to a particular crack in the sidewalk to see whose penny came closest, or playing jacks, or trading or flipping baseball cards matching heads or tails, or pitching them up against a wall. No longer will you see kids suffer the glorious "Moon's Up" penalty where the losing team would be required to bend from the waist against a wall, drop trousers, and let the winners throw Spaldeens at their rear-ends from across the street. (If you hit a "Moon" you could throw again!!) But somewhere, collectively, I remember through a fond haze a childhood rich with games and friends, and pink "hi-bounce" spaldeens, and cement sidewalks, boxball, and the many uses we had of chalk like grinding it into powder, filling a sock and swatting your friend or enemy across the back (or backside) side with it. I don't remember it all exactly, but I remember it was good. I remember the kids all chipping in a nickel to buy a twenty five cent quart bottle of Hoffman soda ("You don't have to go to a uni-ver-sity to know that Hoffman's is the finest when you're thir-si-ty!") and then passing it around after a game. And I remember how we used the tails of our dirty shirts to "clean" the neck of the bottle, or wiping it with a dirty hand before taking a "Slug." And the soda was good. And we never got sick.

The area in which we grew, the area whose people nurtured us and formed our identity, and the area that, in a way, was the cocoon for our formative years, was called "Our Neighborhood." Now it is "The old neighborhood of hallowed memory." I went back there a few years ago to attend a Funeral Mass for Mrs. Ward. The event left an impression on me that I don't expect to forget. The funeral Mass was sparsely attended. Most of the people were old. The neighborhood of my youth had changed, and with the changing demographics came a new people, with new cultures and a new language. This was evident at the church that day. The Old Guard was giving way to the new. I remember standing in the pew as Mrs. Ward's casket was being wheeled the final time down the aisle. Following that casket were two old women; each one holding a lighted candle in trembling hands. I knew them both. Mrs. MacSwiggan, and Mrs. Craemer were all who remained that day of the vibrant immigrant class of Irish who sailed to "Americay" to marry and raise their families here in my old neighborhood in the Bronx. As I watched them walk slowly by I was struck, not only by the procession of honor for Mrs. Ward, (whose name was Margaret, wife of "Big Hughie"), but I was overcome with the realization that I was truly witnessing the passing of an era right before my eyes. The era when New York was Irish and we danced in the aisles with the old folks at the various County Balls. And the days when we relished the Corned Beef and Cabbage at the St. Paddy's day socials that were held annually in our neighborhood parishes. And how we cheered every year at the expected announcement by our pastor that the "Bishop himself" had given us a special dispensation to eat the corned beef even though it was Friday in Lent.

The Old Neighborhood

I grew up in the 1940's and 50's on Sedgwick Avenue north of Kingsbridge Road in the N.W. Bronx. That is to say I grew up in "OLA." It was an area defined, as was much of New York, by the ethnic and religious background of its inhabitants. Growing up I knew only Irish Catholics and Jews. I didn't know any Protestants at all. It's funny how the folks referred to their neighborhood. Non-Catholics referred to it by it's geographical nickname such as "Marble Hill" or, "Pelham Bay", but Catholics always referred to the Parish they attended. So I lived in "OLA", Our Lady of Angels. The next neighborhood down was "Saint John's", and in the opposite direction, people were from "Saint Nicholas of Tolentine", or just plain "Tolentine." I have no awareness of prejudice while I was growing up. There was separation, though. As a young pre-schooler, and even a little later, my friend was a Jewish boy next door named Bobby Kaplan. I remember first learning to play the game "Clue" at his house. But as we grew older we kind of separated, mostly I guess because all my Catholic friends went on to the parish parochial school and the others to the Public School, P.S. 86. I guess the split was natural as we matured with our classmates. The Catholic kids played in the playground across the street. The Jewish kids played in the schoolyard. As time went on there was less and less interaction. It's sad in a way. I remember almost all the stores being owned by Jews. I never knew anything about the refugees from the War, or about the Holocaust, but I do remember seeing numbers tattooed on some forearms. I was later to learn they came from the concentration camps of WW 2. But religiously or socially we never mixed. I could have learned so much.

I grew up Irish Catholic. All my friends' parents had brogues. Almost all my friends had Irish names. Klumpp, of course, was the exception, but I took comfort that my mother was a Kelly. During the 40's, trolley cars rode on steel tracks powered by overhead wires up and down Sedgwick Avenue. Mr. Harding was a trolley car conductor. He told me how in the old days they would rub an onion on the window of the trolley when the weather was bad to keep it from fogging up. Mr. MacSwiggan was a motorman on the Path Tubes, Mr. Monahan was a fireman, Big Hughie Ward was a sandhog who built the tunnels under the rivers around New York, and Slats Slattery and Tommy Ward drove the subway trains. I lived the New York City that was memorialized in the song "When New York Was Irish." The words told it how it was: "We worked on the Subways, we ran the Saloons, we built all the Bridges, and we played our own tunes. We put out the fires, we controlled City Hall . . . . We started with nothin' and wound up with it all."

Cars were scarce. Automatic shift was unheard of. We could have played in the streets if we wanted to, but fortunately a playground was built right across from my house. I'll tell you about the playground in a minute, but first, when I say house, you might think I lived in a house. No, it was an apartment. Apartment 2A, on the second floor of what was officially called an apartment house. My building was a five floor walk-up. No elevator; regulations state that elevators are required only on building six stories or higher. Six families lived on each floor. With only rare exceptions all the people in my neighborhood lived in apartment houses. We never referred to them as apartments. That was our house. I would go to play in Butch's house or hang out in front of Mike's house. If someone was more affluent they may have lived in what was referred to as a "Private House." In my neighborhood there were only "houses" and "private houses." By today's standards, and by the houses I see going up around me here in Jersey, the apartments we lived in were miniscule. We had a living room, hall, kitchen, bath and two bedrooms. When my youngest sister Fran was small, the three of us kids slept in one bedroom. Barbara and I had beds and Fran in her crib. When she got too old for the crib my parents moved her to a bed in their bedroom. Barbara and I fit into our room with no room for an additional bed. The house only had four closets: one my father's, one my mother's, one for the linens and towels that we called the bathroom closet, and the last closet was in the hall used by the rest of us. We couldn't beat the Monahan's though. Three girls followed by seven boys made up their family in a two bedroom apartment. And Mrs. Monahan always had room enough to have all of us kids up to their house for weekend parties. Try doing that today! I'm reminded of a story I heard years ago. A family left The Bronx for a large home in upstate Westchester County. It was a big roomy home with a nice lawn and plenty of room. One of the kids wrote back to his friend in the Bronx. He said that it was terrible in his new home . . . . he and his brothers were each forced to sleep in their own bedrooms!

Playing on "The Block"

If our neighborhood was defined by our parish, then the immediate area in which our houses stood was known as "Our Block." All the kids in the parish didn't live on the same block. I was fortunate to grow up with a lot of kids on my block. We really didn't need to socialize with kids from another block or those who happened to live a few blocks away. Our geographical awareness and social interaction was mostly dictated by the boundaries of our block. Now I'll tell you about the playground. I was lucky. The playground, a large asphalt and concrete park, was right across the street. It was a large fenced in play area with an entrance that we never used. Kids from Sedgwick or from Webb Avenue found it much more convenient just to climb the fence rather than walk around to the main entrance. Most of us still have small scars on our arms or legs from getting caught on those pointy ends of the chain link fence. The park contained swings, monkey bars, see-saws, sliding ponds (the slides) and a shower pole in the center of it all that was turned on by the Parkies in the hot summer days for the kids to cool off. Most of this stuff we never used once we got old enough to use the basketball court and the stickball field. Stick ball was a major pastime. We played all day during the summer and most of us were pretty good. As we got older and our swings more powerful we established ground rules that said anyone hitting the ball over the fence except to the far reaches of center field between the park entrance and the swings would be called out. (We got tired of chasing the ball down the block or into the sewer.) We would choose up sides each day by a unique method of one guy (picked as captain) throwing the stick to another. The two captains alternated hand over hand from the point at which the stick was caught until they ran out of room at the top of the stick. The captain with upper hand (I guess that's where the expression originated) would then have to show security in his grip by twirling the stick around his head three times and then allowing the other captain to kick it once to see he was secure. Then the picking would begin. "I pick Mike; I'll take Bobby", and so on until we had our teams. No fancy adult supervision or equal opportunity playing time for us. We knew who was good and who was not. All the kids understood that. I remember that I was decent and was chosen mostly in the upper middle rounds, but two guys always stood out. Mike could hit the ball over the fence almost at will, and Bobby was a pain in the ass hitter with absolutely phenomenal control. He could hit to all fields, and invariably hit the ball where you weren't. We didn't play much baseball because there was limited room for dirt and grass fields, but there were a few organized leagues in the City. Mostly church leagues. I was good enough to play on a NYC Catholic League All-Star team in 1957. I mention this now to tie it in with our stickball experience. All my practice swinging a stick hindered my development as a baseball player. I never developed proper timing with my swing because of the difference between a longer, lighter stick, and a shorter, heavier bat. I was always swinging the bat late. I never could pull the ball effectively. (By the way, I think that my interest in watching Kev and Krissy at all their sporting events might have stemmed from my all star experience. My parents were both working, and I donned my uniform and rode the subway to the game alone. Somehow I still remember that I would have liked to have had them see me play in that game).

Basketball was the other park game. All city kids played basketball and we were no exception. We only had one full court so we would play two half-court games at a time to accommodate everybody. Three on a side and sixteen points to win. The winners kept playing until they were beaten, or, if they didn't lose, and didn't look like they ever would, then we would shoot for sides again. That meant all the guys would line up at the foul line and take a shot. The first three to sink their shot were on one team, the next three on the other. The rest sat and made up their own threesomes. (That's another thing I had trouble adjusting to. I played basketball in college and always felt the floor was too crowded with the extra two players on each side). If you showed up at the park on Saturday after 8 o'clock in the morning you were greeted with questions like "Where the hell were you?" That's how it was. We were all active kids. No TV, no Saturday cartoons or video games, and no stay at home activities. No programmed activities or schedules. Just show up and play all day. We managed to take care of our own free time, thank you.

The park was maintained by the "Parkies" who were employed by the City to keep it clean and respectable. Parkies were usually Italians who took care of the grass, the flowers, and kept the area looking good. We never knew their last names. They were Joe, the Parkie or John, the Parkie. Sometimes we kids tormented them though. I remember when John the Parkie was sitting, resting on the sliding pond. Butch lit a firecracker and rolled it down the slide and it blew up under John's ass. John was an old fellow, but you should have seen him light out after Butchie! When it was obvious he couldn't catch him, John threw his pick-up stick (the pole with the nail in the end to spear papers and leaves and the like) and almost nailed Butch in his ass. He cursed a lot, too. Maybe it was good we didn't speak Italian! However, we did give deference to Mr. Russo, the Superintendent. He was the man who would authorize the playground showers to be put on.

School Days, Dear Old Golden Rule Days

When we weren't playing we were in school. I embarked upon my learning adventures when I was enrolled in the first grade of Our Lady of Angels grammar school in September of 1945. All Catholic parishes in those days had a grammar (and sometimes a high school) attached to it. It was probably one of the least heralded benefits to the New York City educational system that so many parochial schools existed to ease the burden of public education of the city kids. All of us to this day have stories about nuns and priests who were influential in our early lives. There were plenty of religious around in the 1940's and 50's to staff these schools, and tuition was generally free on the grammar school level. Catholic high schools charged tuition. Cardinal Hayes High School, which I attended from 1953 to 1957, charged the exorbitant fee of $10 per month!—And if a family couldn't pay, it was reduced to $5. My grammar school days encompassed the years 1945 to 1953. We made our first Holy Communion, our first Confession, and were confirmed during those early school years. My first Confession was a rather traumatic event because at one time I was the "lookout" for the big kids who would occasionally enter the Five and Ten Cent Store to pilfer petty stuff like party favors and what-not. I remember Father Kiniary, our crusty, seemingly ancient, pastor, and it was my luck to line up for my first confession with him. "Bless me father, for I have sinned" I intoned while kneeling in this dark cubicle and talking through a mesh grid. "This is my first confession. I didn't say my night prayers. I talked back to my parents and ate meat on Friday one time. And I've been robbing the Five and Ten on 231st Street for two years." "WHAT?" He practically screamed, "YOU'VE BEEN DOING WHAT??" Oh I was scared. "DID YOU MAKE RESTITUTION?" he yelled. "YOU HAVE TO GO DOWN THERE AND MAKE RESTITUTION—PAY THEM BACK!" I just knew I was going to Hell until I paid the store back. But how much? I had no idea, so one day I had a handful of change. I went down to the Five and Ten and threw a handful of coins on a vacant counter and ran the hell out. Saved! I would be able to make my first Holy Communion! I would go to Heaven!!

I'm not able to remember specifically many of the world events while I attended at OLA. Mostly I remember that all the kids were from the parish and the class remained intact throughout the full eight years. I remember mine was the last class to wear knickers as part of our school uniform. You will probably have to look up some pictures of kids around the turn of the century to see knickers. They were baggy woolen pants that ended just below the knee and were worn with matching woolen knee sox. Thankfully, they were abandoned when I passed into the second grade and relegated to the scrap heap of history. I can remember pretty much all the names of the boys and girls of my class even to this day. And I can remember by name all the teachers I had during those eight years. They were almost all Sisters of Charity, and it is a tribute to their efforts that I remember their names with such clarity. I can't name some of the U.S. Presidents. I guess it goes to show you which one was the more inspirational profession. I remember the precautions we learned during the Cold War years. When the air raid drill was sounded we climbed under our desks. We had to learn to evacuate the school via the fire escapes. I remember that my assigned partner, Barbara, always had cold hands when we all had to walk (but don't run) down those outside stairs during fire drills. Mike Tilton and I drove in together to the old neighborhood a year or two ago and visited our old school. We marveled at seeing that our old classrooms were relatively unchanged and we wondered how we ever fit behind those desks. I'll tell you how long ago that was. Ball point pens hadn't been invented yet, we used a wooden straight pen with a removable nub which we dipped into the inkwell before writing. We weren't allowed to use a fountain pen until the fourth grade. And if you don't know what a "fountain pen" is you'll have to look that up, too.

A Little History

A lot of world events occurred during those years and I'll relate some of the ones I remember for you. World War Two is just history now, but this cataclysmic event that altered the course of history was ending just as I entered first grade. Franklin Delano Roosevelt died during his unprecedented fourth term in office, and Harry Truman became president. Adolph Hitler killed himself in his war time bunker, and the infamous "Third Reich" that he claimed would last one thousand years, crumbled. Germany signed a peace treaty in May, 1945, four months before I entered grammar school. The atomic bomb was dropped on the cities of Hiroshima and Nagasaki in August and Japan officially surrendered to the allied forces in September—the month I started first grade. You can see pictures of the surrender being signed aboard the battleship Missouri in any text book or encyclopedia, but an interesting and little known fact is that the surrender was held up by Harry Truman. The battleship New Jersey—I think the most decorated battleship in history—was in the area, but President Truman was from Missouri and he wanted the signing to take place on the ship that was named for his state. The U.S.S. Missouri was dispatched to the scene and the surrender was finally signed.

It is hard to imagine now, but the streets of New York were criss-crossed by many overhead electric wires as the trolleys plied their routes throughout the five boroughs. The streets were lined with trolley tracks and they were a pain in the neck for us kids riding bikes. Our bicycle tires would get caught in the tracks if we weren't paying attention and over we'd go. There were very few automobiles in those days, and the streets were our playground. I remember when the trolley tracks were paved over and I remember when the electric wires that were part of our landscape were finally buried under the ground and the poles taken down. The last trolley ran in New York in 1947. That was also the first year that TV sets were introduced to family homes.

First Television Sets

Perhaps now is the time for me to pontificate on my opinion of the effect TV has had on our society. Overall I think it has had a detrimental effect. To be fair, it has expanded the awareness of our population to the world in general, and it has enhanced communication with visual effects unknown to radio. TV has aired important news events and produced some high quality shows. It can be argued that TV is a boon to shut-ins by bringing the world into their homes. This being said, however, I claim that the advent of television stunted the development of civil society by bringing entertainment into the home and reducing the need for meaningful social interaction. What I mean is, that folks prior to the advent of television always sought to take part in social interaction outside their homes. I alluded earlier to my memories of people in the apartment houses gathering outside to socialize with neighbors. People joined civic organization and church functions more readily than they do today. I really feel society was more genteel then than now because folks were more aware of the people around them. Maybe its hindsight, maybe I'm looking back through rose-colored glasses, but where I live today I see a lot of fancy, and not so fancy, homes where too many people live in cocoons of self-induced seclusion hardly aware of their neighbors. I see homes with two or three TV sets where family members isolate themselves so they can watch their favorite shows alone without interfering with someone else's favorite show. There has been a breakdown of discourse on many levels. Hell, even the discussions, and often fights, in the bars I used to hang out in on Jerome Ave. were carried on with one eye on the ever present television set. Television has great potential for quality news reporting and shows, but I can argue that many news offerings are simply theater, and many shows are mindless sitcoms or games that do little to titillate any real process of thought. Studies of brain wave activity have shown that brains are more active during sleep than when watching a television set. Many TV proponents claim that they are showing what people want—and maybe that's true given the parameters of what's available. But how does one explain that when an occasional quality presentation or well-covered news event is programmed, viewers flock to it while leaving their favorite junk behind? At the risk of sounding elitist I claim the average programming is the result of intellectual laziness, and the public is the worse for it. So there, that is off my chest. Now on with my story.

Baseball Memories

As kids we gave baseball a very high priority. We collected and traded baseball cards. We always had our pack of cards secured by rubber bands with us at all times. We flipped them against the wall to see who could get the closest—and then keep the cards that were further from the wall than ours. "Leaners" were almost unbeatable—unless a guy could flip his card, and knock the leaner over, kind of like Robin Hood splitting his opponent's arrow when it was in the center of the bulls-eye. We would flip them to the ground matching heads or tails. We would trade them. Almost all my friends today remember their collection of baseball cards, and almost all my friends today remember that somewhere along the line their "mother threw them out." It was the golden age of baseball. The rivalry of the three teams in the city was intense. I was an avid Brooklyn Dodger fan who was in the seventh grade when Bobby Thompson hit what is now called, "The Shot Heard Round the World." The Dodgers had a 13 game lead in August of 1952 which they blew, and a playoff was forced with the rival N.Y. Giants. I was sitting on the curb outside school listening to the radio with the other kids as the game drew to its dramatic close. The Dodgers blew a 4-2 lead in the bottom of the ninth when Bobby Thompson hit a walk off home run with 2 two men on base to win the pennant. I remember that I was so mad I cried, and all the kids, as kids always will, made fun of me and beat me up.

My uncle Ed used to torment me about how good the Yankees were. One day when he had me so riled up he said he would make a bet with me. He would add the runs the Yankees got, game by game, and I would multiply, game by game, the Dodger runs. He said he would come out with more at the end of the season. "You got a bet!" I shouted. I got out my composition book and faithfully multiplied the runs of every game. Two times three equaled six. Then I multiplied my six by the next score, say five, to get thirty. Then thirty times four to get up to one hundred twenty. I was killing Uncle Ed! Then one day, when I had about a Gazillion runs, the Dodgers got shut out. And I had to multiply my Gazillion by zero. The answer? Yep, Zero. And for the rest of the season I had to multiply whatever total runs my team got for that day by that zero. Anything times zero folks, is still zero. Finally I got the picture—I'd been had!! But I never forgot the bet—even as I write about it fifty five years later.

We had endless discussions about who was the best in center field. New York teams had three center fielders that made the Hall of Fame in Cooperstown. Mickey Mantle, Willie Mays, and Snider, the "Duke of Flatbush" all roamed the outfield grass of the Yankee Stadium, The Polo Grounds, and Ebbets Field. Only the stadium is left now. And it is a new Yankee Stadium, completed for the 2009 season. The original "house that Ruth built" in 1927 was torn down with not much regard for the history that the revered old edifice contained. When I was in high school the Giants and my beloved Brooklyn Dodgers fled to the west coast. It's all memory now. All who are reading this will never understand the depth of emotion that ran through the fans of New York baseball during those years.

A milestone was achieved in the game when I was in the third grade. Jack Roosevelt Robinson—Jackie Robinson—became the player to break the all-white color barrier of the major leagues. I didn't know about segregation. I was too young. But I remember Jackie Robinson and how he tormented pitchers with enormous leads off base, how he ran with abandon, and I remember him stealing home on more than one occasion. You can look it up—Jackie Robinson stole home 19 times! He was exciting. But he paid a terrible price for being the first to break the color line. Branch Rickey, the Dodger G.M. who was also brave enough to sign him, told Jackie that he wanted a player not only good enough to play in the major leagues, but one intelligent enough to realize that he represented a momentous change in the sport. He wanted a player, he told Jackie, who was brave and strong enough to remain silent when all kinds of slurs and racial epithets were hurled at him. He wanted a man who was strong enough not to fight back when he was intentionally spiked or thrown at. He wanted a player who would accept these indignities so that those following him would be allowed to integrate smoothly because of his forbearance. Jackie did this, and many believe that the pent up emotion of this fierce competitor affected his health and helped lead to an early death.

I saw many players who will be remembered through the years. Joe DiMaggio, Ted Williams, who gave me and my friend Richie Kurtti the finger one afternoon from left field, Yogi Berra, who was loved by all, and a pitcher named Warren Spahn who fought in WW2 and came back to be one of the winningest lefties in baseball history. Sadly, one of the greatest players that I never saw play died at the early age of 53 in 1948 when I was in the fourth grade. Babe Ruth. Like I say, baseball was enormous and I lived through its Golden Age during those years when I was under the tutelage of the good sisters of OLA.

The Nineteen Fifties

There were other events that I consider to be of lasting importance during those years in grammar school. The United Nations was born in the aftermath of World War Two when I was in the first grade. The Korean War that was officially called "A Police Action", which nevertheless killed 50,000 of our soldiers, was fought for the purpose of containing the spread of Communism when I was in the seventh and eighth grade. And President Dwight D. Eisenhower signed into law the Interstate Commerce Act in 1956 and the highway system as we know it was born. These events just mentioned were to have the most important and lasting effects of my time.

When the Second World War ended there were really only two powers left standing. Europe was decimated. Japan and its dream of empire had been crushed. The United States and her world influence was being challenged only by the Communist Empire of Russia and her satellite nations. Unfortunately, not only the political structure of these two nations clashed ideologically, but the economic vision of the free capitalism of our country clashed dramatically with a communist structure espoused by the Soviet Union. The United States instituted the Marshall Plan to assist European nations to get back on their feet economically while the Soviet Union took steps to solidify their hold on much of Eastern Europe. The distrust grew on both sides and Winston Churchill, then the Prime Minister of Great Britain, coined the phrase "The Iron Curtain" to define the areas of Russian influence from those of the West. The phrase remained in our lexicon, and the foreign policy of the U.S. was influenced by maintaining balance with the Soviet Union economically and militarily for the next fifty years. I write this with no sense or purpose of historical detail, (don't forget I was only in short pants when all these political maneuverings were instigated) but rather to share with you the particular era during the time when much of the world's energy was focused on maintaining "The Cold War." This Cold War lasted from the time I was six years old and in the first grade to when I was well into my fifties. Paranoia waxed rampant in those early years. Communists were claimed to have infiltrated Hollywood, Congress, and even the military before more reasonable heads prevailed. It was the beginning of the atomic era and "THE BOMB" was on everybody's mind. It is kind of humorous to think of it now, but as kids in grammar school we practiced what to do in the event of a nuclear attack. We were instructed by the good sisters (the nuns) to slide beneath our desks and cover our head! We actually practiced that in the Bronx! What good could have come of this training I really don't know. Perhaps we were placed in a better position to kiss our tush good bye. If you are interested in what the world was like politically during my time I guess you could refer to the world events that dominated U. S. and Soviet relations for much of my life.

The second era-changing event that occurred as I graduated from grammar school had to be the passage of the Interstate Commerce Act and the creation of a national highway system. The passage of this act is arguably one of the most important pieces of legislation to affect American life to the present day. I remember sitting in school, taking my state Regents Exam (I scored 100% and won the History Medal at graduation in 1953), and listening to the rhythmic hiss-boom, hiss-boom, of the pile drivers as they were laying down what is now the Major Deegan Expressway (Route I-87) in New York. Considering the importance of the automobile to our mobile society today it is hard to imagine those long distance trips on two lane roads that went through just about every town on the map. I really don't remember any suburbs, or mention of suburbia, when I was a kid. Most people lived in cities. Others lived in towns, but no one lived in suburbs. Outside the city there were farmers and a few other folks who lived in what were known as "Rural Areas." People mostly lived in cities, worked in cities and, as a matter of fact, if you remember how I said we would play in the streets, many families I knew didn't even have cars. My mother and my Aunt Dot never learned to drive at all. It wasn't unusual. State highways connected the towns and travel was slow. The Interstate Highway act passed during the Eisenhower Administration in 1956 changed all that. The interstates we take for granted today all began in the fifties. People became mobile. More cars were bought. Developers found tracts of land and purchased these rural areas from farmers to build houses which, for the first time, afforded families the opportunity to buy private homes. Population expanded throughout the countryside as families left the confines of the city to live and commute to their work via automobile. I remember as a kid in the 1940's-50's our family used to travel to Glen Lake (Glens Falls, a city about 50 miles north of Albany) in upstate New York for vacation every July. Let me take a break here and relate a story about Glen Lake before proceeding with my highway stuff. OK?

Asthma

As a kid, probably until I was 14 or 15 years old, I suffered from pretty bad asthma. I remember the attacks that left me puffing and gasping for breath and I remember my mother saying "Take a pill and go to school." There were no inhalers in those days. I know it broke her heart to watch me from her second story window as I walked through the lots and had to lean on every other tree to catch my breath, but she knew what she was doing. My mother never let me give into the disease or feel sorry for myself. Most of my bad asthma attacks occurred during the summer when we vacationed at the Lake. Here is the story—it is true, and if read with the hindsight of the old European myths and medical ignorance it will make sense—and also show how much more sophisticated we have become since the old days of the 1940's. Each year our family teamed up with my Uncle Frank's family to rent a summer cottage for the month of July. It was an old wooden cottage with fiberboard walls separating the rooms and with a deck that faced the lake. I got asthma bad up there. Twice I was turning blue and was rushed to the hospital for an adrenalin shot to ease my breathing. Once my father was called back from work and drove the seven hours up to take me home. He picked me up and then turned around and drove the seven hours back with me to safety. That's one of the unselfish and unsung things a good father does. Moof was a good father, I've never forgotten it, and I did thank him for all he did when I finally was of an age to appreciate it. Anyway each night the asthma came and I coughed and gasped until daylight when I was allowed out on the deck when the new day started. My relatives, in their ignorance, were convinced that the night air, "The Vapors", they called it, were responsible. They shut me in my room. They closed and sealed the windows and the doors to keep these evil night vapors from my damaged lungs. And still I got sick. It was only years later when I underwent a series of allergy tests that I found out I was severely allergic to mold. And guess what that house that had been boarded up all winter was full of? Yep, and by sealing me in my bedroom my sainted Irish relatives sealed me in with my deadly enemy all through the night. It was only when I could emerge to the deck at daylight that my breathing would ease for the day. Their fears were understandable in light of my improvement during the day, but, boy, were they ever backward in their medical knowledge at the time! And now back to the highways.

Changing America

As I just said, the trip to Glens Falls took almost eight hours to cover the two hundred fifty mile distance. I-87 and the Northway now have cut the time to Glen Lake to four hours. Think about it. People who were previously city-bound now could travel. They didn't have to live where they worked, they could shop in giant malls that were supplied by a network of trucks rather than a warehouse, they could connect to relatives and friends with whom they otherwise could only write, and folks could now send their kids to colleges out of state. They could take vacations; resorts and destination holiday spas were no longer only for the wealthier class. All America was now able to live and travel where they wished. I know it is kind of a heavy sociological concept to consider, but think what your life would be without your highway network or your automobile. I'm mentioning it now only in the context that it was during those years, when I was just breaking into my teens, that all this was just starting to develop. You might say that I was in on the very beginning of this enormous social change. Of course if someone reads this years from now when space travel is a given, and people travel through the skies in individual flight suits all this may seem quaint. But for those years it was huge.

A kind of a tradeoff though, was the breakdown of the core neighborhood groups that stabilized our city existence. Many folks moved out. The social organizations that supported our immigrant groups slowly dissipated as the young marrieds left for the American Dream in the suburbs. We'll talk about that later, but first I need to tell you more about growing up and what happened during my high school years, the years when I started to shave and realize girls were different than boys. This was the Era of "Rock and Roll." My folks had Frank Sinatra and Bing Crosby and the Big Bands to entertain them. We had Elvis Presley and the Doo Wop sound. We had candy stores and lunch fountains, and girl friends and drive in movies. Movies were starting to be shown in glorious Technicolor. (Which just happened to be invented by a graduate of M.I.T., the Massachusetts Institute of Technology. Hence the name "Technicolor.")

Cardinal Hayes High School 1953-1957

I'm afraid I wasn't a very impressive sight when I entered high school. I was all of 5 foot 3 inches and weighed 103 lbs. Remember the asthma? I remember that distinctly because 105 was the cut off point between the upper and lower sports leagues. I tried like hell to join the upper league but always fell just short. That is a far cry from the old bald oaf sitting at the computer now. Now I stand just over six feet, and I am embarrassed to relate, punish the bathroom scale by weighing at 240 pounds. Not all fat though, there is some muscle left on the old guy because last week I completed my eighth annual Avon Marathon 26 mile Walk through New York to raise money for breast cancer research. High school was the real beginning of the transition from little kid to big guy. Check it out on yourself. Look at a picture of graduation from grammar school and compare it to your high school yearbook. But the change was more than physical. For the first time I stretched my fledgling wings and I left the friendly confines of my block. At the age of thirteen I rode the subway into the unknown. The cost of a subway token was fifteen cents in 1953. Every day I would walk the twenty minutes to the subway train and ride the eight stops from the Kingsbridge Road Station to my school. Cardinal Hayes High School was one stop down from the Yankee Stadium on the Lexington Ave. IRT. I mentioned earlier that the tuition at Hayes was ten dollars a month. When my sister Barbara entered high school two years after me, her tuition at Saint Thomas Aquinas H.S. was $20 a month. That was when our mother took a job at Alexander's Dept. Store selling housewares to help with the cost of educating us kids.

My high school boasted of a student body of 2600 boys. There were no girls at my high school. In the fifties all parochial high schools were segregated by sex. Girls went to their schools and guys to their school. We had what were called sister schools with which we teamed up for dances and school outings and such, but I guess the good nuns and priests thought it best to keep us, and our raging hormones, separated as much as possible. The students at my high school came from mostly middle class families in the South Bronx and upper Manhattan. Jackets and ties were required in the classroom. We could leave our jacket in our locker and travel to and from school with whatever coat we wanted. Discipline and accountability have always been the hallmarks of parochial education and Cardinal Hayes was no exception. There was no shortage of clergy in those days, and almost everyone on the faculty of my high school was a religious of some order—mostly diocesan priests.

We had a Dean of Discipline who deserves special note in my autobiography: Father Stanislaus Jablonski—"Jabbo"—to the thousands of Hayesmen over whom he ruled with iron discipline. Hair worn too long? "Jabbo" would notice. "Go home and don't come back without your mother!" Sometimes if the event was really a grievous one "Jabbo" would double the threat. "Don't come back without your mother AND your father!" Late for school? Too bad, "Jabbo" would be standing at the entrance. "Report at 2:35 for an hour in late jug room 119." There was no recourse. No questions were asked. A classroom discipline problem? Get a Jug Slip and report for an hour after school to room 117 and stand silently facing the blackboard for the full hour. "Jabbo" would sometimes sneak in the room from behind us and lurk, silently. God forbid he caught anyone talking. "All right!" he would say, "I heard that! Half hour more for everybody!" He was respected and sometimes feared by all, and he will forever be revered by the Hayesmen whose lives he touched. There was only one "Jabbo"—and we all grew with a sense of purpose, and morality, and responsibility because of him. He kept daily order in a school of 2600 boys who were trying to test their adolescent oats. "Jabbo" personified Hayes. By the way, it was years after my high school years that I was to find out what "JUG" meant. I had assumed it was something like being bottled up in a class after school, but the meaning was even more poignant than that. Would you believe it stood for "Justice under God?"

I had a few personal experiences with "Jabbo". Early on in my Hayes career we boasted of a fearsome football team. (No, I didn't play on it. Do you realize how big and tough you had to be to make a squad of perhaps 40 from a student body of over two thousand?) Anyway, at a game I got excited over a touchdown and threw my cup of soda in the air only to watch horrified as it landed on some priest's head a few rows in front of me. That prompted a request from "Jabbo" to report to his office. While I was sitting there in his presence, with fear as my only companion, he called my home and spoke with my mother. "Is this the Gertrude Klumpp from Sedgwick Avenue? Francis Collin's cousin?" He asked. I was shocked when he laughed and introduced himself again to my mother. It turned out the fearsome "Jabbo" was in the Seminary with my Godfather Francis Collins, and he often visited us at our house when I was a little tyke. He said that no, he couldn't visit again as long as I was a student there because he couldn't show favoritism—and then he explained to my mother what I was doing in his office. He told her that I would be getting a thirty day Jug sentence to begin immediately. Thirty consecutive days of detention—"Jabbo" played no favorites. Justice under God. He also became familiar with my problem with Asthma. It was he who contacted the allergy professionals at Belleview Hospital and arranged early school breaks for me to take the train down to Belleview. With permission from my parents, he had me tested and treated. My asthma gradually disappeared. Today as I write, there are massive problems that the Catholic Church is facing due to the improper behavior (pedophilia) of an astounding number of priests and the covering up for them by the bishops. I want to say this: "Jabbo" was a real *Mensch*—and all my experiences with any clergy during my lifetime have been positive ones. I owe a lot to the clergy of Cardinal Hayes High School.

I failed Third Year Latin. I hated it. My mother thought it would make me smart and told me I had to take it. I didn't have the nerve to tell her that I only passed Second Year Latin because I bowled every week with the bowling club moderated by Fr. Donachie, my Latin teacher. And so, at the final exam that third year, I scored 67 which gave me an average for the year of 64—a point below passing. When I begged, pleaded, and cajoled Fr. Kuolt for that extra point his answer was, "To give you one point in average over ten marking periods I have to give you a 77 on the final. There is no way you know 77% of the curriculum. So, no deal." I went to summer school during the summer of 1956. Two things happened because of that. I got my first tax-reportable job as an usher in the Kingsbridge Theater and I got to go to a school where there were girls in my class.

So, the girl story first. Sorry to disappoint you, but not much happened in the way of romance. The girls, though attractive and presumably as smart as I because we all failed Latin, were, in the parlance of the day, all G.U. Geographically Undesirable. The three girls I remember hanging around with were all from a school named Preston, which was located way away on the East Side of the Bronx. We did enjoy each others company in class though. We enjoyed each others company so much that I think we all failed summer school together that year. After coming close during the school year with a 66% average, and with an additional July and August to improve, I managed a 46% in the summer school final. But I did have fun!

Early Work

A little word about work is now in order. My first job came when I was thirteen years old and in the eighth grade. I worked two hours each day after school and eight hours every Saturday picking up and delivering clothes that were dry cleaned at the local cleaners down the block. My first pay was $7 for the week's work—a dollar a day and two dollars for Saturday. I was in the chips! In case you are wondering how I managed to do these pick up and deliveries without a car you must remember I lived in a neighborhood environment where all necessities were usually within a few block radius. Most people walked or took a bus. I could, and did, walk all over the neighborhood stopping at the various apartments (houses we call them, remember?) carrying bags of clothes to, and cleaned clothes on hangars from, the Gold Ribbon Cleaners on Sedgwick Avenue. Later, when I was a senior in high school, I worked for the grocery next door to this cleaners but I don't want to get ahead of my story. That comes later. The usher's job at the movies comes first.

Because summer school was a daytime commitment, it was impossible for me to get a day job. The local movie theater was perfect as far as timing went. The theater only ran shows in the evening during the week and after noon on the weekends. It was a fun job. I also got to wear a fancy usher's uniform that made me look like a ship's captain with a flashlight. I got to sneak my friends in the emergency exit when Mr. Stearns, the manager, wasn't looking. And I got to be a pest when I would shine my flashlight on the faces of any couple trying to "make out" in the darkened theater. All this for fifty-five cents an hour! Mr. Stearns kept official records, tax documents, etc., and he required that I obtain a social security card as a per-requisite for employment So that was it; my official entrance into the great working class at the age of sixteen years. And paying ever since, but don't we all? Times were simpler and safer then. I remember each night when the theater closed and Mr. Stearns would walk about four blocks to the bank. He carried a paper bag containing the deposit of the day's receipts to the night deposit drop. He would ask the usher on duty to accompany him, but I can't imagine what I could have done carrying only my flashlight. To top it all off, all secrecy was compromised because of me in my ship's captain usher's uniform walking in the dark with a guy carrying a paper bag full of money. But they were different days. Days before the Bronx changed and the streets became mean. I held that job with my friends Tommy and Warren until school started in September.

My senior year in high school was the year I worked at the grocery store. Three o'clock to seven after school every Monday through Friday, and nine to seven on Saturday. My pay was $17 a week and tips brought it up to around $35. I was rich! No kidding. That was a lot of money for those days. I was able to help my sister Barbara out with that money one Saturday when she stopped me on the street and told me she needed help. She had a $20 bill Mama had given her to buy something (a dress I think it might have been) and she lost the money. I asked Nat the Grocer for my week's pay a little early and gave it to my sister and our mother never found out. Barbara has always remembered it though. As brother and sisters go, Sista Barb and I were the best. That was a good job, the S and B Supermarket, and I worked hard and found myself in the best shape of my life. Every day I would pedal that delivery bike, walk up countless stairs with boxes of groceries to be delivered, and later, when the store would close, pack up the shelves, put away the empty deposit bottles which were worth 5 cents for a quart bottle and 2 cents for a Pepsi or Coca Cola bottle, and finally, sweep the store. On Saturday I would pedal and deliver those orders for 10 hours non stop. At gym class in school I could climb ropes to the ceiling like a monkey and do sit ups or push ups long after most would groan and quit. I never got tired. My height was approaching 5' 10" and I weighed 155 lbs entering College. I could run and jump and play ball. That was the year I made the All-Star team starting at first base for the Bronx-Manhattan Team against the Brooklyn-Queens Team for the City Championship. We lost that game. When I graduated from Hayes (our graduation ceremony was held at St. Patrick's Cathedral in Manhattan), I left the grocery store job to Bobby Carroll, a year behind me, who followed me in the tradition of seniors working at the store.

That summer I got a full time job with the N.Y.C. Dept. of Hospitals working as a messenger in Morrisania Hospital in the Bronx. My job was to deliver medical records to different areas of the hospital but once in a while I got hijacked to do some unsavory chores like helping lift corpses on and off gurneys at the morgue. I always tried to grab the feet—I wanted no part of the upper body—I was afraid it would sit up and scare the shit out of me! For a while I was assigned to be the oxygen man and to transfer those big green oxygen bottles that were hooked up to the masks that the sick and elderly wore. Today oxygen is piped in through installed systems, but back in 1957 you had to wheel those big tanks around and use a wrench to hook to up to the patients' tubes. I guess it was a big enough responsibility for a young guy, but I always managed to secure the oxygen properly. I didn't like it much though; I didn't want to be so close to all those sick people. Better to just deliver the paperwork and be done with it. But I thought I was a big man then, and coming of age. For the first time I had a job away from the neighborhood and I received a paycheck instead of cash from the store's till at the end of the week. I even celebrated by going out with the hospital workers on my first pay day. I was under age—you had to be 18 to drink at a bar—but there I was, living large, and hanging out with my co-workers and drinking ten cent draft beers at a local tavern on 173rd street. Ten cent beers! And after buying three, the tradition was for the bartender to "buy one back" which meant a free one on the house. Try that today. Maybe the good old days did have some good points after all! When September came I left for college. That was the end of my jobs until I went to work in earnest upon graduation four years later. And that brings me to the end of what I'll call my Novice Years. Before I turn the page on those days though, I'll tell you a little about my social life during those wonderful years of the 50's. The era of "Rock and Roll", of taking your girl to a secluded park to watch the "Submarine Races" in the evening, of the candy store hangout, the trips with the gang in that classic '57 Chevy, and going to the Proms. And the raging hormones. I was just starting to notice girls.

Time to Reminisce

Every era seems to have some kind of label attached to it. The Roaring Twenties, the Depression Years of the Thirties and the War Years of the Forties are examples. I recall the Fifties having no particular slogan. The Fabulous Fifties, perhaps. Most folks my age look back on the Fifties now with a kind of warm nostalgia. A generation or two of those folks older than I may consider the War Years as their defining time. As for the Depression Years of the Thirties and the Roaring Years of the Twenties, well, I suppose those days are consigned to history now because there aren't many around who could recall them. But the Fifties was my time, the salad days of callow youth. All my teenage years, with their associated growing pains and joys, took place in what is remembered as a quiet time. The war years were over, and except for the Korean War, times were tranquil. Eisenhower was a grandfatherly type President and people said, "I like Ike." Returning servicemen were busy building their lives, getting jobs, buying houses, going to school under the G.I. Bill and, thanks to the Highway Bill of 1954, traveling the new roads which gave access to the new phenomenon of suburban living. Televisions were introduced into homes.

People laugh and deride those early TV programs today. All lily-white suburban family sitcoms showed wholesome children doing wholesome things and projected an idyllic life devoid of much of the reality and pain of normal living. Sex? Not even mentioned. Those TV couples always had their own beds and quite a storm brewed when Lucille Ball of "The I Love Lucy" show was the first woman to appear pregnant on the screen. The shows were broadcast live with none of that imbecilic canned laughter of today. The show was funny or it wasn't. Variety shows were common and many entertainers of the day made their debuts on television. There were talented media giants to enjoy. You would have to find the archives now, but if you're interested in quality programming of early TV, watch The Steve Allen Show and Milton Berle's Texaco Star Theater. Comedy shows like "I Love Lucy" or Jackie Gleason's "Honeymooners" should live forever.

There was an ugly side to this era that must be mentioned: Segregation. Segregation gave the lie to that idyllic time depicted on the tube. Rosa Parks died recently and was honored in the nation's capital. One day in 1954 Rosa was riding a bus home from work in Montgomery, Alabama. The bus was filling up and she refused to give up her seat to a white man and was arrested. She claimed she was tired, but in later years she said she wasn't weary. She said she was tired of being treated as a second class person by white people whose laws enforced a segregated society in the South. Martin Luther King rose to prominence at this time as he organized a boycott of the Montgomery Bus Line that lasted for a year before laws were changed. Blacks fought for the right to sit at unsegregated lunch counters, and to attend schools and colleges with white people. The white southern establishment fought bitterly with clubs, dogs, and firehoses to oppose these changes in their class system. The governor of Alabama stood in the doorway of a school to deny entrance to a colored girl. President Eisenhower activated the National Guard to enforce federal law and gradually, grudgingly, things changed. There are still occasional racial tensions that surface today, but the viciousness of the struggle for the dignity of human rights that occurred in the Fifties cannot be ignored. Truthfully, living in the Bronx in an all white neighborhood during those years, and attending a color-blind Catholic high school, I was pretty insulated from these concerns. However, looking back, and knowing what I know today, I feel obligated to mention this ugly time so you can understand some of the unfair struggle millions of Americans endured during those Fabulous Fifties.

Our social lives revolved around our neighborhood. Guys and Girls started to hang around with each other. The local candy store with booths to sit in and the juke box to play records was usually the meeting place. Parish churches sponsored weekend dances with the priests usually milling around to insure that we wouldn't dance too close. "Make room for the Holy Ghost" was their usual intonation. A girl could usually find out if a guy liked her if he asked to walk her home after the last dance. A guy would know if she liked him if she let him, and a goodnight kiss in the hallway was a good thing. House parties were common, and it was usual for fifteen teenagers to crowd into someone's house and dance and play records. Sometimes a guy would have a pint of whiskey hidden but most times not. Drinking was not a big thing for us in those days. We were more interested in finding a girl who would dance close and hope someone would "accidentally" turn the light out in the middle of the song. We went out with all the girls, we danced with them all, and we matured in our social graces. We learned the rules of dating and we got comfortable with each other before a certain bell would go off in our heads and we found one girl we liked more than anyone else. Then we would decide to "Go Steady", and the girl would wear the guy's high school ring. That's where watching the submarine races would come in; going steady with your favorite girl would mean separating yourselves from the crowd, and drifting off to the park in the dark of a summer evening together to "make out." All the way sex, especially with B I C's (Bronx Irish Catholic) girls, was almost unheard of. This also applied to NATO's. (No action talk only) Getting a hand inside a blouse or under a sweater was like a Home Run and you could tell all the guys that you "got tit!" My first date was taking Betty Jean to a movie and it took a lot of my nerve to put my arm around her in the darkened theater. And I remember going to the phone booth in the candy store to call girls because I was afraid my sisters would make fun of me if they heard me calling from home. But I was generally a cool guy; I even started smoking when I was thirteen when cigarettes sold for twenty-three cents a pack. I didn't wise up and quit until twenty-five years later. Five dollars in your pocket was all you needed for a big night out, or a date with your girlfriend. They were happy days, but I was getting older now, and it was getting time to move on. My high school days ended with graduation ceremonies held at St. Patrick's Cathedral in 1957 and it was time to start thinking about college. My Novice Years were ending.

Intermediate Years

College years, The training ship, Going to sea,
Time to reminisce, Working ashore

Brenda with Jimmy McIvor

THE INTERMEDIATE YEARS

College Years

I attended the New York State University Maritime College and graduated in 1961 with a B.S. Degree in Marine Transportation and a federal license to sail as Third Mate, upon oceans, unlimited. How I decided to go there is a story worth telling. When I was seventeen it was kind of understood that I would attend college. My mother was adamant about the idea, and my father was ambivalent, and I was going along with the tide. Times were different then, most guys from my neighborhood didn't attend college, and girls were hardly expected to attend college at all. It might have been an Irish thing to "get an edication" but my father, from his perspective as a tool and die maker, thought it was just as important to learn a trade. I had no idea what I wanted to do with my life and had no idea of what school to attend or even what courses to pursue. To this day I find it terribly unfair to ask a high school senior what he wants to be. Most don't even have a clue—and at that age they don't have to. While I was faced with this dilemma, my Aunt Anne mentioned that two of her nephews were attending the Merchant Marine Academy at Kings Point. I investigated and discovered that there were two Maritime Schools in the area. One was The Federal Academy at Kings Point on Long Island and the other the State Maritime College at Fort Schuyler in the Bronx. Both schools bordered Long Island Sound and were located right on the water. The idea made sense to me. As far as I could tell, the Maritime Schools covered all the bases. At 18 years of age I was required to register for the draft (which was phased out in the 70's) and I would be eligible for military duty. College would postpone this obligation until I could serve as an officer at a later date. My mother was happy, and even my father saw value in this school because I would learn a seafarin' trade. My sisters were happy because they would have more room in the house, and I was intrigued with the idea of cadet status at a military college and a chance to see the world on the training ship. I applied and was accepted at both. I chose the Maritime College at Fort Schuyler simply because they responded first and I've never regretted it.

The State University Maritime College (all state colleges) at that time was free—as in no cost. We did have to pay for uniforms and room and board which cost my parents $600 a year. I suppose that made my parents happy, but even at $50 per month my folks felt the financial pinch of education. Colleges run into fantastic sums of money. Our children, Kevin and Krissy, were expensive. I estimate that Brenda and I paid around $150,000 before they graduated from college in 1999 and 2000. It would have been much more than that if not for the fact that Kevin was awarded an Air Force ROTC scholarship. But today is not 1957, or even 2000, What college tuition will be for my children's children I am afraid to guess.

The Maritime College at Fort Schuyler is actually a school in a real fort that had been constructed in the 1800's to guard the approaches to New York via Long Island Sound and the East River. The pentagon shaped building with the impressive stone walls was rehabilitated by the WPA during the Depression years of the Thirties, and when the restoration was completed the Fort became the new home of the New York Nautical School. During World War Two its function changed, and the Fort was used to train what were called "90 day wonders"—officers training for the wartime Naval Service.

Allow me to digress a little bit here. When discussing the war time endeavors, the role of the merchant marine is often overlooked. Folks were, of course, aware of our Army and Navy and the many battles they fought during the long conflict. But little noted were the incidentals like how did the tanks and jeeps arrive in Europe, or where the gas that fueled them came from, or bullets for the riflemen. And how did the soldiers get food to eat or uniforms to wear? That was the sometimes overlooked function of the Merchant Marine. Merchant ships and merchant seamen supplied the war effort. Franklin D. Roosevelt realized the value of this supply system when he vowed to "bridge the sea with ships." Shipyards, with the help of thousands of "Rosie the Riviters", launched a ship a day. Ships were bombed, torpedoed, and sunk regularly by the hundreds, and still the convoys fought through dangerous waters to deliver the goods. These ships had to be manned by captains, mates, engineers and crewmen whose casualty rate was exceeded only by those of the Marine Corps when the war ended. It was during this war, and to fill this demand for seamen, that the federal Merchant Marine Academy was founded at Kings Point. The federal academy and the five state maritime colleges are still supplying ships' officers for the modern merchant fleets of today.

After the war ended the school at Fort Schuyler was absorbed into the State University System and in 1948 the name officially became "The State University Maritime College at Fort Schuyler." We just called it Fort Schuyler.

It was a small school. The regiment contained 600 cadets. There were two degrees offered, a B.S. Degree in Marine Engineering with the cadets also receiving licenses to sail as third engineer on merchant ships, and a B.S. Degree in Marine Transportation with a license to sail as Third Mate. Deck or engine cadets we were called. I was a deck cadet. The course of studies included the business aspects of operating merchant fleets and world trade. In addition to the required academic core courses I took courses in areas such as Marine Insurance, International Trade, Ship Chartering, Scheduling, and Admiralty Law. What was unique about the Maritime College was the course load of additional subjects not recognized as academic credits by the State. Professional training such as navigation, cargo handling and stowage, seamanship, and ship construction and stability among others, were taken in addition to our regular academic load. A college senior usually requires in the neighborhood of 120 credits to graduate. We cadets, deck and engine both, carried a load of roughly 165 credits before we graduated. But what did we know? That was just the way it was. The attrition rate was high. Two thirds of cadets entering the school were not around for graduation. In my deck class, 105 started and 36 graduated. The same was roughly true of the engineers. Many left because of the specialized nature of the school. Some couldn't adjust to the military regimen and the fact that we were allowed liberty only on Saturday afternoon after inspection until Sunday night. Living with these restrictions proved too confining for many. And, of course, the academic requirements had to be maintained.

Cadet life was different from collegiate life today. A big night for us would be sitting around in the common room in dorms built as barracks during World War Two and shining our shoes in preparation for "Admiral's Inspection." Admiral's Inspection was carried out each Saturday with the usual military decorum of a parade, trooping of the colors, then standing at attention for about forty five minutes as the Admiral (who was also president of the school) eyed each of us while taking his solemn walk through our ranks. We had reveille every morning regardless of whether classes were scheduled or not. We marched from our dorms to breakfast at the Fort in whatever conditions the gods of weather prescribed for the day, and stood for inspection every morning before class. Our undress whites (bell bottom pants and jumpers with a white sailor hat with a midshipman's stripe on it) were always clean and pressed as only we knew how—by folding them inside out and rolling them into tight balls and tied with string and leaving them in our lockers until the creases were squeezed out. During the winter months we switched to undress blues and our dark pants and wool CPO shirts that we brushed with whisk brooms every day to stay lint free. We also took our turn standing watches on the training ship and school grounds as well as the fire watches in the dorms throughout the night. It didn't matter if you had an exam the next day; When your watch came up you were called awake and you patrolled your assigned two hour tour during the night. The grounds tour was especially unpleasant during cold and rainy or snowy nights when your classmates were snug in their beds. The wind always blew across the Fort from the open expanse of Long Island Sound. So, yeah, we lost a lot of cadets. But those who lasted, the one third of us who stayed, drew close and bonded with a camaraderie we all share even to this day. It was odd. It was a strange college experience but I guess we didn't know any better. It was an educational experience, one I wouldn't think of trading today. I went to our 40th reunion a few years ago. I really didn't know if I would go or not, graduation had been so long ago. But, damn, when we all got together again, I knew I belonged there with them. It made me proud to be part of this special group of guys. The class of '61. If anyone should be curious I can tell you that I graduated 16th in my class. My four year GPA was 2.8

A feature unique to our maritime education was the training cruise we took each summer to hone our nautical skills. The training cruises were an integral part of our education. Fort Schuyler boasted of a training ship that was permanently docked at the college. It was named *Empire State* after the State of New York, and had a number following that designated the training ship you were referring to. My first two cruises were aboard the *Empire State 3rd*. It was small as today's behemoths go. It was 417 feet in length, and previously had been a hospital ship that had seen service in the Pacific during WW2. During my time, the *"Empty State"* was home to three classes of cadets intent upon learning the seafaring life. Each training cruise lasted about 85 days, from the middle of June to the end of August. There was no summer vacation for us! In its place was the opportunity to travel to foreign ports and learn a bit about different cultures and visit museums and other cultural items of interest (if you believe that, then you don't know me very well). No, we aspiring young sailors did manage to take in what sightseeing was required, but then we found the dance halls and bars and savored the delights that were more to our liking.

Our first cruise took place during the summer of 1958. We sailed to Bermuda, Belfast, Copenhagen, Antwerp and the Worlds Fair in Brussels, and finally to Lisbon. Two adventures are worthy of note. While in Lisbon there was a side trip that was offered to the Catholic shrine of Our Lady of Fatima. One of our schoolmates named "Peaches" for some obscure reason came from a very religious family and they were insistent that "Peaches" visit Fatima. They had even bought an 8 millemeter movie camera for him to take along to document his visit for the family. Unfortunately when the time came, "Peaches" was restricted to the ship due to an excessive number of demerits. He was worried as hell what his parents would say when he informed them that he didn't make the holy pilgrimage after all. "No problem" he was told. Some of the guys volunteered to take his camera and record the trip for him. "One church is the same as another. When you get home, show the film like you were there—make up some good stories—and no one will know the difference. We'll have it all on film for you." These were the days before digital. So some of the cadets went with Peach's camera—I wish I could take credit for this but I can't because I wasn't with them—and off they went to the Holy Shrine of Fatima. "Done", they told Peaches on their return. "Just ad lib, and your folks won't even guess. All the churches were beautiful." I really, really, wish I was in Peach's living room when he showed his family the movie. "Now we come to Fatima," he boasted, and the screen displayed a beautiful fifty foot reel of a proud middle aged mother breast feeding her kid on a park bench. In Technicolor.

While in Antwerp some classmates and I encountered a group of kids playing basketball in one of the public squares. We joined them in a make-up game and when we left we made arrangements with them for a full game to be played later. When we reported back to the ship we requested that the captain allow us to bring some athletic wear ashore. We wanted to change into comfortable clothes for our scheduled event. The request was approved. Imagine our surprise a few days later when, upon reaching the site of our game, we found the square filled with spectators waving flags and cheering like it was the Olympics! Having no time clock we agreed to four quarters defined by whichever team reached 24, 50, 76 points, and 100 points would win the game. We started off great. We really did know how to play the game and our first quarter lead was something like 26-12. We led at the half by a slightly smaller margin, and by the third quarter those Belgian kids started to run us ragged, but we held a narrow lead. The end was as exciting as any game I've ever played. It couldn't have happened any better had it been planned, but it really wasn't. The score came down to 98-98 and then the Belgian team beat us fair and square. The crowd loved it. They were cheering, exhorting, and some even groaned over a botched play, but the square was alive. It was exciting; and to show their appreciation the local families split us up afterward and took each of us to their homes to clean up and have dinner with them. I remember that I was with the family of the man who owned the pharmacy. I forget who it was now, but one of my friends went to the home of the owner of the candy shop!! We changed back into our dress blues and said good-bye to some of the nicest people I'll remember. No, I didn't attend a "regular college," but I wouldn't trade my experiences for anywhere else. But it wasn't all fun and games. We worked, we studied, and then we played.

Life Aboard the Ship

To begin with, the living conditions on the training ship were Spartan. During my first cruise I found myself in a lower hold on D deck crammed in with about 40 other cadets. This converted cargo hold/dormitory had no windows, and we slept on pipe racks across which we spread a canvas netting that held our mattresses—a comfy addition about 2 inches thick. We covered these mattresses with mattress covers that we called "Fart Sacks" and washed these sacks clean each week. On nice days at sea selected dormitories would be called upon to air bedding and we would lug our mattresses up on deck to air out. I can't imagine a college kid living under those conditions today. But we did. Don't forget, that was 1958. Think a lot has changed since then?? The cadet corps was divided into three watch sections. The days alternated for each group. At sea one watch section would be assigned maintenance work. For the cadets on their first cruise that meant work involving the menial and mundane chipping, painting, and general labor that was always required to keep the ship shipshape. For the engineering cadets it was the same. They cleaned, oiled, and generally could be found bent over scrubbing the machinery or floor plates in the engine room. We deckies had our own particular chore from hell. Let me tell you about the "Holystone."

Many of the decks of the older ships were lined with planks of wood separated with thin seams of tar. They were subject to all kinds of weather, soot, and general dirt from the ordinary use of people walking over them all day. They had to be cleaned and spotless, so the devil invented the "Holystone". The holystone was a heavy abrasive cinder block. The holystoner was the unfortunate fellow whose task it was to kneel on the wooden deck and grasp the holystone with both hands and rub it back and forth until the deck was shaved clean. This was a painstaking and backbreaking job, as you can imagine, and even the most mild-mannered cadet would curse, swear, and generally could be heard muttering profanities that would make the other sailors blush. Hence the soubriquet "holystone" was born. Yes, I took my turn at it also. I took my turn at painting the vessel also. Sometimes much to my chagrin.

I took my turn with the paint brush under the tutelage of Lieut. George Reiser, a crusty curmudgeon if there ever was one. He was charged with developing our seamanship skills. Lt. Reiser was a perfectionist with a bad temper—a bad combination. I suffered his wrath one afternoon after botching the paint job he assigned me. "God dammit, son!" he exploded, "What did you cut that in with, a swab?" (Swab = mop; hence a sailor is sometimes referred to as a "swabie". Get it?) And then he really exploded on me. "If I ever see sloppy work like that from you again, I swear I'll shove your head up your ass and roll you down that gangway!" I will always remember my "college days."

And especially that little tyrant we all grew to know and love, George Reiser.

Cadets making their second cruise were generally in charge of the work gangs, and those making their third (last) cruise would be assigned as the division commanders responsible for various sections of the ship. That's how it was. "Mugs" (freshmen Midshipmen Under Guidance) would be assigned the lesser details and gradually work up to their last cruise when they would generally run the show under the watchful eyes of a ships officer. That's how we learned the age-old process of learning to take orders before we were entitled to give them. The system works. The cadet corps was divided into three watch sections. While one watch section was rotating on work detail, another section was on watch standing duties. Watches included lookouts, helmsmen, messengers, assistant navigators, navigators and cadet officers of the deck who controlled the activities on the Bridge. The third watch group in the rotation was assigned a day of classroom lectures and hands on practice. This was the routine every day at sea with the exception of weekends. On weekends at sea there was no work detail and classes were only a half day. Weekends were time for lounging on deck and watching the ocean glide by. We liked to listen to John play his accordion while Bill strummed his guitar. Sometimes during the afternoon we would duck under the showers that we created by running the fire sprinklers on the foredeck, and in the evening we watched movies on the large canvas screen that was tied between the king posts on the stern.

The schedule while in port was similar. Those scheduled for class had the whole day to go ashore, the work parties had a half day off, and, of course, the duty watch day wouldn't get ashore at all. Most port visits lasted five or six days so everyone got a chance to get ashore. The summer cruises always went to Europe. Each cruise would have us visiting five different ports of call and we looked forward to each of them. I told you about my Mug cruise. The two that followed took me to Plymouth, Oslo, Santander, Marseilles, Amsterdam, Naples, Rome, Barcelona, Dublin and an exotic port called Funchal in the Madeira Islands off the coast of Africa.

Funchal boasted a unique activity. It is a mountainous island and its steep slopes are paved with cobblestones. Tourists such as ourselves were taken to the top of the mountain where we jumped into two seat wicker baskets with wooden runners. These baskets were to be pulled down the mountainside by two guides whose job it was to scare the shit out of the occupants of the basket. They greased the wooden runners and pulled us down the mountain on rope leashes running as fast as they could over the well worn cobblestone roadway, and then braking on the corners, they whipped us around the turns before we would fly off the mountain. Halfway down there was a rest stop where the runners refreshed themselves, and riders tranquilized themselves, with some good Madeira wine. A sign was posted there in many languages which said "For easy work, one drink—for hard work, two drinks". Needless to say we plied our runners with all they could hold. A bottle of good Madeira wine cost 25 cents and we each loaded up with a few bottles and hooted and hollered all the rest of the way down the mountain. That night one of my friends had to have his stomach pumped but that's another story. There are probably more cruise stories to relate, but it's time to move on. Just remember that as a cadet I had a really good time even though I didn't get a tattoo. OK, one more story.

It was in Amsterdam that we all decided we would get our tattoos. When the fateful day arrived I found myself restricted to the ship because of excessive demerits. If you had more that five outstanding demerits you were restricted to the ship until they could be worked off at the rate of one hour's work per demerit. I think I had about 8 or 9 at the time, so I had to stay aboard to knock off at least 3or 4 demerits before I could get ashore. When I finally got to run up the street I looked high and low for my classmates. I never found them and was a little put out when they all returned with their "tats" and I didn't get one. Frank Wicks got an enormous windmill done on his arm and was known as "Windy Wicks" from then on. He eventually became a professor of engineering at a major college. I wonder if his students knew what he had up his sleeve! To this day I kind of wish I had found them and got myself marked for life. I said before, my college days were unique but I wouldn't trade them for anything. So far I've brought you to June 1961. Now, finally, after sixteen years of schooling I was 21 years old. I was in great shape. I stood six feet and a half inch tall. I weighed 195 pounds and now it was time to go to work.

Going to Sea

There wasn't any question about what I was going to do. I had a brand new Third Mate license and I was going to sea. Shortly after graduation I landed a job with the Gulf Oil Corporation. I reported to a ship called the *Gulfspray* while it was in a shipyard in Baltimore. I remember thinking what a pretty name it was until I discovered that all Gulf's ships of that 29,000 ton class were named after Gulf products. Gulfspray was the name of their insecticide! The "*Spray*" would be my new home for the next seven months. I signed on as Junior Third Mate. Junior Thirds did not stand a watch; they were assigned to day work with the Chief Mate and were usually given jobs that taught them about the workings of the ship and the process of cargo transfer. Just as well. At that time, while I knew navigation and general duties of standing a bridge watch at sea, I knew next to nothing about working on an oil tanker. I had to learn the various combinations of piping systems through which the loading and discharge were carried out.

It has been forty years now since I worked cargo on an oil tanker, but I assume the process is pretty much the same today as it was then. The tankers I sailed on were usually divided into four separate sections. Each section contained six or nine separate tanks and each tank was controlled by a system of valves that regulated the flow of cargo. When loading or discharging, the oil was piped through what is called the manifold to which the shore hoses are connected. Each hose connection on the manifold feeds a separate section of tanks. When cargo is loaded it passes from shore up through the manifold and down into the tanks through what are called “Drops”. When a cargo is discharged, the return valves from the tank to the pump room are opened. The pumps push the cargo through the pump room and back up to the manifold and ashore. (You have to make sure that the drop valves are closed or else all you that you would be doing would be circulating the oil.) That’s how the piping on a tanker is laid out—in a big circular system that can be controlled by opening and closing valves to individual tanks. There are two interesting things about the tanks. There are about 30 individual tanks in the ship. This serves two purposes. If the ship was not compartmentalized, a partially filled cargo hold would slosh around and eventually could capsize the ship. The second consideration is that the tanks had to be filled to just within inches of the deck plates to avoid the problem I just mentioned. When loading cargo I had to be extra careful when topping off a tank. It is not like a fill-up at your gas station: The cargo is pumped from ashore through hoses eight inches in diameter and, with only inches to spare, if I was not careful I’d have a spill. Did I ever have one? Yes, once. While loading cargo in Houston I let a tank run over. Not much, but a few gallons ran over the side. That was the old days, though. If I did it today I'd have the EPA all over me with fines and lawsuits, etc. As it was, we just cleaned it up and nothing was said except when the Captain heard of it. He said to me at dinner that night, "Now you are a tankerman."

Captain Mobley was a good captain with a sense of humor that he sometimes used to get a serious point across. The Mates always gathered on the bridge at 1000 each day for coffee. One day during coffee time, Capt. Mobley asked me who I thought was the dumbest man on the ship. I didn't know, but just to say something I said that maybe it was Ben, the ordinary seaman on the day watch, because he couldn't read or write. The Captain said no, it wasn't Ben's fault he was uneducated. A person could be smart even if formal education was lacking. "I mean" he said, "who on this vessel, does the most stupid dumb-ass things?" A rain squall had just come up and was wetting down the foredeck. The captain pointed to a pot of paint on the welldeck that was laying wide open to the rain. "I think the stupidest son-of-a-bitch on this ship is the one who left that can of paint standing in the rain". Then he looked at me. It was my paint pot.

I do have one story about my Junior Mate days. I sailed with a big, gruff Irishman named Sullivan who was Chief Mate. He nearly worked me to death. I lost twenty five pounds during the months I worked with him. I remember one trip when we were mucking out the tanks. (Muck being the sediment and scale residue on the bottom of the tanks) One gang was hauling muck with the steam hoist, there being no electric machinery on the deck of a tanker, and I was assigned to hoist my tanks with a block and tackle by hand. During lunch my hands filled with water blisters. When I went back to hauling after lunch the blisters broke. I left the tanks to go to the first aid cabinet to clean and wrap my blistered hands and the Mate caught me. "You'll have plenty of time to doctor yourself after four o'clock" he said to me. A few years later at an Irish hurling match in the Bronx I ran into him again. He gave me a giant bear hug and pulled me into the bar. He thrust a beer into my hand and slapped me on the back. "God Dammit, Junior, you and me together did more work than that whole damn crew!" Thanks, Mate.

The Merchant Marine has changed. It doesn't resemble at all what it was like when I graduated in 1961. When I graduated, there were fifty-six companies flying the American flag on their ships. Sea routes were predictable. If you wanted to ship to northern Europe you went via United States Lines. South America was served by Grace Lines. Robin and Farrell Lines sailed to Africa. There were tramp ships such those of Isbrandsen and Isthmian Lines whose ships traveled the world. These companies boasted of fleets ranging from 20 to 40 vessels. The U.S. Government took an active role in subsidizing the operation of the American flag fleets. This subsidy was necessary to counterbalance the cost of operation vis-a-vis foreign competition whose pay scales, insurance costs, shipyard, construction costs, and inspection requirements were less restrictive than for those operating under the U.S. flag. These subsidies were remnants of the thinking of World War Two, a time when a strong merchant fleet was necessary for national security. Liberty ships were being assembled in the thousands by "Rosie the Riveters" whose goal was to "bridge the sea with ships." Gradually these subsidies were phased out. Predictably the U.S. flag disappeared from the sea lanes of the world.

With all the ships and the whole world to travel, I stayed with Gulf Oil for my whole time going to sea. I don't jump around much, and if I am really honest with myself, I have to say I am more sedate than I usually let on. I enjoyed my time on the ships. In my reverie I occasionally picture myself a young man again and standing a quiet mid-watch leaning alone, but not lonely, out there on the wing of a ship's bridge with a hot coffee in my hand and watching the light of the foremast rolling gently up among the stars. Sometimes I imagine myself marveling again at the pristine waters of the Gulf Stream and the porpoises that I watched playing tag back and forth across the bow. (Baby porpoises are really cute. Their little black oblong shapes bob up and down trying to keep up with their elders. Not many people know this, but I'll pass the knowledge on to you. Baby porpoises are commonly referred to as "footballs" and that's exactly what they look like!) I rode out many storms, I dodged a few hurricanes, and I saw waterspouts. (tornados at sea) Often times I watched mesmerized as that great orange ball of sun slowly melted into a placid blue sea. And I welcomed the pink and golden hues that were reflected on low lying clouds heralding the fiery dawn of a new day. This was all soul food for my romantic appetite.

One of the myths that rose during my sailing days was that I was rich. I guess I was, because I didn't have a lot of bills to pay. But there was another reason I was able to throw the "Benjamins" around. Years ago Congress decided that seamen should be declared a protected species. For years seamen would be shanghaied—banged on the head in some waterfront dive only to wake up on a ship bound for Bumfuk or wherever. Sailors usually had no official residence other than the home address of the company that owned the ship they were sailing on. They weren't qualified for workman's comp and, if they got hurt on the job, well, it was too bad. In 1936 Congress passed the Jones Act which, among other things, declared the seaman to be a ward of the state. His right to sign on and sign off vessels was guaranteed. The length of his commitment to the ship was spelled out in "Ship's Articles." He would have a right to sue for "maintenance and cure" if injured while under these articles, and he would agree on a rate of pay. One of the peculiarities of this act was to stipulate that the seaman be paid in gold—and that was interpreted to mean he must be paid in cash. (A check would be no good to him if he had no bank account and he paid off in a strange port.) That was why my sisters told everyone I was rich. I had lots of the long green cash. The base rate of pay for a third mate in 1961 was $679 per month. The rate for a second mate was $754. My overtime rate was a whopping $2.96 per hour! I spent seven months on the *Gulfspray* before I was relieved and able to go home. I remember the day I got off the *Gulfspray*. The ship had docked at New Haven and I, not knowing that I was scheduled to be relieved there, went home for a few hours to see my family. For whatever reason, I made a pot of strong coffee at home that gave everyone heartburn. "That's how they make it on the ships," I said. When I received a call that my relief was at the ship, my father volunteered to drive me back to New Haven so I could sign off and pick up my gear. He burped all the way, and when I brought him aboard ship the Captain said, "Glad to meet you. How about some coffee? I just had a pot put on!" Dad burped all the way home. Seven months pay in cash was burning a hole in my pocket and when I walked in the door I threw some hundreds around! Brother John had a serious stash and a minor spending spree ensued. I bought the family's first color TV that year. I had never had so much money in my life, and I know my family never had that much either. I guess I did spent a lot, but I had a good time doing it. Like the time I accompanied PK to Europe to pick up the new TR 3 he bought for delivery in Scotland. PK Joyce was a classmate, and since he had just paid off his ship, a rust-bucket called the *Samuel L Fuller,* he was spending money just like I was.

Between Ships

PK and I flew to Dublin and spent a week in Ireland before flying to Glasgow to pick up the car. We played the part—we bought Scottish tweed jackets, tweed hats and even a tweed knee rug for our legs in that open white convertible with red seats. We sang "You take the high road and I'll take the low road" as we motored from pub to pub en route to Edinburgh. We drove down through England and stopped in Manchester where we somehow got tangled up with a British girls rowing team and were asked to finally leave the hotel because we were screwing up their training. We drove to Nottingham for ale and I started calling myself Little John. I am probably the only person you know who answered a call of nature in Sherwood Forest. Yes, ale does that to you, and both PK and I got caught short and had to stop to water a tree in the famous greenwood of Robin of Locksley. One of my more dubious claims to fame! Motoring on we arrived for a time in London. I don't remember anything of London, but I do remember the ride from there over to Dover. And, yes, the cliffs really are there, and they really are white. They stand out as symbolic buffers between Britain and the continent across the channel. PK and I took the ferry over to Boulogne and we promptly ditched the tweeds and bought berets and scarves and trench coats. We were en route to Paris, the City of Lights!

"Gay Paree" is my favorite city (after good old New York, of course). There are two incidents that stick out after all these years. We were living large, spending money like drunken sailors (which we were) at the Lido—the famous night club on the West Bank of the Seine. Terrific show; dancers covered with feather boas or covered with not much at all, served as eye candy for the wandering seamen. Would the messieurs like some wine? But of course!! When our waiter wanted to know if we preferred domestic or imported we naturally said imported—nothing but the best for us! How dumb did we look when the waiter, with a flourish, poured us a nice bottle of New York State Champagne. In Paris, no less. And double the price. PK let me drive the car occasionally. The Paris traffic is much like any traffic that terrorizes you, but I managed until I entered the circle around the Arch of Triumph and couldn't get out. Round and round I went, waiting for an opening to dash onto one of the boulevards. "Damn," I thought, "I really should get a drivers license!" It is more than 40 years since our escapades on the continent. PK, the best man at my wedding, and I are still friends.

When I started with Gulf Oil vacations were counted as eight days for each month you were on the ship. You had to have accumulated at least thirty days before you could put in for paid vacation. When I paid off the *Gulfspray* after seven months I had almost sixty days of paid leave coming. Later the system changed and the schedule was standardized at ninety days on and forty five days off, which suited me very well. I always managed to find something to do with my time off. My friend Thom Cartledge and I would work as Cargo Mates for Grace Lines to keep us in ready cash. Those were the days when the waterfront was hopping with longshoremen hauling slings of cargo from the ships' holds. That's all changed now—most ships are huge and mostly carry containers so that there is very little left of the romance of the cargo ships that filled the North River and Brooklyn piers up to the Fifties and Sixties. Thom and I would hang out at the Jersey Shore during the summer. Whenever our wallet was low we would head up to Pier 57 North River at Fifteenth Street and meet a Santa ship as it berthed. All Grace Line ships were named "Santa" something. "*Santa Elena*" or "*Santa Margarita*" are examples. Usually these ships would be in port about 36 hours or so, and our job as Cargo Mate was to work in the hold and make sure the cargo was loaded in the proper order. (first in-last out) We made sure that separators were in place that isolated one port from another, and we also saw to it that proper dunnage was in place which would hold the cargo in place when the ship would rock and roll during a storm. The hours were long but the pay was good—$3.50 an hour—and after staying aboard the ship for 30 hours we would head back to the shore with $100 in our Bermuda shorts. There were always the rumors of longshoremen pilfering booze from the hold but I never encountered anything like that. One cute story I was told was about a hatch boss who was a real pain in the ass. The longshoremen slapped an export tag on his car, loaded it aboard ship, and off the car sailed to La Guira without him.

Another job I had to keep busy was working as a laborer on a moving truck. A friend of mine from the Bronx worked as an estimator for a moving company. I would go "shape-up" there if I got bored or needed some extra bucks. You don't see shape-up lines anymore except at spots where immigrant labor congregates hoping to be picked up by some contractor for a day's work. I was in shape in those days and quickly learned the trick to balancing heavy lifts to make them manageable without giving myself a hernia. A highlight of that job came one day while I was moving an office downtown and realized I left my wallet home. Fortunately my sister Barbara worked in the area. Unfortunately though, she had just finished telling her friend Monica wonderful things about her rich brother. I approached them for a handout for lunch and train fare home. And Monica married Pappy Ward, my best friend, instead of me.

You would think that being away at sea three months at a time would dampen my urge to travel. But I did travel a lot during my vacations. I'm debating whether to relate this story, but what the hell; I'm not sure who will bother reading this stuff anyway, but I spent a week at a nude beach on the North Sea in Germany. When my mother found out she called me a "Dirty Slob." Anyway, here's the story. John, a friend from the Bronx, and I met up in Germany. We drove way up north to an island called Sylt. On this little isle there are three towns, and the center one, Kampen, sports a nude beach for the hearty souls who dare to challenge the wind and frigid water of the North Sea. Did we know the beach was there? Of course we did, that was the whole purpose of the trip! A couple adventures stand out in my memory of this semi-comical trip for two guys from the Bronx. One was the absurdity of watching the women bathers standing in freezing water up to their waist and beating the water in front of them with sticks to keep the jelly fish away from their boobs. Even more bizarre was when John, who was a fat Irishman, got so sunburned that he looked like a lobster after one day. The next morning I warned him not to go to the beach because he was so burned up. "The hell I won't! I didn't travel this far to miss this!" So John went to the beach with only a black raincoat covering his naked body. (You couldn't make this up)! To see the effect the north wind had on his unbuttoned coat as it flapped open and closed over his protruding red belly was the stuff of song and legend! Did I meet any ladies? That in itself is a tale worth telling.

I noticed this really pretty girl at our hotel. She had a very noticeable limp that was hard to miss, but she was really very attractive. Well, down the nude beach one afternoon comes a girl limping along on the sand. She was wearing nothing but the sunlight in her hair, but the first thing I recognized was her awkward gait. It was she! The girl from the hotel! I don't remember how it happened, but I found myself wearing nothing but a smile and standing alongside her in knee deep water on the strand. She spoke English, and eventually the topic shifted to the jagged scar that zippered down her shin. She told me it resulted from a serious ski injury and our conversation turned to our mutually favorite sport. (Skiing—as if you are thinking of something else!) Anyway, there we were, naked as jaybirds, talking about ski equipment, ski areas, and downhill racing. I told her about the Rockies in the American West and she spoke of skiing in the Alps. Talk about an incongruity. The funny part of the day came when I offered to buy her lunch. I ran up to the Kiosk near the boardwalk and ordered sausages, beers and whatever else I can't remember now. When I tried to pay I put my hand in my pocket for my wallet and all that happened was that I rubbed my bare ass. No clothes, therefore no pocket, therefore no wallet, therefore no cash. I had to run back for my clothes and get my money to pay the bill. People later asked me about the nude beach and I always said you get used to it.

Time to Reminisce

The T2 Tankers that I sailed on were the standard tankers built during World War Two. They were 529 feet long and held about 120,000 barrels of product. After the war most of them were "Jumboized," that is they were cut in half midships and another section was welded to the middle and the two ends were put back together again. These jumboized ships "worked" in a rough sea. I learned it was natural, ships were supposed to bend like that in times of stress otherwise they would break apart. I found it a bit disconcerting though when I first noticed the vessel hogging (the bow and stern bend lower than the mid-section) or sagging (when the ship sags in the middle) and the expansion joint in the catwalk opening and closing under my feet. Gulf Oil jumboized most of their ships and then re-named them after animals. I was 23 years old and Third Mate on the *GulfJaguar*. I could stand a sea watch and navigate by using a sextant to take sights of the sun or stars. I understood the radar. I could plot courses and calculate times and distances, and in port I could work cargo. Loading and discharging an oil tanker took care, and I spent much of my port watch time on deck checking the tanks. I remember once wondering about a big rust colored streak across the back of the winter work jacket that I used all the time while working on deck. One cold and snowy night somewhere up north I was out on deck opening and closing deck valves to control the discharge of cargo. I was too busy to go inside to get warm, so I found myself under the catwalk where the steam pipes lay the length of the ship. I was rubbing my shoulders back and forth across the steam pipes to keep warm. I had found the answer! The mysterious horizontal stain across the back of my coat came from hours of rubbing against the rust of those steam pipes! Not a big deal, I guess, but I just wanted to mention it because it illustrates the uniqueness of my work. People who keep warm in a heated office ashore never have to worry about horizontal rust stains on their suit.

The date was November 22, 1963. I had just come off the 0800 to 1200 watch and had finished lunch in the wardroom before reporting back to the bridge for docking stations. Everyone remembers exactly where they were and what they were doing that day. We were sailing up Aransas Pass which is famous for those Texas mosquitoes that are so big they can stand on their hind legs and screw a chicken. The ship was getting ready to dock at Corpus Christi when Sparks, (radio operators were all called "Sparks" because of the overhead fluorescent light that would flash on and off as the dots and dashes of Morse Code were keyed. Ships' carpenters were all appropriately called "Chips") barged onto the bridge and said the President had been shot while riding in a motorcade in Dallas. Sparks hooked a radio up to the bridge and we all listened in amazement to the account of the tragedy.

I was not a big fan of President John F. Kennedy. I realize that he was genuinely adored by the Irish as "One of their own", and because he was also the first who served in WW2, he was looked upon as their leader for a new generation. He loomed larger than life in the political arena. He spoke of Camelot Days; he was exuberant, and had, in Jackie, a young and glamorous wife. But I think he was mostly smoke and mirrors. Those were the days of the famous Cuba blockade. Navy destroyers patrolled the straits of Florida and the *Gulfjaguar* routinely met them on coastwise trips between Texas and New England. During one voyage trip a Navy ship acted erratically and passed close aboard to our ship. We wondered what the hell it was doing. The problem was solved a few weeks later when I received a letter from my college roommate asking why I ignored him when he was only trying to say hello. He was the watch officer on that navy ship! I gave Kennedy some credit for his handling of the Cuban Missile Crisis but it wasn't widely advertised that, as Russia removed from Cuba the missiles aimed at us, we removed our missiles from Turkey that were aimed at Russia. His vaunted face-down of the Russian bear was, in reality, a draw. I don't remember any legislation passed in his 1000 days in office that can be classified as anything special. "Camelot", the press called his administration. Kennedy had some good ideas and galvanized folks with his vision, but I believe it was the political acumen of his Vice President,

Lyndon Johnson, that managed to enact the civil rights laws and the social legislation that Kennedy is credited with. Kennedy's assassination was a shock to the nation. People were truly moved by the event. Even now, almost fifty years later, anyone will tell you exactly where they were and what they were doing on that fateful day. The event took on weird and mysterious portions because of what happened immediately after the assassination. The alleged killer, Lee Harvey Oswald, was arrested and accused of shooting the President from an upper window of a book depository as the presidential motorcade passed by. Shortly after his arrest Oswald was shot and died while in custody at the police station by a man named Jack Ruby who, in his turn, died shortly after from cancer. A commission headed by Chief Justice Earl Warren investigated the murder and the ensuing events. The Warren Commission then sealed its' report so it was never released to the public. To this day there are still theories about darkly whispered plots assigned to Kennedy's assassination but as far as I know no one really knows for sure what really transpired on that fateful day in November 1963.

I spent two years as third, and then as relief second mate, aboard the *GulfJaguar*. Altogether I sailed for a little more than three years before coming ashore to work for Shell Oil. I paid off my last ship, I believe it was the *GulfStag*, in Port Everglades, Florida. The following day found me lolling on the beach in Miami, and as I watched the "*Stag*" plying her way south without me, I said good-bye to my deep sea sailing days.

It was during my time sailing with Gulf that I found out a little about myself that wasn't very flattering. I'll mention it now just for the cause of honesty and to put a little more of myself into these pages. Meg was my girl friend through my last year at college and after I continued to sail. We were serious enough, as college sweethearts go, but somewhere along the way I decided I wanted to sail for a while and not be tied down. I sent her a letter out of the blue to tell her I wouldn't be seeing her again. I wrote it all dispassionately and logically and mailed it out to her. Later, with the wisdom of age, and after another girl gave me my comeuppance, I began to understand what a lousy thing I had done. A lot of water has passed under the keel since then, but if I ever see Meg again, the first thing I will do will be to tell her how sorry that I have always been for having written that lousy damn letter. She was special and she deserved a lot better. It was about that time I found out that I had a real problem dealing with situations that were uncomfortable to me. Oh yeah, I can write well enough. I can compose my thoughts and pretty much put on paper what I want to say, but to be able to face an uncomfortable situation and confront it verbally is very difficult for me. I shy away. I can't think on my feet fast enough to handle confrontation, and usually leave with the feeling that "I could have said", or, "I should have said", but I didn't. I don't know if it is fear or what, but I don't like this about me at all. In many cases I've hurt people, or hurt myself, for not standing up when the time came.

Working Ashore

To this day I sympathize with the young folk who are just out of college or just breaking into the job market. Where does one start? How do you successfully interview? And, really, who is so definite on knowing what it is, exactly, that they want to do? I found myself in that situation when I came ashore. Second Mate on an oil tanker? Great! Now tell me what you can do for my company. Interviews were difficult and I wasn't trained for them. I did get lucky though. A classmate of mine, Bob Brand, told me about a job opportunity with Shell Oil, the company he was working for. I was hired as a supply programming analyst with a starting salary of $5200 per year. That was pretty much the average starting salary in the mid-Sixties, so I bought a few suits and ties and began my new shore-side work at 30 Rockefeller Center where the famous tree awes tourists, young and old alike, each Yuletide Season in New York City.

Actually I was well placed. The work was pretty much in line with my transportation degree from the Maritime College and I took to it right away. Our supply transportation department would receive the projected estimates that had been worked up by the sales people. We would allocate these sales estimates to particular refining areas, and then send these projections up to the manufacturing department. They would return with what were called manufacturing estimates detailing just how much of any particular product could be processed by each refinery. Once we had the manufacturing estimates our work could begin. Our department analyzed the sales estimates and compared them to the manufacturing capabilities. We would then set up a supply and distribution pattern for our area. My department was responsible for the West Coast. We had three refineries in our area—one was in Anacortes, Washington. A typical problem would be that Anacortes would fall short of heating oil capacity in the winter while the southern refineries would be short of gasoline production in the summer. We had to be creative. By manipulating production and transportation patterns we could insure the availability of these products anywhere on demand. This could be done by re-working refinery schedules or by arranging trades with other companies to insure the continuity of supply. (For example, a trade could be made with another company in southern California. We would send them our extra gasoline production from Anacortes during the summer, and they, in turn, would send their excess fuel oil production to our northerly locations in the winter.)

I worked at a desk, punching numbers into a calculator and recording them on a lined ledger with a sharpened pencil. It's hard to believe work was done that way, but companies were only starting to dip their corporate toes into the world of information technology. We did have two fellows who knew computers but they worked in parallel with us because no one really was sure the computer could be trusted or tamed to produce usable knowledge. There were no PC's in the Sixties. All computer input was entered with boxes and boxes of cards that had been punched by a key board before they could be read into the main frame processing unit. These big processing units took up enough space that they were located generally in special air conditioned rooms of their own. In my case they were located way down in the basement of the building at 30 Rockefeller Plaza. All I knew was that box after box of punched cards would disappear into the great maw of the computer and info would come out on folded computer paper sheets. If the cards were key punched wrong, or if the input was unreliable, your information would be useless because the computer couldn't tell bad input from good. Hence was coined the phrase "Garbage in-Garbage out." The whole concept of computers was new. I was asked at that time if I wanted to attend special computer classes to learn this new way of doing information gathering. I could have literally gotten into this world at the bottom floor, at the very beginning of the greatest technological phenomenon of our age. I went to a few classes but never got too interested so I dropped out. Who knew? The world was about to change and I didn't recognize it.

Part of the fun of writing this story is to relate certain events that occurred and where I was at the time. New York City suffered the Great Blackout in 1965. Shortly after 5 P.M. all things electrical stopped. The Northeast went black from the Canadian border down through the New England States all the way to New York City. The greatest blackout in history had begun. I don't really understand what happened, but apparently a transmission line from Niagara Falls to New York failed. The excess power that should have gone to New York was then diverted to other New England state with the result that these other lines got overloaded and had to shut down. New York City itself did not have enough emergency generator capacity to cover the massive requirement needed to keep the city operational without burning up so they were shut down also. The time of the event was just as people were quitting work for the day at 5:15 P.M. Fortunately I hadn't left the office yet. Not so fortunate were those who got stuck in elevators around the city. I remember being part of a human chain all holding hands and groping our way down 35 flights of stairs to the darkened street below. The Cold War was on in those years, and the secretary holding my hand in the stairwell kept asking if I thought the Russians were doing this and wondering aloud if we were being attacked. Later the newspaper headlines would read that when the lights went out in the city the New Yorkers shone. It was true. A holiday festive air permeated the city. My sister Barbara managed to get out of the subway train she was stuck in by climbing through an exit manhole to the street above. Black hands reached down to pull her up as she surfaced in Harlem. People were dancing and partying around the streets and my sister says she moved and grooved with a bunch of people she never expected to move and groove with all through the night. It was a weird sight to see well dressed men and women at about 3 A.M. climbing down the manholes in the street. They had partied enough and were returning to their commuter train to try and find a seat so they could sleep while waiting for power to be restored! My friends and I partied all night by bar-hopping and looking for girls to pick up in the candlelight of our favorite watering holes. It was surreal; the only light to be seen was beamed from the headlights as cars threaded their way through the crowded city streets which were made even more adventurous because of the lack of traffic lights. I was dozing in the lobby of 30 Rockefeller Plaza when the lights struggled back on around five in the morning. When the elevators went back into service early in the morning we rode back up to the 35th floor and told the manager we were going home to get some sleep!

My social life was stabilizing around that time. Remember, all through my college years and my sailing days my time was restricted. I couldn't leave the college except on weekends, and naturally I couldn't just leave the ship whenever I wanted without running the risk of getting awfully wet. But now that I was working ashore and living at home again I was able to meet friends, plan trips, and attend Happy Hours on Friday night whenever I wanted. As a matter of fact I was a charter member of the Poets Society at work. Everyone thought how sophisticated we were to entertain interests in poetry and the arts. We proudly wore our Poets button on suit lapels each Friday. Very few people except the "in crowd" knew that our club had nothing to do with following the pursuits of a higher nature. The Poets pin we sported was a classy acronym for "Piss on Everybody—Tomorrow's Saturday", and off we'd go pursuing whatever sybaritic opportunities availed themselves over the weekend. I didn't have any real steady girlfriends during those wild times; I was happy going on trips to the Jersey shore during the Summer and ski trips to Vermont during the Winter. I played a lot, and sad to say, also spent most of the money I had saved from my days at sea. There may have been a reason for my recklessness but I'm not sure, even to this day. Well, there was a girl that I really cared a lot about. Trouble was I was never able to feel sure that my feelings were reciprocated. It was on again-off again stuff and we just never seemed to get our act together. Finally when I returned from one of my three month rotations at sea I heard she was engaged to someone else. It was kind of hard to take, and I guess it took me a long time to feel like committing to another relationship. But, for whatever reason, I busied myself doing things that were pretty non-productive like making the bar scene in Manhattan or just hanging out with my neighborhood friends in the Parkview Tavern on Jerome Avenue.

The Parkview probably deserves a story of its own because I spent so much of my time there. It wasn't that I drank too much; it was just where the neighborhood socialized and where friends met. Kind of the last of the neighborhood Irish bars where I would meet my friends and socialize with their fathers, too. These were the immigrant folks, the older people from the "Auld Country." We have all have gotten married and moved away now but I remember my friends and characters from the bar. The bar was in the shadow of the Lexington Ave. El (for elevated) and I still recall many of my friends' fathers who were motormen for the City Transit System. There were stories about how a train would pull out of the Kingsbridge Road station and come to a stop above the Parkview. The train whistle would blow and a bucket would be lowered to the street. One of the Good Samaritans from the bar would go out and put a beer into the bucket, watch it being pulled up, and then with a little toot the train would proceed on its way. Honestly, that was way before my time. No one would have gotten away with that in the Sixties, but the old timers would tell stories of the old days and, knowing them, I believe them.

Lord knows there were characters there in that old saloon. Old Jimmy the sailor who would get drunk and insist on calling a cab to get him home—even though he lived across the street. The quiet Mr. Clancy who would sit at the end of the bar and smoke those "Guinea Stinkers"—Di Nabolis I think they were called—and smell up the bar. And Slats, who would advertise the condition he was in anytime he broke into his loud rendition of "The Grass It Grows Greener Round BallyJamesDuff." Old and young would stop there before and after wakes at the funeral parlor down the street to buy Mass Cards from the bartender who would be sure to keep the "church money" in a cigar box separate from the nasty profits from alcohol. Beer was 15 cents a glass and you would get a buy back every third round. Nobody even heard of the fancy drinks that permeate the market today, and even if they did, our drinking class would turn our noses up on them. A shot and a beer was good enough for us. And a shot of booze sold for about 50 cents.

We had a social club there at the Parkview. We would attend dances and parties and organize neighborhood activities. One of my favorite events was taking out kids from Saint Catherine's Home, I think it was called. They weren't orphaned; they were kids who had been placed or taken there because their parents had given them up. It was really heartbreaking to see how they attached themselves to us—a rowdy but good hearted group of guys from a bar in the Bronx. The first time we organized the outing we went out to the picnic grounds the day before and cached a few cases of beer behind a big tree at the end of the field. We would sneak away singly or in pairs to the cache all day long and we thought we were pretty clever. That was until we were arranging the outing the following year. That's when Sister Superior told us "It's OK boys, you don't have to hide your beer behind the tree this year!"

I kind of miss those days. It was a time when a neighborhood bonded. There was tradition there, young folks listened and the old folks passed down their history and heritage there. That time is gone for us now. Maybe new immigrant groups are living it. But for us it is lost, gone with our diaspora to the suburbs and our private homes and manicured lawns. But I'd sure like to hear those Irish brogues and songs one more time. Only at New Years now do we sing "Auld Lang Syne". No one knows the meaning of it anymore, but it is old Scottish from Robert Burns. It translates to "The old long ago." If I drank, which I don't do anymore, I'd drink a cup for the old times, and the people gone by.

Work at Shell Oil became pretty routine for me. I would get up, ride the subway downtown and work in the office. I realized early on that I didn't have the temperament or the interest that would attract a lot of management attention. I wasn't corporate savvy but I did realize that I could have a nice, comfortable, safe career with Shell. Kind of like a big womb. I would never be too hot, or never too cold, or never too poor, or never too rich, and never really too excited about giving my life to a corporation that wouldn't know much about me at all. I suppose that I was already too used to being a somebody on a ship. One day an invoice arrived at my desk showing that we had chartered the *Gulfspray*, for a product exchange with Gulf Oil. I checked the numbers and OK'd it and sent it on to my supervisor. The problem arose when his supervisor wanted to know who OK'd it and why it wasn't checked through the marine department for accuracy. I explained that I believed it was valid because the numbers jived with what I knew about the capacity of a vessel. I knew the ship, knew the type of cargo it normally carried, and I had personally turned every valve to load or discharge the damn thing, so I should damn well know what I was talking about. Well, it wasn't enough. The manager called the marine department at Gulf Oil and, after a lengthy conversation, they agreed to meet over lunch to talk about it. Guess who wasn't even invited? That's right, moi. My corporate future was shaky and was decided a few months later by a tragedy. The manager who was so insistent about knowing everything about the Gulf Oil invoice suffered a heart attack and died in his office at work. He was probably in his late forties I would guess. But as awful as that was, and I truly was saddened by his passing, the most poignant effect on me was that his office was just kati-cornered from mine and it remained vacant for months after. I could see his empty chair. I wondered how important he could have been to this corporate behemoth if the job he gave so much to wasn't even filled months later. And, by transference, how important was the work I was doing there either? I started thinking about the boats again. The year was 1965 and I was heading for Puerto Rico.

Porto Rico Lighterage Co.

The long first day, Harry and Lowell, Sammy and the flying fish, Going hungry, The wrong date, Raul and son, Reminisce

LAS AVENTURAS EN PUERTO RICO

I knew that I wasn't cut out for corporate work. My two years at Shell Oil taught me that. However, the only other experience I had was sailing on ships, and I didn't want to spend a life at sea being away for months at a time either. Tug boats seemed to offer a nice compromise. I met with Brian McAllister who was a graduate of the Maritime College a few years ahead of me, and one of the owners of the McAllister Towing Company in New York. Brian advised me that it was very difficult to come to work on the New York boats because the union would not accept new members who hadn't a promise of a job in the industry, and I couldn't be offered a job in New York without experience. He put me in contact with a classmate of his who was general manager of the Lighterage Company in San Juan. Brian thought it best for me to take that job, and then with a few years boating experience, re-apply with McAllister in New York. I left for San Juan in 1965 in what proved to be a pivotal move in my career. I realized that by going back on the boats I would find it difficult to change my mind and try to resume future employment ashore. So off I went, age 26, to a land of tropical breezes and palm trees and new adventures that I hadn't even considered a few years earlier.

Along life's way we occasionally meet people who leave marked impressions on us. Harry and Lowell were two of those people. They were both tugboat captains for the Porto Rico Lighterage Company of San Juan, the company I went to work for after leaving the more civilized and sedate world of corporate America. I'll tell you about them in a minute, but first let me start by relating a bit about how I got the job and my first impressions of the work I was to follow for the next 25 years.

The Long First Day

My first day at work was memorable. When I landed in San Juan, I found a guest house and stayed for the night. In the morning I told the owner that I was going to work, and asked him if I could just leave some of my things until I could get settled with a place of my own. When I arrived at Pier #10, I found all the tugs idle except for the *Catano*. (All their boats were named after sections of Puerto Rico. *El Morro, Fajardo,* and *Cabo Rojo* were some examples. (Catano is a borough of San Juan) When I inquired as to why the boat I was assigned to was the only one looking really busy I was informed that it was due to sail for New Orleans in two hours! I had no idea what was going on. Before I knew it, the *Catano* was tied up between two molasses barges and was heading out to sea. Before the tug reached the famous El Morro fortress at the mouth of the harbor the captain slowed the tug, tooted some whistles, and I watched the barges separate from the tug and glide into their place at the end of our tow line 1200 ft. behind us. It was like magic—I had no idea what had happened. I just knew that, for better or for worse, I was on my way to New Orleans. And it was 1500 miles away and I was on a boat with a crew I knew nothing about. The *Catano* was a stock-built 1500 HP twin screw diesel tug, 95 feet long, with a freeboard (the distance from the uppermost continuous deck to the water) of about three feet. Freeboard was the consideration that intrigued me the most. Prior to this trip I was used to looking at the ocean from the deck of a large ship, not up close and personal as I was now, and when I saw the ocean waves rolling over the rails back aft I wasn't sure if this was going to be a good idea or not! The tug made walking speed. We towed those two barges at an average speed of about 4 knots and it wasn't until sixteen days later that I planted my sea legs on Terra Firma again. The crew proved amiable, the captain was crotchety, and Luis, the cook, was good. I settled in for the ride and renewed my navigation skills as I struggled to take sightings on evening and morning stars to fix our position on the trackless main.

I guess there is a lot you won't know about navigation and towing vessels so this might be a good spot to write a little about that. First of all, the most efficient way for a tug and barge to operate is as one unit with the tug pushing the barge ahead. However, before the advent of what are now called "articulated units," tugs could not push barges in the open sea due to the undulating wave action and resulting stress on the towing lines. In other words, the ropes would break. A barge had to be towed astern in the ocean. The towing line had to be of sufficient length to absorb the undulating action of the waves. It also had to be elastic enough to insure that it wouldn't part when seas got rough. It was this whole procedure of transferring the barges from alongside the tug to finally arriving in this towing position that awed me that first day. In those days the standard hawser (the official name of the tow line) was 1200 feet of 8 inch (circumference) nylon rope. The intermediate hawser between the two barges was about 800 feet. Today hawser work is becoming rare as the tows are getting larger, and the rope is being replaced by a heavy towing wire secured around a drum. Once we were hooked up and our two molasses barges were following like puppy dogs, there was nothing else to do but keep tugging all the way to New Orleans.

Navigating on a tug at sea was a challenge. We didn't have anything like the satellite positioning system in use have today. We used a sextant to navigate with the sun and stars. A sextant is a precision instrument used to measure the exact altitude of a celestial body above the horizon. The frame of the sextant holds a moveable arm that holds a mirror. The end of that arm moves along a calibrated arc that is one sixth of a circle (hence, "sextant"). The other end of the arm is a mirror to reflect the image of the body you are shooting. The frame of the sextant holds a reflecting mirror that is half mirror and half clear glass divided vertically. The idea is to reflect the sun, or whatever you are shooting, into the mirror on the frame of the sextant. Because half of the frame is clear glass you manipulate the moveable arc until the sun's reflection in the mirror is just touching the horizon visible through the clear glass. The arc of the sextant then shows the exact altitude of the object above the horizon. When the navigator knows the altitude of a given object at any exact given time, he can work out a spherical trigonometric equation which will result in one leg of a celestial triangle that can be superimposed on a navigation chart. That leg is called a line of position. The observer is located along this line. When taking sightings on two or more stars the result is two or more lines of position—and where they intersect is where you are. Simple!! The idea though is to shoot three or four lines and see where they intersect. This would eliminate the use of a bad sight which would become obvious if a line didn't meet near the others. By the way, not to get too technical, there is a phenomenon in navigation that allows us to discern latitude by the altitude of the sun. The altitude of the sun at its zenith is equal to the latitude of the observer. By noting the altitude of the sun when it reached its highest point in the sky, the early explorers like Columbus would know their latitude. Also, the altitude of Polaris, the North Star, is always within one degree to the latitude of the observer. If one stood at 90 degrees latitude at the North Pole the North Star would be directly overhead. If you stood on the equator, the North Star would be just touching your horizon. Here in New York the Pole Star can be found at an altitude of approximately 45 degrees above the horizon.

Now back to the tug. I had been a few years out of practice using my sextant and the excessive rolling and pitching of a tugboat compared to the sway of a ship made it difficult to control the mirror image on the visual horizon. My first few sightings were all over the place, but I finally got good at it again. Each evening the captain and I would take stars. Each evening we worked out positions that were almost exactly 2 miles apart—not excessive when you consider the vast ocean—and each evening the captain would erase my position and use his. And each evening I got a little pissed off because, who said his position was the correct one? The captain said, that's who! Tom Cuyler was a crusty old guy who really knew his stuff. He had been sailing since he was 13 and he was in his sixties when I was with him. I was with him when he received the news that his brother, "Kiki" Cuyler, was elected to the Baseball Hall of Fame in Cooperstown. I got all excited and said that he should go up there to the ceremony but he said he had no interest in baseball, hadn't seen his brother for years before he died, and he was happy where he was in the Caribbean. I doubt if Capt. Cuyler ever flew in an airplane. As I said, he was a crusty old salt. He and I stood watches of six hours each. I took the midnight to 0600 and noon to 1800 and we alternated that way to New Orleans.

In New Orleans I went up the street alone when we had some time between the discharging and loading of the barges. I had heard of Bourbon Street, so that's where I headed. I found a bar called "Pat O'Brian's." It looked lively enough. They sold specialty drinks called "Hurricanes" in a hurricane glass with the bar's name on them. They were advertised to be potent but I didn't believe it. I figured I was a bar savvy guy from the Bronx and I didn't plan to be fooled by any tourist drink! And needless to say, pride went before the fall. I remember three things about that night. The first was when I hooked up with a family who was seeing their daughter off into the convent. The more I drank the more I remember trying to talk her out of it while being totally oblivious to the looks of consternation that her parents were throwing at me. They appeared relieved when I finally left their party to go to the men's room. Only I didn't go to the men's room. For some inexplicable reason I decided to forgo the long line to the Loo and found a place to pee behind some bushes in the courtyard. Not wanting to lose my Hurricane, I bent over to place it on the ground behind the bush and then I promptly kept right on going until the top of my head hit the dirt and my butt was still sticking up in the air. "This can't be happening" I thought. "These drinks are only for tourists." Oh, yeah?? Well, after surveying this ridiculous situation for a while, I rolled over on my hands and knees and struggled manfully to rise from the bushes. I decided then that it was time to vacate the premises before I made a complete ass out of myself, not realizing I had done so already. But I wasn't done yet. I hailed a cab. When I got in I discovered that my tongue had somehow morphed into a hockey puck and I couldn't tell the driver where I wanted to go. I got out of his cab and walked the streets until I was in some kind of condition to report back to the tug. Tourist drinks my ass.

If I was expecting a quick trip back I was mistaken. After the molasses was pumped out we took the barges to a dock across the river in Gretna, and there they were steam-cleaned and readied for another load. We loaded the barges with manteca (lard), and proceeded with our newly loaded tow back down the Mississippi to the Gulf and reversed course back to San Juan. My first day at work on the tug boats lasted 45 days! When I finally got back to the guest house the owner was shocked. "Jesu Cris!" he exclaimed, "I thought you was dead!"

My second trip after returning from New Orleans took me to St. Croix, Virgin Islands. This time it was a molasses barge to the Cruzan Rum Distillery in Fredericksted. To show their appreciation the distillery gave us a case of rum to share among ourselves. The rum at that time sold for 95 cents a bottle. "Damn!" I thought, "What a great job this is!!"

I soon learned the routine followed by all the boats in the fleet. When a boat returned from that long trip to "NOLA" (as we called it), it would generally go to the bottom of the harbor list and only be called upon if more than two or three boats would be required at the same time for what was primarily ship docking or sailing duties. This happened rarely, so the returning crew would have a few days rest. Each week a boat would move up the ladder and be more responsible for ship movements until the fourth week when it was likely that they would be placed on the run over to the Dominican Republic. That week was followed by the shorter overnight runs we took to St. Thomas and to St. Croix. Charlotte Amalie is only 78 nautical miles from San Juan, and Christiansted, the port city of St. Croix, only a bit longer at 96 miles. We towed container barges to these islands. The large ships that docked at San Juan's container port routinely off loaded hundreds of these containers. The Virgin Island ports only had facilities to handle a small percentage of these boxes so we would tow only the required ones on specially designed barges to these ports. The routine would continue until it was our turn for the NOLA trip again.

Harry and Lowell

Harry and Lowell were both captains with years of tugboat experience behind them. During my time in harbor service I would ride with either of them and they would share their knowledge of ship-handling with tugs with me. Harry wrote and published a book on precisely that same topic later in his career. As a matter of fact he wrote and published four books covering topics such as marine salvage, towing, and ship handling. While in the harbor, the captains and mates would alternate day on and day off. Usually I reported for work every day because there was so much that was new to me about this business that I needed all the time I could get. Harry and Lowell kind of adopted me and I spent most of my time breaking in with them. At lunch time we would wander across the street from Pier #10 and drink some Corona beer in Colacho's Merchant Marine Bar. Colacho himself was a big, round, jovial kind of guy with a gold tooth and a big hairy chest partly hidden by a sleeveless tee shirt. His chest was always adorned with one of the biggest golden religious medal I had ever seen. We socialized at Colacho's. Sitting around one of the tables with our liquid lunch of cerveza Corona, Harry would usually expound on some of the finer points of towing, but once in a while I would hear stories of the time when he was a boxer in the Washington D.C. area. Lowell was born in Panama and spent his youth in such exotic pursuits as an army paratrooper, Philippine guerrilla fighter, and water skiing instructor who couldn't water ski well at all. You can imagine the stories that flowed from his experiences. Harry, Lowell, and I bonded well. I found that I was with people I liked in an atmosphere I was comfortable with. I never regretted going back to the boats. We established a respect and friendship that endured 40 years until, at their ripe old ages, Lowell and Harry crossed the bar.

I was there in San Juan when Lowell's wife, Bobbie, held a birthday party for him. I remember we watched in amused amazement as the birthday boy proceeded to get smashed and cried all night because he had achieved the ripe old age of 40 years! Harry was a few years older than Lowell. I was always the kid. We called ourselves T T T's. (It was Harry's term) for Typical Tropical Tramps and that's kind of what we were. Times were simpler in the days of my Caribbean sojourn. There were fewer pressures in those days. I guess you could say we all had a bit of adventurer in us, and we operated under parameters that would be frowned upon today.

You may have noticed my use of the term "crossing the bar." Every ship's log records two statistics regarding the duration of a voyage. Bar to bar, and dock to dock. The latter entry records the time a ship leaves the dock to the time that it ties up at the next one. Bar to bar records the sailing time on the open sea. The entrance to every port is always marked by a "sea buoy" that defines the official entrance to the port. The entrance is referred to as the bar (nothing to do with drinking). As a vessel enters or leaves port it crosses the bar. A mariner, when he dies, leaves his home port on earth and "crosses the bar" on his outbound journey for the last time. He will not return.

Sammy and the Flying Fish

One sunny afternoon I was heading out to the beach on my day off. I was dressed only in a bathing suit, T shirt, and sandals when I was intercepted by a car that pulled up to me and made a screeching halt. "Johnny. Get in! We gotta go out and tow a ship back here." "Tell them you can't find me", I replied. "No! You gotta come! Paul is coming, and we got Tomas and Luis, and Sammy is coming too. You gotta come!" So off I went down to the dock and sailed 500 miles north of San Juan to locate the disabled ship and tow it back to San Juan. All of us, with the exception of Paul, and maybe Sammy, were still in our twenties. Paul, the captain, was about 36 years old. The whole business took ten days, and all I had to wear was the bathing suit and T shirt that I left home with. I took sea-showers by standing up in the bow and letting the ocean's salty spray wash me clean. For fun I would lay across the rubber fenders that encased the bow and try to spank the porpoises playing in the waves below me. By the way, I had a book with me on that trip and I'm happy to report that I averaged reading 100 pages a day. By the time the trip was over, and the disabled vessel was safely berthed in San Juan, I had finished *Gone with the Wind.* I enjoyed it.

I was just thinking about the porpoises again. They weren't the only aquatic wildlife I would encounter on these trips. Flying fish abounded, and frequently the crew would scout the decks in the morning to pick up the flying fish that had landed there during the night. These would be fried up for breakfast but I never took even a nibble. That was a little too far from my Bronx-Irish palette to venture. Flying fish are fun to watch. They are about 6 or 8 inches long and they don't really fly, but they propel themselves from the crest of a rolling swell and, with their gills out like wings, they skim a few feet above the water quite some distance until they smack the next swell head on and disappear from view. Sometime they would smack into the side of our tug and fall to the deck. One time a fish flew right into Sammy's head as he was drifting and dreaming while lolling on a deck chair near the engine room door. It stunned and shocked him so badly that he was knocked off his chair. The funny thing was that Sammy was a former championship body-builder, and to watch him get knocked on his ass by a fish why, that was the stuff of song and legend. Out in the middle of the ocean you find your entertainment where you can!

We trolled for fish anytime when we were at sea with a tow. Since we usually towed a loaded barge at around 7 knots (Remind me to tell you what a "knot" is) it was easy for any hungry fish to attack the white rag we had wrapped around a fish hook. We tried to average a fish a day but always fell a bit short—maybe 6 or 7 fish for a 10 day trip. Barracudas were our frequent victims but we tossed them back because we were worried about mercury poisoning. Wahoos were plentiful, but the ones I preferred to snare were the dorado. A dorado is a dolphin (the fish kind, not the porpoise kind) and today the restaurants embellish it with the fancy name of Mahi-Mahi. I guess that is so the uneducated gastronomic dilettantes would not think they were dining on Flipper or Free Willy. The dorado is a beautiful fish. When freshly caught it shines with iridescent colors of green, blue, and gold. Sadly, the colors fade quickly when the fish dies. I enjoyed many dolphin steaks while sailing in the Caribbean and never had to pay for any of them!

I remember a trick we played on Boggiano, the assistant engineer. We had a simple but effective method of knowing if we had a fish on our line. We would lash a boat hook to the quarter bitts of the tug and run the trolling line from the end of the boat hook. That way the line wouldn't get caught in the propeller when it was streamed. We would tie a separate piece of 21 thread line (about half inch diameter) between the trolling line and the boat hook. This small intermediate line had a slip knot with a large loop tied into it. The reason for this ingenious, but primitive, device was this: the hook and bait (usually just a white rag) were not heavy enough to pull the loop closed, but it would close if we were pulling the weight of a large fish. Well, one afternoon Boggiano noticed the slip knot was tightened and he started pulling in the line. It was heavy and he yelled for help. Then he yelled to slow the boat down. Then when no one came to help him he started to swear and strain and pull the line harder. He sweated and called all the crew horrible names and swore we would get none of his fish! No one helped him until his "fish" was almost pulled up to the boat. Then we relieved the exhausted engineer and pulled up the bucket we had tied to the end of the line when he wasn't looking. He was really pissed. His face got beet red and he took off into his room and we didn't see him for hours afterward. When he came finally emerged he really wasn't over it, and he stayed a little mad for a few days. We all felt a little bad and never did the bucket trick again.

Going Hungry

One of my more interesting adventures in the Caribbean was the time we were charted out to the Reynolds Metals Co. to tow bauxite ore from Guyana on the northeast coast of South America to a deep-water loading port in Venezuela. Bauxite is the ore used to make aluminum. The problem was the continental shelf shoals up about 50 miles from the Guyanese Coast, and a normal draft sea-going vessel would go aground before reaching port. Tugs were used to tow shallow draft barges of bauxite ore to the Gulf of Paria where there was a Venezuelan deep water port for sea-going vessels to load. One time early in the trip we were told there was no berth available for us so we would have to anchor offshore for a while. Capt. Cuyler dispatched Luis Ramos and me to take the small motor boat we carried and get on the barge and wait for his signal to drop the anchor. When we climbed up the side of the barge I said to Luis, "What's the signal?" Luis had no idea and neither did I!! When Capt. Cuyler flashed his searchlight from the tug I thought, "That's it!" and I let the anchor go. Then we heard it from about 500 feet away. "Stuupid Bastaaad!" I turned and said to Luis . . . I guess that wasn't the signal . . .

We shuttled down there for about four months. We purchased our supplies, fuel, and food while docked in Puerto de Hierro, Venezuela, because it was a large port and supplies were available. We avoided buying anything in the poorer ports of Guyana. Well, one day while we were en route to Guyana we were notified that the trip would be our last. The Reynolds tugs were back from repairs and overhaul and were to take over our run. The problem arose when we remembered that we planned to take provisions aboard during our next stop in Puerto de Hierro, and now we weren't going there. We wouldn't buy in Guyana, so we sailed for San Juan alarmingly light on food. That's when I learned some comparatives in Spanish. At first Luis the cook called the situation "Pobre" (poor) then a few days later it was up to "Mala" (bad) and finally "Critica" (critical) before we finally ran out altogether. That's when we fished for our dinner. Fish and cornmeal and water did the trick for a few more days until we arrived at out home port of San Juan. But you know what? I've said it many times before: I wouldn't trade those adventures for anything. The adventures suited me, and to my way of thinking sure beat the ordinary work-a-day at the office. Possibly I short-changed my abilities. Possibly I could have achieved success in a corporate environment. But I really believed—and still do—that it wouldn't be me. I liked the boats.

The Wrong Date

I liked the time a yacht that was owned by the Bank of Peru was tied up for overhaul at the pier next to us. When the yacht was ready for her shake-down cruise the captain asked me if I wanted to take a ride with them over to St. John's. The deal was sealed when I asked him if I could contact a girl I was dating in New York to see if she could join me. The "Tomato" (that was Margaret's nickname) flew down to San Juan and off we sailed on an idyllic voyage to the Virgin Islands. This was the life! We were gliding silently under full sail. A full Caribbean moon was casting its reflection on the placid sea. This was a night for romance. What could go wrong? We dropped anchor in Caneel Bay and everyone attacked the giant punch bowl that held a position of prominence on the deck amidships. Around midnight the party was getting a little out of hand; clothes started to come off and it was time for a little drunken skinny dipping in the moonlight. "Be right back," the Tomato said. She disappeared below decks and then surfaced almost nude—except for a giant orange life preserver that covered her from shoulder to knee (almost). "What the hell are you doing?" I asked. "I can't swim," she said. What kind of luck is that? This girl had a spectacular set of big bazooms and I couldn't even get a peek! Millions of girls to date in New York and I picked one that couldn't swim.

Raul and Son

Big Raul and Raulito, his son, were inseparable. Very close. Raulito was his father's deck hand before he applied for a license of his own to go into the pilot house as Mate. Unfortunately he was turned down due to poor vision. He tried to enlist in the Coast Guard, then the

Navy, and finally the Air Force with the same result. Poor Vision. But not the Army! The Vietnam War was raging and the army needed all the men they could get. So, off Raulito went to war. At his going away party we all joked and told him to "choot" at anything he heard because we knew he couldn't see "chit." When Raulito left for the army Big Raul approached me about going to work with him on the tug boats in the Mekong Delta of Viet Nam. We could make a lot of money—a ton of it—and he would be near to where Raulito was. I was single and adventurous, and I thought it might be a good idea. I had never been to that part of the world, and up to that time the Vietnam situation hadn't yet risen to the disaster it became for the U.S. The story may have become interesting but it never materialized. Shortly after arriving in Viet Nam, Raulito got wounded. He was coming home, and my adventure with Big Raul was off. The story really does have a happy ending. Raulito recovered, thank God, and knowing his boating prospects were limited, he took a job as a management trainee with the Lighterage Company and forged a successful career, rising as I seem to recall, to director of Caribbean and Florida operations. And, fortunately for me, that Vietnam adventure went by the boards. Shortly afterward I admired my tan, trimmed my *begote*, and left Puerto Rico and returned to the Bronx.

Reminiscing

As I write this I am stunned by the fact that all this happened so many years ago. Where does time go? I remember Super Bowl One when Vince Lombardi's Green Bay Packers played the Kansas City Chiefs. I flew from San Juan to my neighborhood bar in the Bronx that day just to watch the game live on television. I lost a fast $50 on the outcome and flew back to San Juan that night. I remember Harry and Lowell, I remember Colacho's Merchant Marine Bar next to pier # 10, I remember getting yelled at by Captain Cuyler, I remember catching a shark with Tomas, I remember my sports car—an Austin Healey Sprite with no top so I got wet almost every day, I remember the martini cocktail hours with Paul and Sammy whenever we were underway on a trip and in whatever weather we encountered, I remember how the company used to joke that the tug *Cabo Rojo* only navigated on the outbound leg of our voyages. (To get home they claimed that all Paul, John, and Sammy had to do was to follow their olive pits!). I remember awesome Caribbean sunsets and the comforting tropical trade winds, and I remember the coconut palm trees that all bent at the same angle at the beach at Luquillo. Even now, sometimes on a sultry summer evening in New Jersey, I am reminded of those soft Caribbean nights with white puffy clouds reflecting the lights of San Juan. I was in my mid-twenties and had the world where I wanted it. To this day I remember what Lowell used to call our "Salad Days," and I'm grateful for them.

There is one last thing. I asked you to remind me to tell you about "knots". A knot is a measure of ship's speed using the linear measurement of a nautical mile. At 6080 feet a nautical mile measures a little longer than the 5280 feet that we call a land mile. I don't know how a land mile is determined but I do know how a nautical mile is determined. A circle has 360 degrees. The equator circles the center of the earth and is divided into 360 degrees of arc. There are 60 minutes in a degree, and therefore there are 360 x 60 minutes of arc around the equator. A nautical mile is the distance of one minute of that arc as measures along the equator. It translates to 6080 feet for each minute. A ship measures its speed in knots rather than MPH; that means that a ship traveling at say, 20 knots, would be traveling at roughly 23 miles per hour. Now you know.

Vietnam

History, The Draft, The National Mood, The End Game

THE VIETNAM ERA

I left San Juan during the month of January. I missed the cold weather, and I missed the ski trips I used to take each weekend when I worked at Shell. There is one last amusing anecdote I can share about leaving the islands. Joe Leoncy was the assistant engineer on the tug I worked on. He was a native West Indian from Saint Lucia and had never seen snow. I asked him if he wanted to come north with me for a while and visit a ski area with me. His reply was priceless. The answer in his West Indian dialect went something like this; "John, don' be getting me all vex. I remember de time I went to South Carolina in de winter time and got de chap lips dat almos' keel me!" Joe wasn't eager to risk his lips on a snow covered mountain in sub-freezing temperatures in Vermont. I came home alone.

The Vietnam era was a very big event in the history of the United States. Even today, almost fifty years later, feelings and opinions still run high regarding American viewpoints on the war in Southeast Asia. The best I can tell you would be to read up on it yourself with the 20-20 hindsight of history.

History

Prior to World War Two, colonialism was very much a Geo-political fact. France controlled the vast regions of Southeast Asia which today include Cambodia, Laos, and Vietnam. It was referred to as French Indo-China. This area fell to the Japanese during the war, and consequently gave rise to a guerrilla faction of Vietnamese who fought to contest the Japanese control of the area. When the war ended, the

French government tried to reclaim control of their former colony. The French battled the Vietnamese guerillas that had been their allies during the war, but who now declared Vietnam a free state under a leader named Ho Chi Minh. When the French were finally defeated in 1954, the United Nations divided the nation in half at the 17th parallel. Forces loyal to Ho Chi Minh were concentrated in the north and a former governor, Bo Dai, was installed in the South by the Western governments. The reason was Ho Chi Min. He was a leader of the resistance on our side during the war but unfortunately he was an avowed communist. It was the beginning of the Cold War era and it was the United States policy was to block any communist expansion. Free elections to determine the fate of Vietnam were scheduled for 1956, only they never took place. Bo Dai rigged elections that were held only in the South and declared himself, with the blessing of the West, to be president of the country called South Vietnam. A civil war ensued and the U. S. under President Eisenhower sent American military advisers to assist the army of South Vietnam. That was how the mess started. Things didn't go well for Bo Dai, and the United States continued to send military advisers under the Kennedy administration. Kennedy was assassinated in November 1963 and was succeeded by Lyndon Johnson who then inherited this escalating situation as more and more "advisers" were being sent in to assist the unpopular Bo Dai and his successors. Johnson realized that this effort was not good enough and Ho Chi Minh was positioning himself to win the war. He decided that a communist Vietnam was unacceptable and planned to install American combat units in Vietnam. Politically he needed a pretext for doing this. The pretext came in 1964 in the Gulf of Tonkin when Johnson declared that North Vietnamese gun boats attacked two destroyers of the U.S. Navy. Accordingly, in 1965, American combat troops arrived to fight a war in Vietnam. (The only problem was the Gulf of Tonkin incident never happened. Years later, long after the war ended, the truth came out. Johnson and his Defense Secretary James McNamara invented it to influence public opinion to support a war. Read McNamara's book entitled *Bright Shining Lie*. As American involvement escalated, and the death and casualty tolls mounted, the public grew more and more restive.

The Draft

In those days we had the universal draft and all men at the age of eighteen had to register for the draft. As more troops were sent in more were needed, and many soldiers, the unwilling victims of the Draft Board, were sent to Vietnam. As the public watched more and more of its young men sent to fight in a war whose purpose was murky, more people turned against it. In many cases, especially on college campuses, demonstrations were held against what was perceived as "Johnson's War." (Hey, hey, LBJ, how many kids did you kill today? was a popular demonstration chant.) Other problems arose with the draft. Many of the college kids, including myself, received deferments to finish school while many of the poorer minorities were forced to serve. This inequality was somewhat alleviated by a new selective service system of lottery draft numbers that was intended to equalize the education and income gaps. The draft was finally eliminated by President Nixon in 1973. I'll just take a little break here to tell you about my military status during those years.

I entered the Maritime College in the fall of 1957, well before the expanded involvement in Southeast Asia. When I registered with the draft board at eighteen I applied for and received 2-S status which meant a student deferment. After graduation I reverted to 1-A status which again made me eligible for the draft. JFK was president at the time and the situation in Vietnam was heating up. However, by virtue of the fact that I possessed a federal license as a merchant marine officer, (Third Mate) I had the option of enlisting in the U.S. Naval Reserve as an Ensign. As long as I sailed on my license as a merchant marine officer my time was concurrent as my Navy time. While ashore I was affiliated with an active reserve unit called the Convoy Commodores Squadron which was made up exclusively of officers who had sailed on merchant ships. Our job in that squadron was to run exercises regarding vessel convoys to supply a war effort by sea. My Navy commitment never took me to the Vietnam Theater and I was just as glad it didn't. I was discharged from the Naval Reserve with the rank of Lieutenant in 1969.

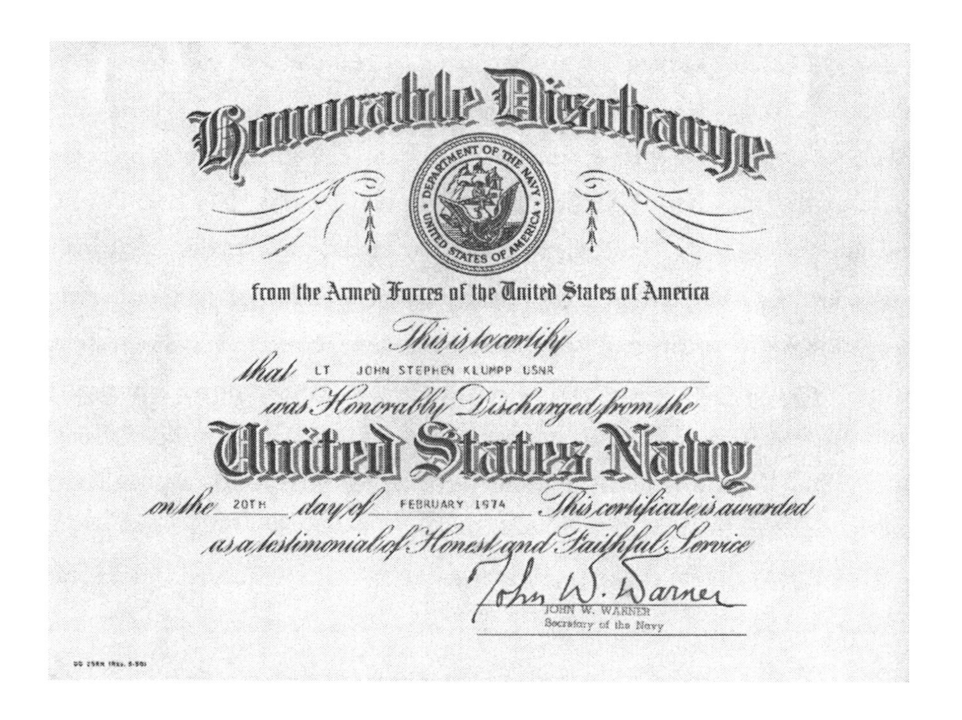

Honorable Discharge

DEPARTMENT OF THE NAVY · UNITED STATES OF AMERICA

from the Armed Forces of the United States of America

This is to certify

that LT JOHN STEPHEN KLUMPP USNR

was Honorably Discharged from the

United States Navy

on the 20TH day of FEBRUARY 1974 This certificate is awarded

as a testimonial of Honest and Faithful Service

John W. Warner

JOHN W. WARNER

Secretary of the Navy

The National Mood

Vietnam was basically a jungle guerrilla war. Our soldiers were caught up in a situation where friend or foe was never clearly identified and atrocities were documented to have been committed by both sides. The U. S. Army was involved in a nasty situation at a village called My Lai where many civilians were massacred by our soldiers. The enemy, called the Viet Cong, sometimes used civilians, often women and children, to bomb, destroy, or ambush, and then disappear back to the safety of their villages. The civilian deaths, given these circumstances, could be understood but not condoned. Colleges here at home were rife with protests as young students resented their obligation to military service. They marched, they burned their draft cards, and reviled the soldiers returning from that awful guerrilla war in the jungles. The returning soldiers who had seen comrades die in rice paddies for a war no one believed in anymore were stunned by their reception at home. Many Americans who witnessed these demonstrations revolted, in turn, against the students that they perceived to be spoiled appeasers and downright un-patriotic brats. Battle lines were drawn that finally erupted at a college in Ohio called Kent State. Nervous National Guard soldiers called to keep order found themselves surrounded and harassed by students chanting and waving flowers and, in some cases, trying to insert flowers down the barrels of the soldiers' guns. Something sparked the tinder, and when the soldiers stopped their firing, four students lay dead and many others lay bleeding on the grounds of their university. The nation was appalled at the pictures that were flashed by the newspapers of college coeds kneeling beside their dead friends. The ground in the photo was strewn with the now forgotten flowers while the upturned faces of the sobbing coeds seemed to be voicing a silent and agonizing "Why?" The Kent State Massacre it was called. The public battle lines had been drawn. The returning soldiers bore the brunt of it, and many never came to grips with the reaction of their fellow citizens as they returned home to a polarized public who sometimes blamed them. But now the floodgates were opened. More demonstrations and more confrontations followed. Johnson proved intransigent. He remained committed to a losing cause because, as he said, he refused to be the only U.S. President to lose a war. And so more people died, and more people turned against the soldiers who were fighting it. The national mood was ugly as anti-communists and supporters of American military power clashed with those who basically opposed the war on moral grounds. I saw bumper stickers pasted on automobiles that read "Kill them all and let God sort them out." But I also saw peace symbols on windows and graffiti paintings on building walls. The fabric of our American culture was being ripped apart by the hippie credo of free love and peace that was now clashing with older veterans of other wars and "The Establishment" who just didn't understand the 60's generation.

The End Game

In 1968 the North Vietnamese unleashed a surprise offensive on the Vietnamese holiday of Tet. It was a successful blow to the U.S. war effort and Johnson finally announced that he would not run again for president. Richard Nixon succeeded him in 1969. Nixon ran on a platform that he claimed had a secret plan to end the war but would not divulge it at the time. Upon his election Nixon expanded the war by bombing enemy supply lines through Laos and Cambodia. The peace protests escalated and questions were raised about the legality of the bombing missions to neighboring countries. Returning soldiers faced more hostility at home and suffered psychological effects lingering to this day. When Nixon took office with his secret peace plan, 28,000 soldiers had already been killed in action. When a peace treaty was finally signed in 1973 (after months of haggling over the shape of the negotiating table), an additional 30,000 had died, bringing the cost in lives for this misadventure to 58,000 soldiers—enough to fill Yankee Stadium with bodies. And yet that wasn't the end of it. When the U.S. left the country a civil war between North and South erupted and would last another two years before the country was finally united in 1975—under Ho Chi Minh. We had accomplished nothing.

The sixties were a tumultuous generation. I witnessed the assassination of President JFK and his brother Robert, the murder of the civil rights giant Martin Luther King, and the resignation in disgrace of Richard Milhous Nixon. I witnessed the rise of the hippie and drug culture in America, and the national movement toward racial equality. The year was 1968. I was 29 years old, and I was coming home to face this upheaval armed with a mustache and a beautiful tan from the Caribbean.

Deckhand

Back at Sea, Mullins Practices Medicine, Finally the Harbor, Ropes and Stuff, Playtime

STARTING AS A DECKHAND IN NEW YORK

I left San Juan in early 1967 and headed directly for the wintry slopes of Vermont to ski for a few months. I had been missing that. I started to take skiing seriously and enlisted the aid of a professional instructor from Austria. "Bend Ze kneeze. Ten dollars, pleeze" and spent time with him learning the technique. Knowing what I know now, and considering the changes in equipment and technique required to get optimum use from all the new design changes, these early lessons now seem hopelessly out-dated but they served me well at the time. I stayed in Vermont for a few months. No broken bones, but I did develop a lingering staph infection which resulted in a series of painful boils that kept recurring around my thighs. I suppose it was due to the long johns and heavy pants that replaced the lightweight summer stuff of the Islands. I only mention it now because on my first trip with my new towing company those boils caused me quite an unusual problem that I'll relate to you later.

Back at Sea

I went to work for the McAllister Towing Company in New York. It didn't take long to get back to sea. The company flew me down to El Salvador in Central America to join the tug *J.P. McAllister*. I relieved the mate on the "*J.P.*" because his wife had just had a baby, and he was scheduled to go home. So there I was, living in the tropics, then living in snow country, and then returning to the tropics again. My body didn't know what the hell was going on! The tug had just delivered a dredge that was to remain there for harbor expansion and we were to return home light (without a tow).

Once again at sea, I discovered that the Gyro compass was not working. The advantage of a Gyro is that it will always give you true north without any magnetic interference. The magnetic compasses work fine, but you have to know the inherent errors before a true course can be followed. Variation is the primary error because magnetic north is not the same as true north on the globe. Magnetic north is, in reality, a huge magnetic mine field in Northern Canada that attracts the compass magnetic needle to it. The error produced by the location of magnetic north in relation to true north can be readily read off the nautical chart at your location. The second error, called Deviation, is caused by the effect of the surrounding steel structure of the vessel itself. A trained compass adjustor can shift the compensating magnets of the "Navigator's Balls" (the two round metal balls found on either side of the compass—what did you think they were?) in order to minimize the magnetic effect of the iron of the vessel. But in my case, on my first trip on this tug, no one knew what the errors were—and without knowing this, the compass was useless. Here is a little tip I told you about earlier: The altitude of the North Star is within a degree of your latitude. Since we were sailing at around 8 degrees latitude at the time, the North Star was visible only 8 degrees above the horizon—low enough for me to rig a dummy compass and then steer the boat to the four points of the compass while using the North Star as a reference. In this manner I was able to roughly gauge the resulting error on the compass we were to use on our trip north. As cadets we learned to correct the compass by applying the rule: going from compass to true course you would apply deviation (East or West) to the compass to get a magnetic course, then apply the variation found on the chart to get to a true reading. Compass Deviation Magnetic Variation True. CDMVT (Can Dead Men Vote Twice) Of course the reverse is opposite, and to a sailor's mind, easier to remember. TVMDC (True Virgins Make Dull Company!).

Mullins Practices Medicine

The trip north was un-eventful except for the boil situation I referred to earlier. I developed a large and very painful boil right on the "Taint." For those not familiar with colloquial medical terms from the Bronx, the "Taint" is that part of the body where your legs join at the crotch. Right there in the middle, where it Tain't Ass but it Tain't Balls either. Anyway, it hurt like a son of a gun and it hurt when I sat and it hurt when I stood to balance on the rolling deck. One of the deckhands volunteered to come to my rescue. John Mullins had a recipe he claimed came down from "His Sainted Grandmother in Ireland." He mixed a poultice he called a "Drawing Salve" from sugar and brown soap. Then he had me bend over while he slapped it on my boil and covered it with gauze and tape. The idea was to leave it on a few days until the lye in the poultice would eat through the skin and allow the boil to break and expel the poison onto the gauze pad. Nothing happened for a few days until one day I had to do a "Number Two." While balancing on the rocking and rolling commode I discovered that the fool had taped my rear-end shut! Tears of rage and pain fought with gales of laughter as I ripped that obstructing tape from under the sorest part of my body. Ah, the adventures of going to sea! I eventually had to get to the hospital in Panama (yes, I rode a tug boat through the Panama Canal) to have the thing lanced. But from then on over the years, as I saw John on and off other boats, he would always greet me with, "How's your ass-hole!" As I said, my work environment was not your run-of-the-mill variety but I wouldn't change it for anything. Like Lowell used to say, "You can't civilize a boatman!"

Finally, the Harbor

When I returned to New York my education as a boatman began in earnest. While working in Puerto Rico I learned to steer a tugboat and do ship work in the harbor. I learned to make up to the barges that we used to tow containers to the Islands. What I didn't realize at the time was the restricted nature of my education. Ship jobs were pretty much confined to cruise ships at Pier #3 in Old San Juan, and the container ships to their berths in Puerto Nuevo. The container barges always went to St. Thomas and St. Croix with an occasional trip to Rio Haina in the Dominican Republic.

I had no idea of the scope of towing operations in New York. All kinds of non-descript vessels had to be towed. I got to be familiar with coffee barges that were off loaded from South America that had to be towed to processing plants in Jersey City and Hoboken. Derricks, cranes, and lighters had to be maneuvered alongside ships that were docked at the Manhattan and Brooklyn piers. We moved deck scows for piping and building material, copper barges to and from the smelter, oil barges, sand scows, and trap rock barges from quarries upstate, railroad car floats to transit freight cars across the North River, and, of course, the ubiquitous scrap iron scows that held scrap metal and the rusted engine blocks destined for the Orient to be recycled. Each of these units required knowledge of the best way to make up (tie-up) the tug to the barge to be towed. Hundreds of docks and terminal facilities had to be learned. I had to learn the handling characteristics of various units in order to assist the man in the pilot house get under weigh and land tows when his visibility was restricted. I had to lasso like a cowboy and learned to throw lines on and off the bitts, bollards, and cleats used to fasten vessels to a pier. And of course, I had to clean and paint the tug to keep it "Ship-shape and Bristol fashion." There wasn't much in my academy background to help me learn all this. I had to get down and dirty. There is simply no way one can be an accomplished tugboat captain without serving his time on deck first. Was I an accomplished deckhand? At first, a resounding NO! The union pay scale for deckhands in 1967 was roughly $65/day. I wasn't worth it. I must have caused a lot of grey hairs for the man in the pilot house until I learned, first, what was expected of me, and second, how it was done.

George Carpenter, the captain of the "*JP*" was very patient with me, but even he finally recommended I be transferred to a smaller tug where I would be able to better practice my craft. He was right. The "*JP*" was a larger boat and spent a lot of time towing oil barges to ports outside of New York. I needed to learn the Port and most importantly I needed to be able to throw and splice lines or I'd be no use to the captain of the boat. Did I learn? Yes, I suppose that I got fairly adequate. The two years I spent as a deckhand benefited me in other important ways. I developed an appreciation of the deckhand's job. I learned what could or could not be done on deck and applied these considerations when I went steering again. Peer pressure was an important factor. I was accepted into the fraternity of boatman, not because I was a Maritime College graduate with a license, but because I was willing to spend the time on deck learning my job just like the others. It was called "Learning the ropes".

Ropes and Stuff

I suppose that this is as good time as any to tell you a little about boats and ropes. First of all, they are not called "ropes" on a boat. They are called "lines." Lines come in all sizes, usually measured by circumference, and by now are made up mostly from synthetic material. The old hemp or sisal fiber ropes have long passed into history. Nylon, Dacron, and Polypropylene lines have taken their place. Each line used aboard a tug is suited to a particular purpose. Most of the barges that are towed at sea today are done by hooking up to a towing cable of 1 1/2 inch wire. However, when I started, few wires were in use and we towed with what we called a "Hawser." Usually a hawser is an 8 inch (circumference) nylon line 1500 feet in length. Nylon is good for this purpose because it stretches, and its elasticity will absorb the stress created by towing in rough seas. When not in use the hawser is always neatly coiled in a rectangular shape on the stern deck aft of the towing bitts. Wire bridles are shackled to the end of the tow line and these bridles get hooked up to the barge in tow. The inboard end of the hawser is shackled to a chain that is used to rub across the stern of the tug. Were it not for the chain the hawser would be sawed through in short order. The inboard end of the chain is, in turn, shackled to a Dacron towing strap that is made fast to the towing bitts of the tug. Sounds complicated, but it's not, really. The Dacron towing strap, rather than the chain, is what connects the hawser to the boat. This is a safety precaution because if the barge sinks for some reason (it happened to me one time en route to St. Thomas) the strap can be chopped loose and the tug freed from the barge.

On larger tugs an 8 inch nylon (because it is lighter than Dacron) line is used when doing ship work around the harbor. When the tug comes alongside the ship, the deckhand throws up a heaving line (a small ½ inch line with a ball called a "monkey fist" weighted on the end of it) and the ship's personnel haul it up along with the attached ship line. When the job is done, the ship's crew should lower the line down to the tug. I can tell you from experience what a pain in the ass it is if the ship just drops the line into the water. The deckhand has to haul it up hand over hand out of the water and back onto the boat and those lines are heavy as hell!

In my experience around New York Harbor most of the dock to dock towing is done with the barge towed alongside. Dacron lines of various thicknesses are used in lieu of nylon because you don't want these lines to stretch. The tug has to remain tight to the barge in order to control the barge underway. Usually three lines go out; the tug pulls the barge along with a towing strap from the side, sometimes called the "hip", of the tug to the barge, and a head line and a stern line hold the tug in place. The headline and stern lines are usually doubled or tripled up to eliminate stretch.

Various other types of lines and hook-ups are employed depending on the type of unit towed and what the captain wants to do with it. Shifting scows in narrow channels or around docks, for example, smaller lines are used that can be thrown on and off easily. I won't bore you with any more details because there are many, many ways a deckhand performs his required functions. But I guess you have the general idea. I didn't even mention jumping on and off docks, or trying to wrap frozen lines around bitts, or crawling over or around old scrap iron or rock scows in all kinds of weather. It is physical work and I was in pretty good shape after a few months on the job. But as I said before: my work environment was not your ordinary run-of-the mill variety

My friend and shipmate Captain Harry Reid wrote several books about towing. In the preface of one book he wrote about what he called the "Brotherhood of the Sea." When Harry autographed a copy of his book for me, he wrote of our times sailing together and our drinking bouts at Colacho's Merchant Marine Bar. But he also wrote, "To a good friend, a good shipmate, and definitely a member of the Brotherhood." I'm proud of that. Really.

So there I was at the ripe old age of 28, with money in my pocket, a good job, and a schedule that allowed me to work one week on and one week off the boats. (Just so you know, the week on meant that I actually worked, ate, and slept, aboard the tug for the entire week. The work schedule was six hours on, six off, for seven days. We received the equivalent of 84 hours pay for our week on and nothing for our week off. It still averaged out to a 42 hour week.) Now the question I will address is what I was doing with myself when I wasn't throwing ropes on the tug.

Playtime

Most of my friends from the old neighborhood were married by now. The old neighborhood bar wasn't the same anymore. I'd stop in once in a while. The old Irish denizens that frequented the Parkview Bar on Jerome Avenue were still there; they were fun to share "jar" with occasionally, but there wasn't enough action there for a single guy. Don't ask me how 'cause I don't remember, but my social scene shifted to the many pubs and gathering places that dotted the East side Midtown. I'm not bragging or even justifying it, but drinking was the primary recreation for us in those days. The bars were always full. I had my favorites like Joe's Place, Paddy Quinns, the Salty Dog, and the

Recovery Room, but the hands down favorite was Rumms on Fiftieth Street and Third Avenue. The place was always packed with young working singles. Guys and girls in their twenties and thirties would mingle there with friends or try their luck meeting new friends and maybe getting a date. We all knew literally dozens of single people and always found activities like ski trips, summer houses at the Hamptons, or whatever activities Jimmy McIvor cooked up. McIvor. Any of us could probably write a book just about him. Jimmy was one of the owners of Rumms, the guy the place couldn't operate without. He knew everybody, introduced everybody to everybody, and livened up our world by his presence. A natural bar-owner and raconteur, everyone knew McIvor. I don't know how we met—I just did. Jimmy and I went to the same high school, and every so often during a dull moment we would get the urge to sing our old school song at the top of our lungs. (Especially the part when we sang FIGHT-FIGHT-FIGHT!)

We went to the Hamptons out on Long Island in the summer and to McIvor's ski house in Vermont almost every weekend in the winter. These ski trips played a critical role in my future as you will see later on. For now, though, you just have to know that I was having a pretty good time drinking and partying and going on weekend getaways with a bunch of friends. I was of average age of our group—we were all around thirty at the time. Dating wasn't critical; most of us had no driving urge to settle down. During the sixties and seventies many young people got married soon after graduation. Those that didn't, however, generally were in no rush and remained single until their late twenties or early thirties. It could have been different with me. Shortly after graduation from college I wanted to get serious with a certain girl but because of a series of mutual mistakes, misunderstandings, and bad timing, things just didn't work out. I didn't have a serious girl friend for many years after that but changes were on the horizon. One afternoon at the Cove Point Inn at the Hamptons I noticed a particularly pretty girl playing cards with some friends on the lawn. A really pretty girl whose name, I found out later, was Brenda. You are going to hear a lot about Jimmy and Brenda and some of these friends later, but for now it is time to get back to the tugboats. I was not decking anymore. was promoted to a job steering in the pilot house. I was promoted to Mate aboard the tug *Catherine McAllister.*

In The Pilothouse

Learning on the *Catherine,* The Reciprocal Date, Offshore voyages, Bahama sojourn, The Voyage from Hell

IN THE PILOTHOUSE

The "Bell Boats" are all gone now, and another piece of the sights, sounds, and lore of tug boating has passed into maritime history. I'm going to tell you now about the days when I was steering a tug boat, but first I'll mention those old Bell Boats. I never steered (the man in the pilot house operating the tug is "steering") a Bell Boat, but I decked on a few of them. The times were changing even then. Today pneumatic throttle controls in the pilot house have replaced the symbiotic relationship between captains to engineers that existed earlier. The bell boats were fitted with two types of bells that rang in the engine room, a big one that "clanged," and a small "jingle bells." The captain steering the tug would signal the engineer the speed and direction ahead or astern he wanted by one of the bell pulls located in the pilot house. The captain and engineer worked as a team: the engineer anticipating the bell signal, and the captain anticipating the time required to turn over the engine. The signals were not complicated, but you had to pay attention to what you were doing. One clang from Stop meant Half Ahead. Two clangs meant Half Astern. Are you with me so far? OK, the jingle bell would indicate an order for either Full Ahead or Dead Slow from that Half Ahead (or Astern) position. One clang, followed by jingle bells, would indicate Full speed ahead. One clang, followed by a double jingling of the bells, meant Dead Slow ahead. Sometimes, even today, I slip and refer to someone who is dawdling or dragging their feet as operating on a double jingle. They don't know what the hell I am talking about, but now at least, you do. The whole litany of the bells, their clangs and jingles all meant something that you don't really have to know now. In fact you could almost count on one hand the captains and the engineers who have used them today.

Why am I telling you this? I don't know, maybe I am just trying to impart to you some of the old ways, the old color, or the old sounds of bells and clanking machinery that one hears no more. Just picture these sounds coupled with the billowing steam erupting from those tall stacks, the smell of wet rope coupled with the miasma of the morning river, the big rope fenders dangling like giant mustaches from the bow, and hear the thumping of the propeller with the accompanying gurgle of the wheel wash. Listen for the occasional shouts to the deckhand. Or the raucous cry of a herring gull overhead. Watch as the work horses of the harbor push their giant charges into safe berth at one of the finger piers that used to line the North River. Imagine you hear the "peep whistle" as the captain pulls on the cord to toot the little whistle above the pilothouse to let the pilot on the ship know his orders were heard. Imagine the sun is just rising over Brooklyn Bridge as those first early rays pierce the cross-town voids between the concrete canyons of Manhattan. Squint your eyes as you imagine the sun peeking into your pilot house window as you lay your tug alongside the steel side of a ship in that early morning stillness order to guide it into her berth in the North River. Your picture is complete. Let the sights, and the sounds, and the smells of the harbor overwhelm your senses. This is the romance of tug boating.

Learning on the *Catherine*

The old *Catherine McAllister* was a converted steam tug with a wooden pilot house and those fuzzy rope fenders hanging over the side. It was a great boat to get started on. It didn't have more than

1200 horsepower (compared to some of 5000 HP and more today) but it was useful as a shifting tug engaged primarily in moving scows and other non-descript vessels around the port. As a deckhand I was aware of the tides and currents of the area, but it was not until I started steering that I realized the full impact of these elements when handling a tow. The *Catherine* was under-powered; and consequently she felt the effects of these forces to a degree greater than the bigger boats. It was ideal for me though, because learning the physical capabilities of the boats I steered was an important part of my learning curve. It was not without trepidation or embarrassment that I initially fumbled my way around the port.

I was scared to death to get the early morning orders, "Go to the Erie Basin in Brooklyn and see Paulie for shifting." Paulie was one of the pier superintendents responsible for loading and getting the ships to sail on time. He was a short, round guy with a voice you would expect to hear on the docks of Red Hook, Brooklyn. Much of the cargo was stored in the sheds that lined the piers, but a lot of it was laded off scows that had to be shifted alongside the ship. Paulie would shout at me to pick up "Hughes # 364," or whichever scow he needed and place it "Starboard side to alongside #2 hatch." When that was done I would sometimes get a crane or derrick to place alongside another hatch while the first scow was off loading. The trick was you had to be quick—and I was never quick enough for Paulie. Later I learned there were tricks to handling these scows. I learned to shift them with only one line instead of the normal make up of three. I learned how to spin them around in those confined spaces so the correct side would lay against the ship. I wasn't afraid to take one from the ship and let it loose to drift while I fetched another—I knew I was getting quick enough to retrieve it before it got into trouble. I learned all this by doing—there is no other way. Paulie, with his yelling, didn't help me. But eventually, I learned. I learned the language of the pilothouse and the deckhand and I formed a team. Shifting, making up tows and doing creek work got to be fun for me.

Speaking of creeks—it seemed like every creek in New York Harbor contained a scrap iron dock. And every scrap iron dock was inhabited by a mangy junk yard dog or two. The dogs, especially at night, would come running and snarling with the arrival of the boat. Not to worry, though. The dogs would have the uncanny sense of stopping on the stringpiece right abreast of the galley door. All the boatmen fed these dogs from leftovers and the dogs knew it. The mangy mutts were our buddies. Many times I would be walking through these scrap yards only to be accosted by the snarling sentinels who lived there. They would run up until a few feet from me, and then they would stop and sniff and smell the boat and diesel smell on my clothes. When their inspection was complete they would become docile as house pets and would trudge right along beside me to the boat to receive their "treat." One time though, a rather portly cook who was new to the boat didn't understand these rules of engagement. He got scared as the dogs ran to him and he backed up so quickly that he backed right off the pier into the dirty, sloppy, oily water of the creek. He was a lousy cook anyway and we debated whether or not we should help pull him back aboard. What a job we had pulling him out! Only his pride was hurt, but after that week we never saw him again.

Ships are different today, and you don't see many deck scows either. I liked the waterfront in the days when the ships worked the cargo booms and longshoremen with their hooks loaded the rope slings heavy with break-bulk cargo and stowed it in hatches that always smelled of old dunnage. (Dunnage was old wooden pallets or other material the carpenter would use to shore up the cargo so it wouldn't shift in the seaway.) The ships were small by today's standards, but they all had 4 to 7 hatches and a corresponding set of cargo booms and winches that would lift cargo from the pier to their hold. Ships would be in port a day or two before sailing to far away places. Each ship would be worked by gangs of longshoremen that were assigned to each hold. The port was always bustling with the sound of winches and the hum of cables and the raucous shouts and oaths of the men working the ship. Not so today. Super cranes load and discharge thousands of sealed containers aboard giant ships in a matter of hours. The old North River and Brooklyn piers are abandoned now. Ships are too big, and the transportation facilities around the old piers do not have anywhere the room needed to transport and store the thousands of containers handled daily. New ports are built up in the more spacious area in Newark Bay. The old ships are gone—and so is a lot of the color and romance of the old waterfront.

The Reciprocal Date

I remember I met a girl at one of those midtown watering holes I told you about. It turned out that she was from Detroit and was working as an art teacher at St. John's University. I guess I regaled her with enough sea-stories so that she eventually became interested in my world. And I in hers. She spoke of art, and I confess I didn't understand much of it. But I did develop an appreciation for the knowledge that she shared with me. We eventually arranged a reciprocal date. I would take her for a day down to the docks and she would spend a day showing me the Museum of Art. It worked out really well. I took her to the piers at 23rd St. Brooklyn. We visited the docks and then got to board a Farrell Lines ship. We drank beers at the neighborhood bar and ate hero sandwiches with the longshoremen and had a good old time. And she did take me to that museum. I remember her asking me what I thought of a particular painting. The painting appeared to be nothing but all black. I told her I thought that I could have painted it. She laughed and proceeded to show me that there were various shades and textures of black that were placed on the canvas and arranged in such a way as to unconsciously draw a viewer's eyes to a small focal point that was noticeably the blackest. I really wasn't too impressed, but I did appreciate the fact that there was a lot about the art world that would pass unnoticed unless someone would spend the time explaining it to a philistine like me. I guess I didn't wow her too much . . . she went back to Detroit.

Offshore Voyages

Eventually I got more comfortable steering the tug around New York. The *Catherine* was my regularly assigned boat but I found I was still in demand because, as an academy graduate, I was one of the few in the company who could navigate. Most of the boatmen were fathers and sons who grew up with the boats. They were unsurpassed with their local knowledge and boat handling, but had little experience navigating the open ocean. McAllister would often take me from my boat and assign me to a trip away from my normal bailiwick of the harbor. Whenever I tell people that I worked on tug boats I often get the response, "Oh! It must be fun to push those big ships in the harbor!" I try to tell them that towing involved much more than pushing ships in the harbor, but either the recipients of my revelation either ignore it or don't really comprehend the scope of the towing industry. I'll tell you more as we go along, but for now I will just tell you about some of the off shore towing trips that I took while with the McAllister Towing Company.

I already mentioned that I transited the Panama Canal when I told you of the great boil caper; but I also transited the Welland Canal. Unless you want to sail your boat over Niagara Falls, (which I wouldn't recommend) you have to find another way to transit the Great Lakes between Lake Ontario and Lake Erie. The Great lakes are all of different heights above sea level and are interconnected by a series of locks. You can check me on this, but I believe the Sault St. Marie Locks transits 10,000 vessels per year between Lake Superior and the Lower Great Lakes and is known as the busiest series of locks in the world. Twice I was up in that part of the world and had bad experiences each time.

McAllister purchased a tug that operated out of Toledo, Ohio called the S.*M. Dean*. In her earlier life she was engaged in the coal trade transporting coal barges on the Lakes. I was part of the crew that was sent north to bring it up the St. Lawrence Seaway and around to New York. About three days into the voyage the asthma I suffered as a kid resurfaced with a vengeance. I simply couldn't breathe! Coal dust was everywhere, permeating the atmosphere from every nook and cranny of the boat. Coal dust in the lockers, coal dust in the mattress, coal dust in the pilot house chart drawers—and I got a bad reaction from it. I really couldn't breathe. Fortunately we had an engineer with us who suffered from emphysema. Bad for him—but good for me. It turned out that the medication he took for his emphysema was identical to the medication I took years before for my asthma. He shared his Tedral pills with me so I could live until we returned home.

The second trip up that way was even more adventurous. We teamed up with a tug from Montreal to tow a dredge and two mud dumpers out the Seaway to New York. The Montreal boat had the dredge and we, on the *JP*, were towing the two dumpers. It was late fall, the end of the shipping season on the Lakes, and the weather was predictably bad. We took a terrible beating all the way down the Gulf of Saint Lawrence and somewhere around the Prince Edward Islands most of our electrical equipment shorted out. We had no radar and no Gyro to guide us. We managed to duck into the Canso Canal between Nova Scotia and the Cape Breton Peninsula and there we went weatherbound for a week hoping the storms would abate.

It was bad. A ship was reported to have sunk off Nantucket, and we knew that we had no business being out there with a tow. What pissed me off was the company refused to send electronic maintenance men to repair our equipment while we waited on weather. "Wait 'till you get to New York," we were told. Well, after a long stay in Canso, the captain decided to give it a try and we headed back out to sea. The weather was still not good, but it wasn't awful, either, so we bumped and rock and rolled west along the coast of Nova Scotia with our barges in tow. Then things turned to shit. The wire bridles that attached the tow to our hawser parted. We were also sailing through a down-east fog at the time and we lost the tow because we had no radar. With no radar we had no choice but to call and have the company send out a salvage tug from Halifax to locate and hold the barges.

By the way, we were lost also. (Remember no Gyro?) The Foundation Towing Company of Canada specializes in sea rescue and recovery. They located our tow and found us as well. They gave us a magnetic compass heading to Halifax so we headed there to go in for repairs while they held our tow safely for us. After a harrowing trip sailing blind along the fog shrouded and rocky coastline of Nova Scotia we managed to locate Halifax harbor and what do you know!! All the repair men that we needed and asked for at Canso were waiting for us right at the dock! Now it was costing the company money. We were told to get fixed up quick and get back out because the salvage tug was costing them by the day. I really got pissed then and, honestly, I was still shaken up from the lousy foggy trip finding the port, so I said bullshit on this and quit right then and there. I had thousands of sea miles under the keel by then, but that trip shook me up. I have to admit that the reason I didn't want to go back out was I was a little scared. Mad too, it's true, but a little scared, also. Anyway, there I was, on the dock in Halifax with my bag in my hand and a $5.00 bill in my pocket.

I checked into the first hotel I could find, went to my room and then promptly located the bar. A few martinis calmed me down. I ate dinner at the hotel while I charged the drinks and food to my room before I called New York (charged to my room) and told my mother to send me money in Halifax before I went to jail! Remember, there were no credit cards in use in 1969. She sent up a Western Union money gram and I paid the hotel, boarded a plane, and flew home. Then I went to Vermont for a few weeks to get my head together.

I guess the story has an epilogue; The Captain did sail with the remaining mate and he had to go weather bound again for another week before the storm finally played itself out. I stayed in Vermont for a few weeks and then came home and called the operations manager in the office expecting to hear that I had been fired. "No, dammit." he said, "You're a pain in the ass but you were right—the weather stayed bad. They're not back yet. Just go back on your own boat and shut up". So there I was, back on the *Catherine*, bumping and banging scows as I continued to learn my trade and the vagaries of the Harbor.

Bahama Sojourn

There's more. Sometime around 1970 the Bahamian Oil Company (BORCO) was building a deep water loading port in Freeport in the Bahamas. Large oil tankers were to use these facilities and BORCO had contracted with the Netherlands for four new tug boats to service the docking operations when the port was fully operational. This time I found myself on the *AJ* (JP's brother) *McAllister* doing ship work for a few months in the Bahamas. It was a peculiar time. The Bahamian government had recently declared that they were no longer an English colony and a tide of nationalism was sweeping the Island. Foreigners were only allowed to work in the Bahamas until a native Bahamian could be trained to replace him. There were a lot of bad feelings toward us and we pretty much stayed on the tug—we weren't welcome anywhere else. When we finally left the Bahamas I resolved never to return, and I haven't. By the way, I heard later from unverified sources that one of the Dutch captains who relieved us got his throat cut by a native. Knowing the attitudes there at the time I could believe it. I don't want to bore you; but just in the interest of explaining that I did more than "push ships" I'll take this opportunity to tell you that during this time I also delivered another tug, the *Neil McAllister* from New York to Puerto Rico and stayed there with the boat a few weeks until turning it over to their subsidiary operation in San Juan.

The Trip from Hell

Whenever anyone asks me if I ever had any adventures on the boat I always respond that adventures are bad. I didn't want adventures. I wanted a nice, calm, uneventful voyage. But yes, I've had adventures. While I was with the McAllister Towing Company they purchased four new higher horsepower tugs. These boats were built in Pittsburgh of all places, and floated down the Mississippi River to be outfitted and delivered to us in New Orleans. I was part of the crew that flew down to bring these boats home. Most of the trips were uneventful except for the "Marjorie". That was one of the adventures. Apparently the glitches hadn't all been worked out when we left New Orleans on her maiden voyage. We had two new mud dumpers in tow and we were looking forward to a nice calm trip so we could arrive in New York in time for Christmas a little more than a week away. Well, we missed not only Christmas, but almost New Year's as well. The first indication that things would not go swimmingly was when our electric power failed in the Mississippi River and the boat took a hard left and drove right up into the cypress trees lining the bayou. We could only watch in astonishment as our barges slid on past us and knocked down a few trees of their own. The weirdest thing was, because we had no electric we had no radio, we couldn't call anyone to tell them we were literally up the creek. Would you believe we waved handkerchiefs at passing boats? It wasn't hard to get their attention because it was kid of unusual to see a tug and two barges hung up among the trees on the riverbank.

Well, back to NOLA for a few days and then we tried it again. This time we made it all the way across the Gulf and turned the corner around the Florida Keys where we picked up the Gulf Steam flowing north. I might as well tell you that the *Marjorie* rode lousy in the seaway and rolled like a bastard (a really stupid metaphor). But I think she would have rolled on wet grass. And I didn't think much of the brilliant minds in Pittsburgh, either. I guess someone forgot to tell the architects that this wasn't to be a riverboat. We had figured that out pretty quick, though, when we left Southwest Pass and sailed into the Gulf. The giant refrigerator-freezer had not been secured and it rolled right off the bulkhead and toppled doors-down right on to the Galley deck! And can you imagine the fun we had watching all the chart drawers in the pilot house, and the cupboards in the galley, and the drawers in our rooms sliding open and shut as if by magic with each roll of the boat? Well, we survived; and no one got crushed by the falling refrigerator.

Now we were at last on the East Coast with our bow pointed North toward home. It was Christmas Eve when we looked back and found an empty tow line trailing behind us. What the hell? Where was the damn tow? We reeled in our wire towing line and found that the splice that held the thimble to which the towing bridles were attached had pulled apart. It didn't part—it just pulled apart and our tow was loose! Hello Coast Guard??? You can imagine how happy they were to be roused out of Miami on Christmas Eve to babysit our tow while we sailed into West Palm to find an old Norwegian who, we were told, had the talent and equipment to splice wire. I remember that he charged fifty bucks for the job. I asked him why so little. He (figuratively) had us by the balls. We needed to get the wire spliced. And we needed to get back out there and relieve the Coast Guard who were bouncing around watching our tow drifting North with the Gulf Stream Current. "Fifty bucks is plenty for this job", he said. I guess they don't call them "Squareheads" for nothing!

Are you tired of this gloom and doom yet? Too bad, there's more. We tailed those barges for a few more days up the Gulf Stream until the weather moderated enough to get close enough to them to re-attach the shackle to the bridles. And guess who had to make that timed leap through the air between the boat and the scow to do this? Right, Moi. OK, job done, we missed Christmas after all, but what can you do? We damn near missed New Years, too!

This time our adventure happened off the Delaware Capes. We had a new second mate on the boat and he got tangled up with an inbound freighter. The freighter really had the right of way, but the mate believed the ship should make way for the tug and tow because we were less maneuverable. I guess he had a point, but you never take anything for granted. The ship didn't change course and the new mate stopped the tug. When the ship cleared the mate slammed the throttle back to full ahead again. Big mistake. The heavy towing cable sank to the bottom when the tug was stopped. When the pissed-off mate went full ahead the cable came off the bottom with such a jerk that it parted. The barges were loose again. Hello New York??? Please send down a rescue tug because we have a broken towing cable and no spare towing line on this maiden voyage from Hell. For two more days we bounced around our tow until we were relieved. Finally we headed north again, sans tow, and arrived just in time for New Years Eve. I swore I would never sail on that boat again and I'm glad I didn't. A few years later she was lost with all hands in a storm off Cape Lookout off the outer banks of North Carolina.

By the way, the captain for all these trips I mentioned was the same captain that I quit on later in Nova Scotia. Like I said, we had a lot of water and adventures under our keel before that trip. I guess the captain knew me well enough by then to cut me some slack when I finally walked off. Maybe I finally had one adventure too many, but after that time I started to resent the trips. I felt I was being punished because I could navigate oceans. I really wanted to do harbor and ship work and wanted someone else to get called upon for these trips for a change. I guess I started to get a poor attitude, and started to criticize the company too much. Finally, after four years I needed a change. And I guess so did they. I was still young, still single, and perhaps a little more independent than I should have been. All in all, McAllister was good to me. I learned a lot and made a lot of friends. And I began to be known as one of the boatmen in the harbor. But in 1972 I left them and went with the Turecamo Towing Company. I stayed with them for the next twenty years.

You may have noticed that I have made mention of the "North River". All New York boatmen refer to the Hudson as the "North River". The origin dates back to the exploration of Henry Hudson, and was counted as part of the dividing line between the early settlements of the Dutch and the Swedish settlers to the South. The Hudson River was called the "North" and the Delaware River was known as the "South River". Now you know.

The Sixties

Storm clouds, LBJ, Winds of Change, Martin and Malcolm, The Women Rule, Topsy-turvy World, The Good Life, Brenda, Steamboat, The proposal, A Little Bit of Me

Red Setter Crew, Jimmy, Alex, Brenda and John

SOME THOUGHTS ABOUT THE SIXTIES

"May you live in interesting times" is an old saying when you want someone to experience a certain amount of upheaval in their life. Before going on to more tugboat tales, I want to switch gears now and tell you about the "interesting times" of the late 1960's and early 1970's. Societal upheaval was the norm in those tumultuous years. Wars, assassinations, civil disturbances, and the rise of a drug culture permeated this era. Sociologists sometime explain this phenomenon as a natural result of the torpor of the 50's, when the nation was catching its breath after the Second World War. It was a time when President Eisenhower guided our newly assumed role as the world's superpower vying for supremacy over the communist aspirations of the Russian Bear named Joseph Stalin. International relations were being redefined. On the domestic scene, grandfatherly President Eisenhower was unfairly portrayed as playing golf (a game he loved, but played poorly) and generally letting the nation ease into the era that is still referred to as "The Fabulous Fifties." Singers were called "Crooners," and their songs, if they weren't downright silly like the one about the monkey's honeymoon, spoke often of love and affection. Gentlemen wore suits and ties to baseball games and took their hats off in elevators if there were ladies present. Sneakers were only used for play. The American Dream of a house in the suburbs with a television set, family cars, and family vacations, were realized for many. And kids behaved themselves and were "all above average." It couldn't go on.

Storm Clouds Gather

The overriding storm cloud that signaled the demise of this idyllic existence was the Vietnam War. I wrote of this war in a previous chapter so I won't re-hash the grim tale again. It is important to realize however, that I, and many others, consider this disastrous event to be to be the lightning bolt that preceded the civil thunder that followed in its wake. Once unleashed, the dogs of turmoil were not to be contained. These dogs bore names like Lyndon B. Johnson, Robert F. Kennedy, Martin Luther King, Richard M. Nixon, Haight-Ashbury, Stonewall, Kent State, and Montgomery. Note the caveat that this is not to be considered a definitive history of the era, but merely the times as I witnessed them. I'll share them with you now.

L B J

Lyndon Johnson succeeded to the presidency with the assassination of John F. Kennedy. Johnson was quirky, and liked all in his family to share the same LBJ monogram. His wife Claudia was called Lady Bird Johnson, and his daughters were Linda Bird and Lucy Baines. Even the family dog was LBJ (Little Beagle Johnson). Some wags contend that there was a "Looney Bird" somewhere up there in the closet but I'll let that pass.

I liked much of what Johnson accomplished. Much of his legislation took political courage. Unfortunately his initiatives were instrumental in creating the great divide that split the nation during his tenure. Race riots in such diverse areas as Newark, Los Angeles, and Detroit, fanned the flames of discontent, and racial baiting was common during those Johnson years. Martin Luther King, the eloquent Baptist minister, had successfully pushed for change to the "Jim Crow" laws of segregation in Alabama and Mississippi. The successful bus boycotts of Montgomery, the March on Selma, his "Letters from a Birmingham Jail," and the lunch-counter sit-ins that King organized brought the question of civil rights to the attention of the nation. President Kennedy in 1961 and Lyndon Johnson in 1964, to their credit, authorized the Civil Rights Bills that outlawed segregation in schools, public facilities, government, and in housing. Johnson followed this up with the Voting Rights Act which granted African Americans the right to the polls. Upon signing this landmark legislation he was known to have said that the Democrats will have lost the South for 100 years.

Johnson was a political animal and a Democrat who, when he nominated Justice Thurgood Marshall to be the first black to sit on the Supreme Court, proved himself to be a leader who rose above politics to do the right thing. Social programs such as revisions to the Social Security Act, and the initiation of Medicare programs reflected his desire to foster what he called a "Great Society". But his blind spot, his Achilles heel, was his handling of the Vietnamese War.

When Johnson, a member of the Evangelical Church of Christ, was sworn in on a Catholic bible found aboard Air Force One after Kennedy's death, the total involvement of American personnel in Viet Nam numbered 16,000 advisers. It escalated to over 500,000 during his tenure. He fabricated a story about Vietnamese gunboats firing upon U.S. ships (The Gulf of Tonkin incident) as an excuse to escalate the war. He allowed our generals to mis-represent body counts to show progress when there was none, and he slavishly refused to alter his failing policies by saying that he would be damned if he would be the first American President to lose a foreign war. Hubris is an apt description for his motives. Excessive pride . . . you can look it up. Years later his

Secretary of Defense, Robert S. McNamara, wrote a book about the Vietnamese War entitled, *A Bright Shining Lie*.

When asked one time why he kept certain people on his staff when things were going badly, Johnson referred to his deception obliquely by saying that he would rather, "Have them in his tent pissing out, than outside his tent pissing in." With the country in turmoil and his reputation undermined by massive protests in the Capitol and elsewhere, Johnson declined to run for a second term. This paved the way for the ascendancy of Richard M. Nixon and his impeachable (not to be confused with "impeccable") administration.

Before Nixon, however, I will try to tell you something about the turmoil that gripped the nation in the form of riots, marches, and other demonstrations. It seemed as if every minority group had finally had had enough of the seemingly peaceful façade that presumably gave the lie to the reality of simmering submerged prejudices. In reality, there were many oppressed minority groups that chose the 1960's to vent their frustrations with the civil order of the Country. A case may be made that the catalyst for this upheaval was the growing dissatisfaction with the Vietnam War.

Martin and Malcolm

Martin Luther King was a towering American figure in the fight for racial justice in America. At the young age of twenty-six he organized the successful boycott of the public buses in Montgomery because of the racial prejudices that required blacks to give up seats to whites and to ride only at the back end of the bus.

I want to editorialize a bit here: How the hell could those practices still exist in America 100 years after the Civil War? What the hell were we thinking about? Skin Color? I didn't grow up in a racially mixed neighborhood, but black students were common in my high school. And none of us saw color. Perhaps we didn't grow up to be taught that way compared to some Southern parts of the country, but those who perpetuated this awful prejudice by passing it down to their innocent children deserve the back of my hand.

The "Jim Crow" laws. The very name should shame the history of the United States. Separate water fountains? Separate bathrooms? Separate hotels and dining areas? Separate theaters and baseball teams? What in God's name were they thinking? Who the hell did the advocates of these laws think they were? And don't tell me that white society just didn't know any better. Bullshit . . . They had to have had. I was sailing out of Port Arthur, Texas, on oil tankers during the early 1960's. There was no segregation on our ships; but when we docked, the segregated taxis were there waiting to carry us to our respective parts of town. I saw segregation first hand.

There is a song I remember from the famous musical, "South Pacific." It goes something like this: "You've got to be taught before it's too late, before you are six or seven or eight, to hate all the people you're relatives hate. You've got to be carefully taught". Ecidujerp is prejudice spelled backwards. Either way it doesn't make sense.

And now, during the 60's the kettle began to boil over. Newark, NJ and Los Angeles went up in flames. Martin Luther King forced the nation to face its dark side. He demanded Americans accept what the Declaration of Independence declared 200 years earlier: "All men are created equal". He led the Poor People's March on Washington in 1963 as hundreds of thousands gathered at the Reflecting Pool and the Lincoln Memorial to hear his message of hope for all Americans. Yes, I was there that day, with my oldest friend Pappy Ward. And I'm proud of it. Read Martin Luther King's "Letters from a Birmingham Jail," and listen to Martin Luther King's "I have a Dream" speech and understand the cry of black America during those days of the 60's. King was feted in Washington by President Kennedy and various civic associations, but I have the feeling that his acceptance by white society was predicated on his platform of non violence.

There was another charismatic black leader of the time who rivaled Dr. King. Malcolm X took a more aggressive posture and was generally as hated by the whites as King was accepted. Malcolm had some good points, though. I remember he was quoted as saying "If the White Man sics the dogs on you, shoot the dogs." Malcolm derided the protests of his people as self-defeating. No more was the motto to be "Burn, Baby, Burn" as neighborhoods went up in flames. Malcolm taught, not black integration, but black pride. He said, "Earn Baby Earn!" (And when you have a pocket full of money watch how fast the whites accept you.) Both men met the identical fate during those tumultuous 60's. They were both assassinated for their beliefs. Ironically both men, who only met once during their careers as civil rights leaders, were swapping their position on racial matters.

MLK was treading on the toes of the military establishment by decrying the imbalance of poor blacks serving in Viet Nam as compared to the white college kids with deferments. He was mulling over the possibility of a black boycott of the draft which would have hamstrung the U.S. military effort at the time. He drew the ire of J. Edgar Hoover, the demagogic head of the FBI, and the white intellectuals who were suddenly uncomfortable with the growing militancy of his message. In 1968, at the age of only 39, he was killed by a rifle shot while chatting with supporters on the balcony of a motel in Memphis, Tennessee. Malcolm, on the other hand, adopted the Muslim tradition. While on a trip to Mecca, he was amazed to learn that there were white Muslims also, and that not all "Blue-eyed Devils", as he called whites, were bad. As his militancy mellowed, his hard-core supporters deserted him. He was shot in 1965, also at the age of 39, by his former Muslim associates while giving one of his conciliatory speeches at the Audubon Ballroom in New York.

As I said, these were intense times. I'm trying to pass on to you the story of my life and the times I lived through. I lived in interesting times. But there is more. Robert F. Kennedy, brother of the late John, was assassinated by a bullet to his head in 1968 after a campaign speech in California. He was only forty-two.

Betty and Gloria

Perhaps because they were emboldened by the effects of black militancy, Women's advocacy groups began to stand up for their own equality. "Women's Libbers" they were dismissively called. But they had Giants of their own espousing their cause. Betty Friedan, the founder of the National Organization for Women, and Gloria Steinem, a celebrated magazine editor, were equally as influential in espousing women's rights as Martin and Malcolm were in theirs.

The women's cause was not new or unique to the 1960's. As early as the 1920's they demanded, and won, the right of suffrage. For the first time women became an organized political force in the country. The second phase of their liberation came during the sixties and concentrated more on personal rights rather than political ones. They fought for what they called their reproductive rights. The right to control their own bodies led to the famous or infamous (which ever way one sees it) Roe vs. Wade decision in 1973 insuring a woman's right to an abortion. Paradoxically they also fought for the right of maternity leave. Domestic violence was discussed openly as well as was equal opportunity in the work place. Equal pay for equal work became an issue. Many battles were won during those turbulent sixties, and many continue to be fought today. The women's movement can now be considered to be in the third phase. The battle has shifted to economics. Women are demanding the end of stereotypical male-only positions and they are finally cracking the "Glass Ceiling" that prevented them from rising above a certain executive level. And we can see the end of sexual bias in hiring and promotional practices. They made their presence felt by integrating former all male institutions like West Point and Annapolis. Title 9 legislation has been initiated to guarantee equal funding for athletic scholarships at major colleges. Women's athletics were promoted by the arrival of nationally known talent such as Billy Jean King in tennis, Nancy Lopez in golf, and Althea Gibson in track and field. Perhaps most importantly it was during this era of the 1960's that little grammar school girls became aware that their careers were not restricted to the traditional fields of nursing or education. It might be difficult for you to understand now, but this was quite a revolutionary movement in its day.

A Topsy-turvy world

The placid Fifties were being turned on its head. Things were moving fast. Gays and lesbians fought for their recognition as individuals under the law. Riots again wracked New York when police raided a bar catering to gays in Greenwich Village. The bar was called the Stonewall Inn. The ensuing riots marked the inception of the militant gay demand for acceptance, and relief from the mores of a society that rejected them.

The Stonewall Riots signaled the birth of gay pride activism. On the other coast a drug culture sprang up as various self-styled "Gurus" such as Timothy Leary advised youth to "Turn on, tune in, and drop out." Marijuana (pot) and LSD and other hallucinogenic chemicals became the drugs of choice of what came to be known as the Hippie or Beatnik generation among disaffected youth in San Francisco.

The cigarettes and beer and whiskey of my generation were now passé. The Fifties were passé. The old ways were history—we were living in "interesting times." Love songs were out. Crooners were out. The famous Doo Wop music of the 50's that I really enjoyed was fading. Folk singers like Joan Baez (*We Shall Overcome*) and Judy Collins and Pete Seeger sang songs with social and political messages. Folk Rock groups were in, and their songs reflected the angst of the times. I'll give you a couple of examples and then move along in my narrative. From the Kingston Trio: "Where have all the young men gone—gone to soldiers every one. When will they ever learn?" And from Peter, Paul, and Mary: "If I had a Hammer, I'd hammer for justice and freedom all over this land!" And from the Mamas and the Papas, "If you're going to San Francisco be sure to wear some flowers in your hair." Harry Belafonte summed up the pathos of the times with his song. It ended like this: "They helped a lot of people but it seems the good die young. I just turned around and they're gone. Has anybody here seen my old friend Bobby? Can you tell me where he's gone? I just saw him walking out over the hill, with Abraham, Martin, and John."

To be fair, I guess you could wonder what the hell I was doing when all this shit was hitting the fan. The answer would have to be I that wasn't doing much. I was too old to get involved in campus and student unrest, I wasn't going to Vietnam, I never took drugs, and I really didn't spend too much time worrying about women's or gay or lesbian rights. N/A. Not Applicable. As I write this now, I realize that I've matured some over the last forty years, and have come to feel deeply about our responsibility to respect one another. What I was doing at that time though, was keeping busy working week on week off on the tug boats and spending my free time doing the singles thing and hanging in bars in Manhattan. I had some fun times dating a lovely airline stewardess (during those sexist days when stewardesses had to be young, slim, and pretty). Her name was Danny (Danielle), and she shared an Eastside apartment with other Stews that happened to be dating friends of mine who were cops. Between the girls' schedules, the cops' schedules, and my weeks off, one could never tell when a party would spontaneously erupt when one of the girls arrived home after a flight. Many were the nights I never made it home and I'm sure my folks got tired of hearing I was visiting a sick friend.

The Good Life

Jimmy McIvor's bar in Manhattan was called "Rumms". During the week it became my hangout. There was always a line outside Rumms to get in because it was one of the "in" places to go, and I kind of enjoyed just cruising past those lined-up hopefuls outside and taking my place among the regulars who had special access to the social scene. Jimmy and I became good friends, but he claims he is still mad at me for yelling at him and making a (drunken) scene because he threw a hooker out of his establishment just for plying her trade at the bar. I guess I must have just returned from that march on Washington, or something, because I claimed he was prejudiced! Weekends we all traveled to Vermont to ski and to continue partying at the ski house named "The Red Setter." Jesus, if the walls of that ski house could talk, what stories they could tell! Dinners at the massive kitchen table for twenty five revelers at a time were prepared by the house chef, and chief alcoholic, who we called Chink. Chink's crowning moment was when he discovered a mouse swimming in the stew he had prepared. Don't get me wrong. Chink prepared two or three course meals for us and they were really good. He knew what he was doing, because he was also the full time cook at Rumm's during the week. Roasts, pork loins, steaks, and chops, all with the usual accompaniment of vegetables and salad, were the usual Saturday Night Fare for the hungry skiers. After dinner, the table was always cleared for the giant bottle of Grand Marnier. We would sing the same songs every weekend till the wee hours and nobody seemed to mind. Jimmy could always be counted upon for a little ribaldry with some snippets of songs like "Up with your petticoat and down with your drawers . . . . I'll show you mine if you'll show me yours." These bacchanalia were tradition at the Red Setter. And so were the Alpine and cross country ski races that Jimmy organized throughout the Winter. We knew how to "party hearty." Now, in my yellow-leaf years, maybe I have calmed down a bit. I don't drink anymore.

Ray and Jimmy were partners in the house. Ray was the practical one. One time he purchased a washer and dryer so we could clean up our ski clothes. Jimmy, who really is one of a kind, then promptly went out and bought a rubber raft shaped like the Loch Ness Monster for the pond outside. Even though the pond was frozen! You couldn't make this up!

And of course, since there were guys and girls holed up together in these riotous quarters, it was not unexpected that raging hormones occasionally took effect. Two funny stories I'll have to share with you and that's all. I don't want to leave too bad an impression of me and those crazy, wonderful, and for the record, intelligent (sometimes) friends I hung with in those days. There was a quiet and dark side room in the Red Setter with a cozy fireplace and a comfortable couch alongside of it. Charlie Long, who was a rather pompous fellow, wanted to sleep there but found the couch occupied by Young Johnny Farnham who was a guest, rather than a member, of the house. Charlie told him to get up as he was a member and John was not. Young Johnny Farnham looked up at Charlie and said, "Oh yeah? I got one of your members under me right now, so get the hell out of here!" Young Johnny Farnham eventually did marry his partner of the evening so I guess it is OK to tell the story.

Jimmy tried his luck one evening too. He squired Elaina up to the bedroom that he shared with Ray Smith. "I can't do anything here," Elaina whispered, "Ray is sleeping in the next bed!" Jimmy said not to worry. He said that Ray slept like a log and wouldn't hear a thing, and besides, he couldn't see worth a damn either. Things seemed to be going along smoothly when Elaina stiffened and said, "He's moving. He's waking up!" Jimmy tried to calm her down by saying Ray probably couldn't see them anyway. A little while later Elaina leaped from the bed and bolted for the door. "Where are you going?" Jimmy asked. "He is putting on his glasses!" she shouted over her shoulder, and then she vanished from sight. We called Jimmy's room "The Honeymoon Suite" every day after that.

Brenda

A pretty girl named Brenda was the best girl skier in the house and was part of this gang also. You'll hear a lot more about her later because now that pretty girl is my wife. Maybe this is the time to tell you about how Brenda and I got together. It's a good story and, if nothing else, it will show you that she is quite possibly as crazy as I. Jimmy always claimed he was after her, but now he says that he got even with me because I married her! Jimmy, "Uncle Jimmy" now to our kids, no longer owns the New York nightlife, and he's slowed considerably, but we three have remained close friends all through the years. My story with Brenda began the day I told Jimmy that I would pick him up in Manhattan and drive up to Vermont with him. I forgot, and he was left alone, holding his bag, on the corner of Lexington Ave and 89st Street. I didn't realize it at the time, but for me it was to be a life-altering event.

I left Jimmy waiting for me in Manhattan. I forgot, and drove directly to the Red Setter from my home in the Bronx. The Red Setter is located in Manchester, Vermont, about a four hour drive from New York City. When I arrived I was surprised to see that so few people came up that weekend. The house seemed empty; there were probably only five or six people there when the usual crowd numbered at least twelve to fifteen on any given weekend. I asked Brenda out to dinner that night because there was no sense in cooking at home for so few. Of course I knew who Brenda was. I had noticed her a few summers earlier at the Hamptons while she was playing cards with some guys at the Cove Point Inn. (Another hot gathering spot) She didn't notice me, and we never spoke, but I remember she was an extraordinarily attractive girl. A few months later we did meet at a party in Manhattan, and later in Vermont I had a chance to give her a ride back from the mountain to the house my sporty Gremlin. (The Gremlin was the new American Motors car that looked like it was chopped off behind the back seat. It was so cheap that I remember it did not even come with a door to the glove compartment because I didn't order the "deluxe" model.) So, it is fair to say that I knew Brenda as a member of the ski house, and she knew me at the time.

We went to a nice steak place in Manchester called The Five Flies and don't ask me why it was called the Five Flies because I don't know why it was called the Five Flies. On the way out of the ski house I grabbed my ski jacket with the famous red setter logo. Brenda's jacket had been ordered, but it hadn't arrived yet. She grabbed Jimmy's jacket on her way out to the car. Now, these jackets were special. If you had one, that meant you were one of the heartiest weekend partiers in Southern Vermont. Brenda and I enjoyed our steaks, and I enjoyed the opportunity to talk with her and get to know her better. After dinner we drove to the Roundhouse Disco for some more drinks and dancing until I ran out of money around midnight. (I still had money in the house but not on me just then.) When I mentioned to Brenda that maybe we should head home, she excused herself and said she would be right back. Upon returning, she threw a handful of money on the bar and said we could stay a while longer. I asked her where she got the money, and she calmly told me she sold Jimmy's ski jacket to Baltimore Bob. I was astounded! She sold my friend's coat for beer money! I thought, "This is the girl I want spend my life with!" Brenda and I had a successful evening; we had a nice dinner and got to know each other better, and Baltimore Bob, the nudge, got the coat he never would have gotten any other way. We were all happy except Jimmy, who was going to be pissed.

We started dating regularly after that weekend. I guess we became what is called, "An Item." It was unusual to split off from the group, but I suppose it was getting about time. I was 34 years old and Brenda was 28, so maybe subconsciously we decided that serious dating wasn't as scary as before. People started to notice. John and Brenda were being mentioned in the same breath. It all came together on the Red Setter ski trip to Colorado. Jimmy had planned a ski trip to Steamboat Springs. It so happened that the trip coincided with my sister Fran's wedding in Aspen and I asked Brenda to be my date where, coincidentally, she would meet my family. Everyone loved her; and I was starting to get some ideas, too. After the wedding Brenda and I drove from Aspen to Steamboat to meet the others.

Steamboat

Steamboat was relatively new. People had been sliding on sticks for thousands of years, but recreational skiing, as enjoyed by the public at large, was a fairly new phenomenon in the U.S. Steamboat Ski Area opened for business during the Sixties and we arrived in 1974. We carried our madness with us. Jimmy ordered thirteen Tequilas to accompany our beers during a little après ski bacchanalia with the caveat that the waitress must have one with us. She was a tiny girl, and as was our wont, we gave her a nickname for the week. Big Red. Big Red explained her dilemma to her manager and rather than lose the sale he gave her the OK to imbibe with us. Jimmy was in top form. He went on to meet the infamous "Margo from Oneonta", and borrowed a hundred dollar bill from me to ply her with cocktails and regale her with tales of his skiing prowess (among other things). Margo from Oneonta proceeded to roll him of his dough. Jimmy asked me how long he had to have the money in his possession before it was officially a loan that counted. When I related the story to the others it was agreed that, since the money actually changed hands, he still was in debt to me. Guess what. He still is.

The week in Steamboat was great . . . Except for my roommate Gruber. I didn't know much about him but, I said yes when Jimmy asked me if I would room with him. The first night in Steamboat he told me he was cold and would it be OK if we kept the window shut? I prefer an open window, but to be a good roommate, I agreed. I went down to meet the others at the bar and when I returned Gruber was already in bed. Shortly after I climbed into mine he woke up and said, "I have the runs, and I am passing a lot of gas. Do you think Tums will be good for the runs?" I glanced over at the shut window and thought, Jimmy, you bastard, you did this to me on purpose!

We had never skied out west before and were really surprised by the difference from the crowded icy slopes of Vermont. Soft snow meant that we didn't have to "ski by sound" while attempting to edge into a turn. I guess I was impetuous, but I purchased a condo right out there on the mountain on that very same trip. The price I paid was $32,000 if you can imagine that today. I really thought that I might be able to work on the tug two weeks on and then two off and live in Steamboat. I would commute to New York on the first of the month and return to the mountains for the last two weeks. Brenda, it seems, had other plans.

We continued to date when we returned home. We remained an item and subject of speculation among our friends. We hadn't been dating long, but our friends all saw a lot of potential there. Brenda and I didn't have to pretend much—we couldn't, because we were both known so well by our peers. If the saying is true that you can tell much about a person by the company he keeps, then we both had a pretty good read on one another. Our friends thought we were a natural—except for one evening at a bar called Puddings in Manhattan. That was the final stop and head count for all of us returning from a Vermont weekend. Brenda and I were very late arriving back in Puddings after one trip because the driving was dismal. The roads were wet, the sleet was coating my windshield, and my windshield washer fluid wasn't pumping well. We had to stop every few miles to manually wipe the windshield clean so we could see. When we finally did arrive in Manhattan, Brenda innocently announced to all that "John's spritzer doesn't work." After a few seconds pause to digest this information, one of the guys said to her, "Why are you going out with him for, then?" Nobody, but nobody, escaped the cutting wit of our crowd.

The Proposal

Brenda and I survived, however, and a few months later Brenda told me we should think about getting married. First she primed me with quite a few Grand Marniers in order to soften me up a little. To this day I insist that Brenda proposed to me but that isn't exactly the case. Close, but not exactly the case. I guess I better tell you how it happened. You deserve to know how John finally abandoned his life of carefree bachelorhood and committed to a life with the beautiful Brenda Manning. We were at Puddings again. Out of the blue Brenda looks at me and says, "If we keep going out together we should consider getting married." I was taken by surprise. "You would think of marrying me?" "Yes", she said. I fumbled around then for the right words. They came out something like this: "I'm not asking. But if I were asking, what would you say if I did ask which I'm not asking." Brenda said that she would say yes. While my befuddled brain was being overloaded, Brenda excused herself and made a visit to the ladies room. When she returned I blurted out, "Well then, would you?" Brenda said, "Would I what." "Oh for Chris-sake", I remember saying, "Don't make me go through this whole thing again!" Well, Brenda said yes again, and that meant we were going to be married. I'm such a romantic.

A Little Bit of Me

I know that I can tell a lot of funny stories. Anyone who is reasonably perceptive can tell you that comedy often hides much that a person is afraid to share. Why did I take so long to finally marry? It wasn't for lack of dates. I know that there were other girls who may have married me had I asked. Why hadn't I? The simple inescapable reason is that I was unable to really, really, expose enough of my inner me to establish a completely healthy relationship. It was a tragic failing. I would date someone until things were serious, and then cowardly bail out. I know I did this, and I'm not proud of myself. But I'm very introspective, and I was unable to let anyone see into the real me. My flaws and my fears of confrontation, my inability to develop what I could call a personality forceful enough to succeed in competitive situations remained locked inside, and I knew I could never be truly intimate with anyone until those barriers to my inner me were broken down. I just didn't have a lot of confidence in myself. When the time came to either shit or get off the pot I got off the pot. Before Brenda I had a lot of opportunities. I let a lot of girls down who deserved better, and I'm ashamed of myself. Why am I telling you this? Because Brenda was different. I joke about her asking me to marry her, but the way she broached that topic left a breach that I could charge through. I'm not sure I could have ever been sure enough of myself to propose marriage to Brenda. I knew that I wanted to marry her, and when she brought it up I knew it was the time to finally scale that wall. Did all my inhibitions disappear? No, of course not. I still write better than I talk. I still leave situations thinking I could have said, or should have done, but now at the age of 71 they don't seem so important. After 37 years of marriage and with two children we raised I guess Brenda has me figured out. And she stays with me anyway, so I think I'm finally all right.

We were married at Sacred Heart Church in Hartsdale, New York, on November 16, 1974. That was about ten months from the time we started dating. Brenda was twenty-eight and I was just two weeks shy of my thirty-fifth birthday.

Transition

Starting Life With Brenda, President Richard M. Nixon, Watergate, The Investigation, The End of the Line

TRANSITION

I am reminded of a conversation I had with a girl whom I met on one of the eight marathon Avon Breast Cancer Walks that I made every year for charity. She was partaking in the New York Walk, as was I, to help raise money for Breast Cancer research. I'll tell you more about that later. We met casually, and as we walked along First Ave an amiable conversation ensued. Whitney is a Jewish girl from Kansas City, Kansas, who was the caregiver for her elderly grandmother. Her grandmother, she told me, was an immigrant who left the upheavals of the Shtetls and the infamous pogroms that wrecked havoc on the Jewish societies of Eastern Europe around the turn of the century. She told her grandchildren many stories of life in Russia when she was a girl and how families fought to maintain their Jewish heritage under trying conditions. Her stories were so real, and depicted a life that witnessed such joy and such sadness that the grandchildren taped them so they could be replayed. Whitney told me that as her grandmother lay dying, her request always was, "Whitney, play me my stories." We thought about that as we walked along together, and decided the reason her grandmother derived such solace from those tapes was because it was affirmation that, as long as her story existed, she would never truly be gone. So maybe, in a small but similar way, I write this for the same reason.

I'm going to call this chapter "The Transition." I was married and my single bon-vivant bachelor days were over. My life was changing. Brenda and I were getting used to each other; we found an apartment and began life together as newly married couples do. By the way, do you know what the first thing newly marrieds do on their honeymoon?

They unpack their bags and then they "Put their things together." Pardon the poor joke . . . Anyway, these were our early days together, the days when we were both working, when we had plenty of money, and were thinking of buying a house. We enjoyed our vacations, and we enjoyed each other as we looked ahead to the life before us.

Starting Life with Brenda

Our first (and only) apartment was located at 280 Bronxville Road in the quiet village of Bronxville, New York. I don't remember how we lugged our furniture up to the eighth floor. I think Jimmy helped, but settling in to our new apartment is a blur today. I do remember it was a pretty neat place because it was one story higher than the surrounding roofs. We had a door from our living room that got us out to a balcony on the roof and we had a great overlook to the village. We also inherited a pet of sorts. The bird could be found napping every day until twilight time: then we would watch it awaken and soar to the skies over our building. He would dart in and out of our line of vision in search of flying bugs, moths, or whatever flying insect that he could swoop into his gaping beak. I bought a bird book and we identified our evening companion as a Nighthawk. We kind of made him our mascot, and we called him simply, "Hawk." Brenda and I enjoyed our evenings up there on the roof. I used a little ingenuity by creating a little roof top Eden for ourselves. We grew tomatoes, peppers, and eggplants in dirt-filled five gallon buckets that I lugged up from the street when the elevator was working—which wasn't often. That's another story, but believe me, many were the days that Brenda and I trudged those eight flights of stairs leading to our new home.

We were living large in those days. On my crew change days I would arrange to meet Brenda at five o'clock when she finished work. We would have dinner down in New York. Frequently we would wind up for a few drinks with the old crew and Jimmy McIvor at Rumm's, his establishment on Fiftieth Street in Manhattan. We both were making good salaries at the time; Brenda and I were each earning roughly the same, about $25,000 per year. That was enough to take care of what little bills we had, have some fun, and still save most of what Brenda made. Try doing that today!!

We took a cruise to Bermuda with my best man, P.K. Joyce and his wife, Kathleen. We straddled our rented motorbikes and scooted around the island searching out exotic locations and admiring the pastel colored homes and pristine waters that were blotted up by the famous pink tinted beaches that lined the southern shore of the Island. We found Jobson's Cove and had a swim in one of the more beautiful spots you'll find. We traveled a lot in those days: Colonial Williamsburg, the famous Skyline Drive over the Blue Ridge Mountains, Cape Cod, and, of course, our annual pilgrimage to Colorado. Yes, Brenda and I were living large. We weren't simply in love . . . we really liked each other, too. BK and I had fun together and Life was good.

Working as I did, with one week on, and one week off, the boats gave me a lot of free time during the weeks that I was off. That's when I would lug the five gallon pails up to our roof, paint the apartment, or try my misguided hand at some craft that was beyond my talents. Like carpentry. The windows of our apartment opened up to the roof of the adjacent ells of the building. Anyone could walk across the roof and climb through the window to our bedroom. It made Brenda nervous—especially when I was away on the tug. So I got to work. Hammer, nails, plywood, and saw were put to use as I cleverly constructed a bookcase that fit into our window frame. "Not bad for a guy from the Bronx", I thought as I stepped back to review my handiwork. Brenda was happy. Then the whole God-Damned thing fell out of the window, books and all, and landed on our bedroom floor one night a few weeks later when we were asleep. It scared the hell out of us. We thought we were being invaded via the roof! I nailed some wood back there, and thereafter left that home handyman business to those who know something about it. I'm a reader and a writer and a dreamer—that's what I do best—and I have a little story about reading to share with you now.

I volunteered my time at The New York Lighthouse for the Blind on 59th Street. My job was to read to the blind patrons that came to the lighthouse. Often the clients would arrive with textbooks to be read, or possibly some research papers to complete for graduate work.

Sometimes the work was as mundane as simply reading the New York Times or some trip itineraries for their information. One person puzzled me, though. I often was assigned to read to Bob Rodriguez, and he always came armed with a load of books containing what I took to be fairy tales. College academics I could understand, but fairy tales every week? When I asked the supervisor about this I was surprised by her answer. She explained to me that it was Bob's job, "He is one of the world's foremost authorities on national cultures as illustrated by the type of fairy tales and sagas prevalent in their culture." I thought about this for a while. I thought about trolls living among the rocks and crags of Norway, of billy goats lurking under bridges, or of the lost children stolen by evil witches in the dark woods of the Black Forest of Germany. Bob's work was interesting once it made sense to me. I did that work for a few years and it taught me to reappraise my thinking of the talents and abilities of those we would call handicapped. Somehow I believe that I sometimes see things clearer now because of my association with those who are unable to see. I'm happy I did that volunteer work. I got more than I gave.

While Brenda and I were busy living our idyllic existence troubling events were darkening the national horizon. This will be the time to tell you about Richard M. Nixon

President Richard M. Nixon

The news of the day was filled with events playing out in Washington D.C. as Richard M. Nixon fought to preserve his presidency and then ultimately lost it. 1974 is a year that will be remembered by many, not because Brenda and I got married, but because it was the year that saw the only resignation of a sitting President in the history of the

United States. Richard M. Nixon was an intelligent and sometimes effective president, but with a fatally flawed character. I never liked him. Most people didn't. He was seen by many as an opportunist and not above manipulating events to suit his own agenda. He burst on the national scene after a particular nasty campaign during which his questionable insinuations helped him defeat his opponent for senator from California. Seeing how the wind was blowing during the witch hunt that was described as "The McCarthy Era," Nixon proclaimed himself a staunch anti-communist. At that time the only two rival powers still standing at the end of World War Two were vying for hegemony in a fractured world. His rise was rapid and he was chosen as Dwight Eisenhower's vice president during those early years of the "Cold War." His relationship with Ike was cool. The Eisenhowers never allowed the Nixons to their private rooms in the East Wing of the White House. Once, when asked what contribution Nixon made to foreign policy, Ike replied, "Give me a minute and I might think of one." Nixon wasn't stupid—I have to believe he knew that many people didn't like him—and it fed his natural tendency to distrust people and to get them before they got him. This unfortunate tendency is what eventually destroyed his presidency. His philosophy was aptly summed up by the sign reportedly displayed in his White House office. "Once you got them by the balls their hearts and minds will follow!"

His paranoia was further fed by his close loss (0.2% of the popular vote) to John F. Kennedy in the 1961 presidential election. It was alleged—but was never proven—that Kennedy actually stole a few key states with a little help from his old man's money. Nixon subsequently ran for Governor of California and lost again. This prompted him to indulge in a little self-pity when he told the press that they "Wouldn't have Dick Nixon to kick around anymore." However, he made a comeback in 1968, winning the presidency by taking advantage of the unpopularity of the Vietnam War by announcing he had a "Secret Plan" to end the war. There was no secret plan—Nixon exacerbated the national ire by ordering carpet bombing of the enemy's supply lines as they snaked through the independent countries of Laos and Cambodia—countries with whom we were not at war.

To give the devil his due, Nixon showed himself to be a capable and far-sighted head of state. He successfully competed with Russia by establishing a mutual spirit of Détente (cooperation) with them, and he also displayed exceptional vision by establishing relations with China. Nixon is also credited with the longest long-distance call on record when he dialed up Neil Armstrong when he made the first landing on the moon! On domestic issues President Nixon's record was surprisingly liberal. He established OSHA to oversee safety in the workforce; he adjusted social security payments to inflation, and was an effective proponent of affirmative action programs. He is seen in history as a flawed and tragic figure that held such promise, but he was undone by his personality in the scandal called Watergate.

Watergate

The Watergate is the name of a prestigious hotel in the Capitol. The Democratic National Committee had its main offices there in 1972. Five overly zealous Republican partisans, one of them a strange macho man named G. Gordon Liddy (who once held his finger to a flame to show friends how stoic he could be while withstanding pain) broke into the Democratic offices for reasons which have been never fully explained. One theory was that the Democratic committee might have held info damaging to Nixon's re-election chances. The ensuing investigation revealed the existence of a "Dirty Tricks Team" that the Republicans had organized to create political sabotage on people who had been placed on their enemies list. Two un-savory characters named E. Howard Hunt and the aforementioned G. Gordon Liddy headed up this dirty tricks group. These guys did jail time later. It is another reason I don't like the affectations of folks who initialize their first names. The activities of this group fit Nixon's paranoia and his philosophy of "Get them before they get you."

Investigation

The Watergate investigation turned up information about a possible connection between the burglary and the Republican Committee to re-elect the President. This caused folks to wonder if people higher up in the organization could be implicated in the plot. When the names of the Attorney General and two highly placed White House Aides, one of whom was Nixon's Chief of Staff, surfaced, the scent was picked up by two young reporters on the Washington Post. After unearthing a highly secret and reliable Mole called "Deep Throat," Bob Woodward and Carl Bernstein delved into the terrible secrets of the administration of Richard Nixon. As more and more names fell under this investigation, people were now asking what the president knew, and when did he know it. Nixon stonewalled. A special investigator was named. Elliot Richardson, the new Attorney General who replaced the disgraced John Mitchell (who later went to jail), resigned rather than obey the President's order to fire the special investigator. Things remained at a stand off until the "Smoking Gun" was revealed.

The End

It was finally disclosed that Nixon had secretly installed a system for taping all conversations in the White House. The judge, Robert Sirica, demanded that the tapes be made public. Nixon refused, and the groundswell of public opinion turned on him. Under pressure he submitted partial and edited transcripts but the clamor for the tapes persisted. When finally, under duress, Nixon released the tapes they were found to have an eighteen minute gap in a crucial conversation in which he was involved. His secretary claimed to have erased the tape by mistake, but no one believed her. When further examination of the tapes revealed that the President himself discussed the possibility of short-stopping the investigation only six days after the break-in, the question of what he knew and when he knew it was solved. He was taped discussing with his Chief of Staff the possible use of hush money to be paid to E. Howard Hunt. Also discussed on the same tapes was the possibility of having the CIA testify (falsely) that the investigation had to be discontinued because it involved a matter of national security. His fate was finally sealed. The lies, the evasions, and the foot dragging of two years were over. His support evaporated; and faced with the certainty of impeachment by the House, and conviction by the Senate, Nixon resigned his Office. Richard M. Nixon was brought down by his own inclination to secrecy, and by the paranoia that drove him to see enemies on all sides. He was forced to resign in disgrace, the only American President to do so, in 1974.

Family

Lake Mohawk and the Kids Arrival, Brenda, Mooma and Moof, Kevin and Krissy

FAMILY

Brenda bought us a house in 1976. I had some sort of vague idea that it was probably the best thing to do, but had no real plan about where to live or what to buy. It seemed like most of my friends followed a pattern of getting married, and then buying a home and moving out of the Bronx to someplace in the suburbs. People from Brooklyn or Queens generally moved out to Long Island while the Bronx folks gravitated to Westchester County north of New York. I had rarely given it much thought. I guess I was surprised that I had even gotten married in the first place, never mind making as drastic a move as deserting my comfortable Bronx cocoon. New Jersey was never on my horizon. No one I knew ever moved to New Jersey on purpose. Sheila, Brenda's sister, and her husband Rudi advised us that if we were thinking of entering the housing market we would be better off doing it sooner rather than later as the home prices were increasing at a rate faster than we could save. Brenda and I agreed. She traveled out to Jersey later in the week when I was away on the tug and Rudi drove her around the area and introduced her to various realtors willing to show them what was available. When I arrived home at the end of the week she greeted me with, "Hello, home owner!"

Of course Brenda prefaced the transaction by saying it was contingent upon my approval, but that was already a given. She knew I would agree to her choice, especially since I had no real preference of my own. But New Jersey? I have to admit that it took me many, many years to admit that I lived in New Jersey. I shed my Bronx skin slowly. I never forgot William B. Williams, a famous disk jockey of radio days, who is credited with saying, "When you're not living in New York you are just camping out." To her credit, and with Rudi's sage urging, we purchased our house in the community of Lake Mohawk. It might shock you today to read this, but the purchase price of our home was all of $41,250 with a mortgage, including taxes, of $333. per month. Brenda's sister, Maureen, never noted for her sagacity or reluctance to comment on her personal preferences, congratulated us on our "cute little starter house." I am sitting at my computer desk writing from our "starter home" 34 years later. We haven't moved, and at this point we never intend to move, either. Our roots are firmly planted in the community of Lake Mohawk. I guess I better tell you now about the place where Kevin and Krissy were raised and where Brenda and I passed from being young marrieds to the senior citizens we are today.

Lake Mohawk is located in Sparta, New Jersey. Sparta is what I suppose one would call a "bedroom community" in Sussex County in the northwest corner of the state. A bedroom community is, by definition, a community in which most of the inhabitants work elsewhere and commute daily to their place of employment. They return home to eat, sleep and prepare for another commute the following day. It is not a bad thing, and is fairly common, given the central location of business enterprises and the availability of commuter transportation such as bus, rail, and auto over a convenient highway system. Lately, more people are now "cyber-commuting." That is the new term for working from home utilizing the internet, conference calls, and other modes of high speed technology that are being continually introduced to the business community. But for now, at least, I can say that Sussex is a laid back rural county in an otherwise hectic state both in terms of population, income, taxes, and industry. Lake Mohawk is an oasis in this teeming beehive of activity. The lake country in this area of the state is noted for its tourist attractions. Notables from far and wide including Thomas Edison and Babe Ruth, availed themselves of the relaxation afforded in a setting that encouraged swimming, boating, fishing, hiking, climbing, and the thrills of a now defunct amusement park located on Lake Hopatcong. (Ho-Pat-Cong—Don't worry, I couldn't pronounce it when I got here either.)

Lake Mohawk was formed in 1927 right in the center of a pristine area when the headwaters of the Wallkill River were dammed and a depression between two mountain ridges consequently flooded to create a lake three miles long and about a mile wide. A boardwalk and a club house that are still in use were constructed at the east end of the Lake. The little town that sprang up around these facilities was built to resemble an Alpine Plaza and still catches the eye today. It was the first view of the lake that convinced me that Brenda's choice was perfect for us. Our house is located about two miles down the lake from the Village Plaza at 472 East Shore Trail. We didn't move in immediately, we still were enjoying the "DINKS" lifestyle in New York and felt no immediate need to vacate our Bronxville apartment and our proximity to the City. DINKS, for those of you curious enough to wonder, is the acronym for dual-income-no-kids. It is kind of out of fashion in today's conversation because now most families require two incomes just to make ends meet, kids or not. We worked, we saved enough of Brenda's salary to pay half down on the house, and we managed, to indulge ourselves on a cruise to Bermuda. We were like the young kids we complain of today. We wanted everything, NOW!

Brenda came home from work in the evening around Christmas time 1976 and at dinner she smiled at me and then told me yes. "Yes what?" I queried. Yes, she nodded and smiled again, and then it hit me. We were going to have a baby! Nine months later I remember spending an extremely nervous night at Lawrence Hospital in Bronxville August

30, 1977. Kev was slow in coming. Brenda was in labor all night. At one time a modern sensing machine couldn't detect our unborn baby's heartbeat and it scared the daylights out of us. We were reassured when the machine proved faulty and the heartbeat was still strong when we heard it through less sophisticated instruments. I remember I told Brenda that I would rather be in a plane than the delivery room. I was afraid of planes at the time. The appearance of forceps that resembled early instruments of torture unnerved me, but I was assured that they were necessary to turn the baby for normal delivery. Brenda was a hero. She proved steady as a rock under all that pressure and I was a wreck. I was in the delivery room the whole time trying to be helpful by wiping Brenda's brow until she said, "enough, already!" And then around six thirty in the morning we were blessed when our son Kevin entered our world. We were Dinks no longer; it was time to move to our house at Lake Mohawk and begin raising our family.

There were some renovations we wanted to make to our new home. An unused garage was converted to a living room, and a small bedroom wall was knocked down to make one larger bedroom for me and Brenda. I remember that most of the rugs were the shag carpet type and during the course of these renovations much of the plaster and sheet rock dust settled into the shag. I attempted to cure this problem by taking the rugs out, hanging them over a line, and beating the crap out of them with a stick. Simple but effective. I had to laugh when our neighbor Ted Ford came over in the middle of my workout. "What's the matter?" he asked, "Don't you like the house anymore?" We liked the house alright; it was just that we wanted to add our own personal touch to the dwelling. Many more changes were in the hopper but another blessed event overshadowed our new move and usurped our projected alterations.

Maybe I was more virile around Christmas, or maybe my aim was better or something, but it happened again. This time Brenda and I were visiting my sister Fran and her husband Jinx at their home in Aspen, Colorado. Brenda suspected she was pregnant again and Fran wouldn't let us leave Colorado until we knew for sure. Yes, the answer came back; we were to be parents again! Krissy was the only one of us to be born a native of New Jersey.

Some things you don't forget, and sitting here at my computer I still recall the details of how Kristine Michelle, now simply known to one and all as Krissy, blessed us with her arrival. Brenda woke me in the wee small hours of the morning of September 27, 1978 to inform me that the baby was coming. Remembering the long vigil that that slow-poke Kevin put us through thirteen months earlier, I asked her if she was sure the baby was coming. Brenda said yes, she was sure, and I gallantly replied, "Well, in that case, I better get my sleep!" Brenda re-awoke me around breakfast time and said she wasn't kidding. We had to get to the hospital immediately. Brenda was getting frantic and it didn't help when I pulled into the parking lot of our local Seven-Eleven to get my morning traveler, a sixteen ounce coffee to take out. And Brenda grew even more frantic as we got tied up in the A.M. rush hour traffic on route 80 and I refused to drive on the shoulder to avoid it. We made Saint Clair's Hospital in Denville and Brenda was wheeled up to the room. When I parked the car and ambled up to see how she was doing she told me to get the nurse. I told her I had just seen the nurse and she said there was still time. "GET THE NURSE!" Brenda finally yelled at her dawdling husband. So I did. She wasn't kidding. Brenda made it to the delivery room and Krissy slid into our world with only minutes to spare. I helped a little on this one; the doctor let me cut Krissy's umbilical cord. Later Kris was known to have said that Pop made her belly-button! And I never got a chance to finish my coffee traveler.

This story has quite a bit to go because I have a lot to relate. But I'll take a quick moment here to insert a quick but heart felt editorial comment. Marrying my wife, Brenda, and the birth of our two children have been, for me, the luckiest and finest aspects of my life. I have been blessed with a wonderful, kind, and caring, and still beautiful wife who has put up with my foibles these last thirty-seven years. I have been blessed with Kevin and Krissy, now in their early thirties, for the adults they have become. It is they by whom I can judge the value of my time on the planet. I can put my feet up now and know that I did all right. And that is a very good feeling . . .

Brenda

Up to now my narrative focused primarily on my favorite subject. Me! Just kidding, of course, but now it really is time to tell you about

Brenda, my wife, my friend, the girl I love, and truly the better half of my nature. Brenda just seems to fall naturally into this part of the story because, with the birth of our children, the tale of our family becomes paramount. And the role of mother and caregiver looms ever larger. When the children were infants I didn't know much about caring for them. Brenda became the most important person in their young lives and she was superbly fitted to the task. But she is much more than a mother. She was, and still is, the beautiful and talented, and intelligent woman who led a lively and fun-loving life long before she met me. She had forged a successful career of her own, and now it is time to tell you about the girl I just call Bren, or maybe just, BK.

I found it hard to write this section. I spent a really long time trying to figure out just how to go about writing about someone other than myself, or some historical event that occurred in my lifetime. Brenda's story is intensely personal. She is an important, and valued, part of my life and I want to do justice to the girl I have been happily married to these last 37 years. First I have to tell you that she is 100 percent a "people person." Brenda thrives on company and interaction with others either in person or via telephone. Makes no difference—BK relates to people in ways that astound me. I know that Kevin and Krissy will agree with me, but if by chance some grandchildren or great, great, grandchildren ever read this, they better know that no one, absolutely no one, could work a crowded room like my BK. We took a test one time that would indicate our personality traits and found that I would wear down quickly interacting with people, while Brenda was energized by them. We complement each other, I guess. I call her the Saint of the Old People. Brenda has a heart of gold for the old folks; my parents, our elderly aunts, and even some neighbors were all in some way touched by the caring spirit of my wife. But don't just picture her sitting around serving tea to geriatrics—picture her instead with the moxie to sky-dive from a plane 10,000 feet over Sussex County because she wanted to do something special for her 50th birthday. Picture her as the best girl skier in Jimmy's ski house in Vermont. Picture her racing down NASTAR courses on various slopes to win a bunch of medals that she liked to show off on her ski jacket. Picture her falling out of a moving jeep after a few too many drinks with McIvor. That event, by the way, earned her a plaque from the Budweiser Company as "Brenda Manning, Miss Saloon Girl, 1974." And finally picture the look on her face when our kids, when they were little, found that plaque while rummaging around all the accumulated junk in Jimmy's ski house. "Mama, was that you??"

Brenda graduated from Mercy College, Dobb's Ferry, in 1969 and went to work for AT&T. Computers, the tool that no one seems to be able live without today, were just in their infancy and Brenda was asked if she would be willing to train on these new fangled tools of the future. She was trained pretty much from the ground floor of the technology boom and when I met her she was holding down a good job with the accounting firm of Peat, Marwick, Mitchell in New York. Her job was developing technical courses and teaching CPA's how to utilize this technology in their practice. I told you she is gregarious, and I told you she is adventurous, and I told you she is fun. Now I'm telling you that Brenda is smart, too. And she was, (still is) pretty enough for me to have taken notice of her from among the crowd one summer weekend years ago at the shore. She was playing cards with a bunch of guys, so I only stared at her from afar. Little did I know that a few years later she would consent to be Mrs. Klumpp.

Brenda deserves much more credit than she would ever ask for. My job on the tug boats dictated that I would spend one week away on the boat followed by one week at home. Kind of an odd schedule, but my family never knew me to do anything else. The point is, Brenda was alone half of the year while caring for two children only thirteen months apart. I wonder how many young mothers in today's age of nannies and day care would have maintained the schedule that Brenda accepted without complaint. I don't think I ever gave her the credit and respect she deserved at the time. Later, though, I came to realize all she has done for our family. Without my wife's help our financial situation would surely have overwhelmed us. Not that I didn't make decent money—I did—but all the family extras and vacations we enjoyed were subsidized by Brenda's earnings. Even today, thirty years later, Brenda's earnings are helping with the expense of Krissy's wedding. We are a team, Brenda and I. My wife received her Master's Degree in technological education from Rutgers University and taught evenings at the local community college. When economic times were tough during strikes or lay-offs, Brenda and I, together, opened an office cleaning business a few evenings a week. (And she would work it alone when I was on the tug.) But her real avocation shone through when she entered the personnel employment business. Brenda has been involved finding people jobs for more than a dozen years. She is still contributing.

This month Brenda turns 65 and will receive her first Medicare card to complement her social security check. Seems funny to write that—seems like only a few paragraphs ago I was telling you about the pretty girl I noticed so many years ago. Where does the time go? Andy Rooney was right when he said that life is like a roll of toilet paper; the closer one gets to the end, the faster it goes.

This year Brenda and I welcomed the arrival of the New Year with a rather odd activity that we had done three times before. We drove to

New York City's Central Park, and then along with about 6000 other crazies, we did a four mile Champagne Run through the Park New Years Eve at mid-night. It really isn't as looney as it sounds. People come from far and wide and the camaraderie among the adventurous is palpable. There was dancing in the park from Ten P.M. on, and a costume parade that took place just prior to the run. At midnight the run began and we dashed off under a terrific fireworks display that illuminated the wintry evening with dazzling color. The roads through the park were lined with well wishers as we jogged along, and I remember thinking how happy I was that BK and I were running in, rather than watching, the event. I thought to myself, "Life is not a spectator sport!"

Thirty-seven years have passed into our history. And for all these thirty-seven years I have remained humbled and grateful for Mrs. Brenda Klumpp sharing my life. Brenda is truly a beautiful woman. Beautiful inside as well as outside.

But wait . . . I forgot to mention her culinary expertise. While we were dating, Brenda asked me up for a wonderful dinner of Chicken Divan. Later I was invited to savor her Chicken Kiev, all tasty and buttery, with just the right seasoning. My gastronomic taste buds were later titillated by a wonderful London Broil. Wow, I remember thinking, this girl knows her way around the kitchen! Later, when we were married, BK served up Chicken Kiev, followed by Chicken Divan, followed by London Broil, followed by Chicken Divan, followed by Chicken Kiev, and followed again by London Broil. I began to see a pattern emerging . . . . Then one day she asked me how long should she nuke the hot dog in the microwave. I knew then that I was in trouble.

Mooma and Moof

I suppose the best way to tell you about my parents is to write about them as a couple rather than separately. And they were a couple, having been together for over fifty years. Mom and Dad knew each other from early on. They grew up next door to each other on Woodycrest Avenue in the Highbridge section of the Bronx. If any one wants to know where that is, all they have to do is find Yankee Stadium and see the hill that rises behind it. My folks were married in 1937. My mother, Gertrude (she didn't like that name) Kelly, a Catholic girl from Irish parents, married Carl Klumpp, from a German family with no particular religious affiliation. In those days inter-marrying among different ethnic groups was not common; the exception being the German-Irish combination, which was. Because my father was a non-Catholic, they were not allowed to be married in the church; The ceremony was conducted by the priest in his parish house, or rectory, as it was then called. I never wondered about it, but one day, long after my mother passed away, I asked my Aunt Dot why my mother's wedding picture didn't have her wearing the traditional white gown. She explained to me what I just told you; because they were not to be married in the church proper a white gown was deemed inappropriate. My two sisters and I were raised catholic. My father never converted. He was, I guess, what you might call a mystic. At the waning days of his life he always said he believed in life after death and, as he got older and frailer, he often spoke of "Going on his next adventure." Wherever his "next adventure" took him, it was to a good place; He was a good man. He was baptized once but I don't think it counted. My little sister Fran, when she was about 7 years old, was so worried Dad would not go to heaven without being baptized that she took matters into her own hands and poured water all over his head when he was napping on the couch after playing a Saturday round of golf with his friends.

My mother was like a rock. It was her family. Dad worked and Mom ran the house, did the shopping, prepared the meals, did the wash, and clothed the kids, and made sure we did our homework. I'm sure an editorial comment is due at this point, but I'll leave it alone except to say that it was true that women were pretty much expected to fulfill these roles, and most did. However, there was more to it than met the eye. The old saying that "Dad rules the roost, but Mama rules the rooster" was pretty much true, including my family while I was growing up. In my younger days I related better to my mother than my father. She was always there when the kids needed her. She did the homework with us. (Even though she threatened to kill me one night because I couldn't learn fractions. Even today I have trouble coming up with correct answers four out of three times.) She always had our school clothes ready, made our lunches, and generally was available if we got hurt playing some game or other. She would give us our chores, like going to Nat and Sy, the local grocers, with a list of what we should buy and the instructions to tell Nat to "put it in the book." She would come and pay it later. Many times she sent us to retrieve the wash from the washing machine located in the basement. We would put the wash on the dumbwaiter and Mom would pull it up to the apartment. We had one lone machine that served the 30 families in our apartment house, and you better be there when the rinse cycle ended because someone else was standing by to use it. The clothes dryer was the clothes line up on the roof or the wire frame that was suspended from the ceiling in the bathroom. And if you don't know what clothes pins are, you can ask someone my age to tell you.

Mom had a fairly set routine which never varied much. She never learned how to drive a car. She would take the bus to the A&P on Fordham Road, shop, and then join her coffee klatch of friends at the sweet shop for an hour or so most afternoons. I remember that I would wait for her to get off the bus around three o'clock and I would help her upstairs with the bundles. She had a great sense of humor and was a great mimic. It was fun to hear her relate stories of people she knew or met. One of her classics was when two ladies, Flossie and Josie, who lived with their families upstairs, witnessed an armed robbery at the local supermarket one afternoon. Josie couldn't see very well—she really needed to wear glasses—and Flossie tended to stutter. As Josie was checking out, an armed man busted in and put a shotgun on the counter and demanded money. Josie pushed him roughly aside and told him to wait his turn, and while he was at it take his umbrella off the counter. Flossie, who was on line behind Josie, was spitting all over herself trying to tell her it was a "st-st-st-st-stick up! We'd laugh every time she told the story. It was an interesting neighborhood that we grew up in. One time Franny found Bernie the pharmacist tied up on the floor behind his counter in the store. He was all tied up with surgical tape and Franny left him there and ran home and then waited for our father to get home from work so she could tell him! Bernie was on the floor for quite a while.

When we all got a bit older and we could care for ourselves Mom got a job in the housewares department of Alexander's Dept. store. She never failed to get home with another story from some customer or other she encountered that day. Perhaps that is where I get it from. I seem to find the bizarre or the humor in situations that may, perhaps rightly, go unnoticed by others. Mom did have a temper though, and sometimes it showed. She's gone now so I can relate to you the time she picked me up and pushed my head over the gas stove and told me to "stick your tongue out dammit!" She was going to burn it off because I told a lie. (She really didn't burn me, but it scared the hell out of me so that I didn't do it again.) I also made (once) the serious mistake of smelling the spaghetti Mama served on my dinner plate. Her hand flew out, grabbed the back of my head, and mushed my face into the food. "How does it smell now!" she yelled. I didn't do that again, either. In 1947 there was a major snow storm, a blizzard really, in the City. Somehow or other I made Mom mad again. My sister Barbara still has a small scar near her mouth where my mother hit her in the face with the shovel that she was swinging at me. I ducked. And she could hold a grudge if the issue warranted it. She never forgave Sister Gertrude, the fifth grade grammar school Nun. My little sister Franny was a high-spirited kid who always was happy and liked to laugh. Sister Gertrude took Fran one day and made her kneel in front of the class and told her to pray aloud because that stupid Nun told my little sister that she was possessed by the devil. Mom tore into that nun and anyone else around and took Fran out of the school. She never set foot in a Catholic church for about 40 years until she met Father Dan Murphy, the pastor of our church here in Jersey. She was strict but fair and sometimes we didn't realize the attachment and love she had for all of us. Franny's problem with the nun probably had a lot to do with her self-esteem and later problems with alcohol and it affected both my parents deeply. Every once in a while my mother's bitterness would surface. My father frequently mentioned his sadness for Fran.

I mentioned that as a child I suffered from severe asthma. Some mornings I would find myself gasping around the house and Mom would yell at me to take a pill and go to school. Then she would sit and look out from the second floor window and watch me lean on tree trunks while trying to catch my breath as I walked to school. She never let me cop a plea or feel sorry for myself—but my Aunt Dot would tell me later how my mother was hurting inside but was afraid to let me know it because she was afraid I might give in to the disease. And I already mentioned that my father drove seven hours one way to take me home when I was sick.

Mom seemed to have found her nitch at the kitchen window. If we were out late during our teen age years, there would be Mom sitting at the kitchen window smoking her Camel cigarettes until we were home. This, of course, would embarrass Barbara and she would always tell her dates that there was some crazy lady who lived on the second floor who stayed up at the window smoking every night—until one time she took her date home and the date blurted out, "You're the Crazy Lady!"

Mom took care of us. She was the foundation of the family. Her job was to see the home was run the way it should be. Sometimes, and this is one of them, it is difficult to write about my mother. She was always there for us; whenever we needed her, she was just there. We got to expect that, and when I try to write about her it all comes out in one giant image. She was Just Mom.

It was some years later that I realized that it was Dad who showed us things. In word and deed he was the teacher. He was quieter than Mom and I'm afraid that we took it for granted when he got up and went to work every day to support our family. It was obvious that Mom took care of the house, but Moofa's contribution was more subtle and I didn't fully appreciate it until I grew older. It was Dad who showed us how to work and to be responsible. The only time I remember him using bad language was when I was in my twenties and I arrived home late for dinner because I stopped at the bar for a few beers after work. I never got into that habit because he came down on me in no uncertain terms. He told (yelled at) me, in front of the whole family, that he wanted no more of that shit—and to stay out of the f**king bars after work. It was probably one of the most important lessons I learned from him—and I never forgot how seriously he meant it because of the use of the "F" word. I don't know that I ever remember him using that word again except once more when he was old.

He was the guy who let us grow and develop confidence. When I was a little boy he taught me not only how to shift the gears in his 1937 Plymouth sedan but he also took the time to explain to me just what the gears were for, and how they worked. He even let me drive the car when we were up at my Grandfather's farm when no one was around. I remembered that, and I did the same thing for my kids when the time came. I taught Kevin and Kris to drive on a gear shift automobile because that is how Moof taught me. Dad brought me to the sporting goods store—I still remember the store name (Vim's on Fordham Road) and I remember exactly where that glove was located in the store when he bought me my first baseman's mitt. He taught me how to catch a ball and I taught it to my kids. Dad taught me and my sisters the four step approach for rolling a bowling ball even though it would piss mom off because we were rolling it in the apartment. Mom and Dad complemented each other; Mooma was the homemaker and caregiver, Moof was the breadwinner and the teacher. We never owned bicycles, but my father would rent them for a few hours on Saturday and taught us to ride. (As a young man he rode motorcycles—even rode all the way to Mexico with his brother and Uncle Gus when he was in his twenties). His passion was playing golf. He tried in vain to interest me in the sport but I simply never got the hang of hitting anything but Mulligans off the tee. Long and wrong, that was me. He enjoyed the game for years; he even took great pleasure in taking his grandson Kevin out to hit a few balls around.

Dad was a tool and die maker. He worked in machine shops all his life. Mostly he had an aversion to working in large corporate factory settings so he stayed in small plants usually working in the jewelry or watch case line. He always said his goal was to make $100 a week—then we'd have all the money we needed. How times have changed! But, because most of the shops were small many of them tended not to survive, and he was forced to find another shop. One day I guess he had enough and he took work with a large corporation (ADT) and belatedly found out they were pretty good to work for after all. For the first time he had security, he had a pension, and had regular raises. I guess Dad was pretty much into his 40's when he found out that big wasn't bad after all. But he was pretty much a blue collar man and I guess he was mildly socialist in his philosophy. He didn't trust college boys and bosses and always encouraged me to find a trade. My folks never even had a checking account when I was growing up. Mom went to the post office for money orders to pay and mail the bills. Our apartment rent was somewhere around fifty dollars a month.

One funny story about my father and his lack of financial acumen happened when he suddenly inherited $10,000 from an Uncle Harry in Philadelphia. No one even knew an Uncle Harry—he was my grandmother's relative of some sort. All of a sudden Dad becomes a capitalist. Now he was reading the *Wall Street Journal.* Finally he gives up and tells me he doesn't know enough about money and investing so he will just deposit his inheritance in the bank and let it get interest. Only three weeks later, as he was riding home on the El, he saw fire trucks pouring water into the bank where his money was. "Gone," he said when he got home all ashen faced and trembling, "The money's burnt up!" He really didn't know how a bank worked. I had to explain to him that his inheritance was safe.

As my folks grew older it was nice to see the contentment they shared. By this time they were no longer Mom and Dad, they were known as Mooma and Moof. Sister Barbara married Geir Hjorth who emigrated here from his native Norway. Barb had kids before Fran and I did, and in Norway grandparents are identified as coming from the mother or father's side. Forget the spelling . . . I don't speak Norwegian . . . Famu and Fafa are the father's mother and father's father. On Barbara's side Mom and Dad became Mooma and Moofa, or just plain "Moof." The names stuck. Mooma and Moof finally left the Bronx and moved out to a townhouse apartment near me and Brenda and the kids. Mom still did the cooking and took care of the house like always, and then she would sit in her favorite lounge chair and settle down to watch her programs on TV. She wasn't a reader, and politics bored her. Her interests were directed toward her family and her group of friends. Dad was the reader. Dad was the thinker. He read a lot in is older retired years because, as he said, he didn't have the time when he was working. Mom would die every time he would get excited and say "Listen to this, Gert" and start to read to her. She hated that, but it seemed like that was the only friction that ever came up between them. They had their fights when I was young, but it was nice to see them settled as they aged. They were comfortable together and enjoyed watching us kids raise our own brood. They held hands a lot and often my mother would refer to him as "My Fella."

Then Mooma got cancer. She didn't develop it all of a sudden. She fought various cancers all her life. As a young woman she had some cancerous bone in her finger cut out; later, when I was starting high school, she had another operation for something in her insides—she never told us what—and finally, later in life developed the breast cancer that took her away at the age of 79. We watched her get sick and how well she handled the illness. She taught us kids a lot throughout her life, and it is fair to say that her final lesson was how to end a life with courage and dignity. It was hard on Dad. He remained the staunch caregiver and Mooma's long illness wore him out. When she died he was so tired. Something left him then, but he was always upbeat and willing to be helpful for me and Barbara. Despite the old age ailments that also took its toll, he survived Mooma by six years.

Dad developed a blood disorder that used up his white blood cells and every once in a while he needed a transfusion. A "Pump-Up", he called it. Little by little he aged. He couldn't play golf anymore, and I think that bothered him more than anything. Even when it got a bit dangerous for him to drive his car and I took his keys away, he never complained. But he did say how much he missed playing golf. Sometimes when I was driving him somewhere he would doze in the passenger's seat. I would turn up the heat in the car for him and look over at the old man next to me. Dad just got too old; he couldn't stay alone, and he didn't want to come live with us. He liked to sleep a lot and dream of his old friends, he said. He also said he was afraid that Brenda might be too bossy and make him get out of bed and get dressed every day. Because of his age and his blood condition he was always cold and the heat in his apartment was always pumped up to almost unbearable levels. One day I couldn't stand it because I thought it was so unhealthy. When he went into another room, I opened the patio door for air. When he saw what I had done he lost his temper, something I almost never saw him do except for the time I mentioned before about me stopping off at the bar. And for maybe only the second time in my life I heard him use bad language. He yelled at me to close the door. Yes he did; he not only told me to close the door, he told me exactly what kind of a door it was . . . . starting with an "F." I felt bad, but I always listened and respected him, even when I was a senior citizen myself. But it was nice to know that he was still feisty at 86 years old. Eventually though, Dad was really not able to care for himself and we had to move him to an assisted living facility. I could wish that, when my time comes, I'll go quickly and save the kids the heart-rending difficulty of moving a parent out of their house, thereby forfeiting their physical and psychological independence. Dad passed away only nine days after the move. It was his time; He was 86 years old when he sallied out on his Next Adventure.

Kevin and Krissy

We had, for a few months, two chickens running loose around our house. They were named Coco and Sprite and don't ask me why. They kind of had the run of the place. They would peck away at the food we left out for them and then poop on the floor when the urge arose. Sandy the dog would follow them around with what, for a dog, was a bemused look as if wondering what the hell they were doing in his home. Brenda and I wondered also but the answer was a simple one. We had two kids who brought them home from school one day as part of a project for which they had volunteered. They were to raise the little chicks until they became big hens and were returned to the farm from whence they came. One of the unexpected joys of rearing children. The kids are grown now and they are both fairly launched and out on their own. They have done us proud; as a parent, I guess that is the finest feeling we can hope for. At this writing Kevin is a Major in the Air Force, and Krissy is the assistant principal at her school in Duxbury, Massachusetts.

When Kevin and Krissy were babies Brenda did almost all the nurturing. I only started taking an active role when they were old enough to communicate and share things with. But I have to say that raising our family with Brenda was the most enduring and satisfying accomplishment in my life. Kevin and his sister Kris are gifts for whom I will be eternally grateful. As I write this I am reminded of what Brenda's niece Joanne said of her Uncle Henry after his funeral. She said that that when she was a little girl she spoke and thought as a little girl and Uncle Henry always understood her. As an adolescent she saw things as an adolescent and Uncle Henry always understood her. And as a young woman Uncle Henry understood her, still. Now, as an adult, she understands the real gift of Uncle Henry. He was always there for her. She could talk, and share, and relate, to him at whatever level she required at the time and she knew Uncle Henry understood. That was his gift. What a wonderful requiem, and I hope some day it might apply also to me. It is so important to be able to relate to your kids. There are parental parameters of course; parenting is not about being a friend. Communication is critical. Parenting is a challenging vocation. There are no "do overs." But I think Brenda and I did well. It's a good feeling.

Kids have to learn how to play ball so I invented the "Step-Back Game". I would use a rag ball and toss it to the kids. If they caught it they would take a step back and throw it back to me. If they missed, they would have to take a step back in. Up and back we would go until they were both able to throw and catch whatever came at them from any distance—a useful talent when the object became a baseball or a softball. The kids played on the town leagues that were fun but sometimes painful to watch as kids struggled to learn how to not swing at pitches a foot over their heads. Parents who watched their little athletes throw to the wrong base, or a pitcher walking eight batters in a row during a 12 to 10 nail-biter in the second inning know the feeling. Kevin played first base on Little League teams called the Tigers or Cherokees and Kris played second and pitched for a team called the Penguins. Penguins?? Who's afraid of penguins? Sometimes we were surprised. I showed up at one game in the second inning to find the score already 4-0 in our favor. The guy sitting next to me said that I just missed the kid playing first base who hit a grand slam over the fence into the parking lot at the Dairy Queen. It was Kev—and the coach bought pizza for the team to celebrate his "Grand-Salami." Kev knew how to play; while with the Air Force in Turkey Kevin once asked if he could join in the base softball tournament. He was asked if he could play well enough to make the team. He said he thought so. Later, during the actual competition, he only hit two home runs over the fence, four doubles, and two singles in ten times at bat. Kev wrote and told me laconically that now all the folks on the base wanted to talk to him about was softball.

Krissy's sports knowledge came in handy because she could name the entire Mets batting order before she started first grade. It was her interest in the national pastime that stood her in good stead when, years later, she would meet her future husband after a Red Sox game at Fenway Park. Sports were always a big activity with our family. Don't even mention bowling . . . . we spent hours every Saturday watching kids roll that heavy ball down the alley.

We skied together as a family. The kids learned to ski at the age of five in the "Kiddie Corral" at Steamboat Springs, Colorado. Later when

Brenda and I founded the Reverend Brown Ski Club at the grammar school it was amusing to see Krissy, who was in the fourth grade and really too young for the club, standing waiting at the bottom of the slope for the older boys to catch up to her. This, after they voiced doubts about skiing with a girl—and a girl younger than them to boot! I remember racing the kids down the slopes while puffing and panting and staying just behind them. Then I would always beat them at the last minute. I don't have to tell you that eventually the day dawned when Kev and Kris were on racing teams and could beat me. There was one happy day that we shared in Colorado after running the NASTAR Race in Steamboat. (NASTAR—National Standard Amateur Race) is a race against a set standard time. The whole family won medals that day—Silvers for me and Kev, and Bronze for Brenda and Krissy. We might have spoiled the kids because one time we were driving to Vermont and I told them we would have a good vacation. The little darlings explained that this could not be a real vacation because we didn't get on a plane!

I did my best to expose Kev and Krissy to the world outside Sussex County. I am probably the only parent who took his kids to his old neighborhood in the Bronx to teach them how a fire escape worked in an apartment building. Or to explain how folks would hang their laundry up on the roof to dry. We became regulars at the famous Bronx Zoo, so much so that Kevin in the fifth grade became the tour director and showed the class, and teachers, how to navigate around the Zoo while on a field trip. (As an aside I have to mention that the kids wanted to award me "Chaperone of the Year" for my good work with them on a field trip to Washington D.C. The kids, who were in the eighth grade, were wearing me out. I finally told them to partner up, keep with the group, and go inside the Smithsonian. I told them to be sure not to lose their partner, to behave themselves, and not to embarrass me. They eventually emerged feeling pretty proud of their un-chaperoned selves and found me dozing on a park bench across the street.)

Our kids were interested in travel and far away places. Many evenings after dinner they would exchange meaningful glances and slide their little bodies under the dining room table. When BK and I would wonder where the kids went, the answer would always filter up from beneath us. "We are in China!" Then we would go through the whole routine of how the weather was, were the mountains there very high, or did a lot of people ride bicycles. The kids always had answers and the game went on. Funny how things happen though. Krissy was a junior in high school when she had the opportunity to accompany a medical mission to that very same China of her youth. She spent ten days in Nanchang helping with a project called "Operation Smile," an organization that travels abroad to volunteer operations for children born with cleft palettes or other facial disorders. Her job on that trip was pretty neat. Because the Chinese children couldn't speak English, it was Krissy's job to help prepare them for the operation. She did this by using a doll as a prop and showing the kids the face mask the doctors would use. She would demonstrate on the doll the the needles and tubes that they could expect to see during their operation. Later she showed them a toothbrush and how it was used. All this using a doll as her prop! She even taught one special little girl the "Thumbs Up" sign. When it was time for that little girl's operation (she was Krissy's favorite) the doctors asked Kris if she wanted to accompany her during the operation. Krissy later told us that as the girl was being sedated, she looked at Kris and gave her the Thumbs Up. I think that is a great story. Later, that girl's parents, who had walked 100 miles to get to the hospital, thanked Krissy and gave her some local fruit as a gift when they were leaving.

Kevin, in his turn, visited China while serving as a communication officer attached to the White House. He had respnsibility for supporting the president of the U.S. when traveling on his trips abroad. His job was to be part of the team that always travels with the president (POTUS) during his trip. The group includes the president's personal staff, the secret service security team, and the communications team that insures secure network access and coded transmission systems for the president's use. That was Kevin's job, and it took him to China, Mongolia, Japan, Uraguay and Estonia and other far away places.

As a little aside I could also mention that our little travelers went with Aunt Bobbie to Hawaii when they were about eight years old. Brenda and I stayed home. And we still haven't been to Hawaii.

Later it was I, Pop, who taught them how to drive using a standard stick gear shift. Sometimes it was hard not to get excited when Krissy would back up at 50 miles per hour or Kevin would once again misjudge a left turn and wind up on the grass alongside the road. At times such as these I would struggle not to yell at them. I usually vented my frustration and fear by pounding my palms against the vinyl dashboard in front of me. The kids still laugh about it today . . . . but by the time they took their driver's exam I was sure they knew how to drive. The test I laid out for them was harder than the one they would take with the Motor Vehicles Inspector. Even Moof would get into the mix when he would advise his one and only Krissy as she shifted gears manually. "Listen to the engine Krissy, just listen to the engine, it will tell you what to do." She has never forgotten that lesson. Some of Moof may have rubbed off on me. Kevin bought an English standard shift car for use during the eighteen months he was stationed with the Air

Force in Turkey. I questioned him if it would be difficult to shift gears with the opposite hand from the opposite side of the car. He reminded me that it posed no problem because I was the one who always let him shift from the right seat when he was a little boy. It was just what I was taught to do when sitting alongside Moof many years earlier. From father to son; from father to son; the concept of this transference is truly beautiful to ponder. But the flip side is the responsibility that fathers assume. Like father like son is a fearsome truism. We have to do it right. One of the greatest compliments I ever received came from Moof when he told me I was a good father . . . and I answered, "Thank you Dad; I learned it all from you."

The kids' education was of paramount importance. We started them off as little tykes at the local Montessori school in Sparta. They thrived there. When time came to enroll them in the first grade Brenda and I sent them to our local public school. They were doing OK, nothing special, but Brenda and I were beginning to have our doubts about letting them stay there. Sure, there was no tuition other than what we paid in taxes, but something was missing. We figured it out together while vacationing on St. Croix in the Virgin Islands. I had sailed down there years before and was quite familiar with the Island. We even owned an acre of property at the Buccaneer Estates but never developed it and eventually sold it for a small profit. As was our habit, Brenda and I liked to attend daily Mass at the local church in Christiansted. One day we found the church filled with little kids in school uniforms celebrating the Feast Day of Mary. They were singing hymns that we knew, so like good Catholics, we joined in. The realization hit us both at the same time. Our kids would never wear uniforms like we did, wouldn't attend Mass on Feast Days like we did, and would never learn the songs that we were singing. We went home, took them out of the public system, and after a brief conversation with Sister Philomena, enrolled Kevo and Krissy in Reverend Brown, the elementary school sponsored by the parish that we belonged to in Sparta. We have never regretted our decision. Even when Krissy managed in the third grade to shock us with words about Kevin that she wrote on her blackboard for Brenda to see. "I heard those words on the school bus Mommy!"

They eventually graduated to Pope John High School, and we watched them as they grew. The most common consideration when choosing a parochial high school over a public one is as valid today as it was in 1992. Discipline. The Alpha and Omega of the discussion. Our kids wore uniforms, which to me is a huge deal because it separates school from play. People will argue with me over this, but I know from experience that proper dress affects behavior. In my single days I occasionally worked the door at my friend's saloon in Manhattan. We had a simple dress code; shirts had to have collars, shoes instead of sneakers, and no hats inside the door. The trouble we kept out that way was worth it; There was rarely a disturbance inside. The code worked—and it still works in parochial schools.

In addition there was Father McHugh, the principal and his never forgotten sayings. "What part of NO is it that you do not understand?" Or," Ten O'clock is Ten O'clock." But he wasn't rigid all the time. Kids will be kids and Fr. McHugh knew it. An illustrative story begins when a student flashed a full moon from the gym window at an unsuspecting and thoroughly shocked woman as she drove by in her car. She promptly took a U-Turn directly to Father McHugh's office. "What kind of school are you running here," she demanded. "Where is the discipline and responsibility that you claim to be so noted for?" "I've just been mooned!" Father Mchugh, with his droll Irish humor, rose to the occasion magnificently. "You're right, Madam. This type of behavior has never, and will never be condoned at Pope John. The guilty boy will be punished, you may be assured of that. Now tell me, did you recognize who it was?"

I can't remember how many athletic events I attended during those years. Kev played baseball both for Pope John as well as the independent Fall leagues. Krissy played on the P.J. varsity softball and field hockey teams. They both spent three years skiing on the varsity ski team. I spent a lot of time watching my kids, and I think they appreciated my presence. It is quite possible though, that they were sometimes embarrassed by my loud cheering or loud complaining over an unsatisfactory call by some blind umps or refs. That's tough. The only thing I couldn't critique was their skiing results. The clock treated everyone equally. The only thing I could do for them while they were skiing was cheer as they whizzed by me down the course to the finish line. It was a little scary to watch them sometimes, but they were good racers. But sometimes I was glad I that I wasn't around to see what they were doing. Like the time after high school when they went "canyoning" at Interlaken, Switzerland. Canyoning is a crazy sport where you don a wet suit and helmet and then dive into roaring rapids and body surf down through jagged mountain ravines. Two weeks after they arrived home to tell us about it, an Australian group of twenty kids were killed by a flash flood that overtook them in a mad rush down the canyon's swirling water. That tragic event caused the sport of Canyoning to be banned. A good decision. I can conclude my discussion here by saying that both Kevin and Krissy are intelligent, active, and athletically talented kids and I was their greatest fan. I still am.

There was another consideration for Pope John that I considered important. The key, I believe, is the level of parental involvement. That, and the trained expectation of the students that a good college will be the next step in their education. I noted some friends that the kids had over to our deck one day. The colleges they eventually attended were Boston College, Notre Dame, and Franklin and Marshall. There was no peer pressure or expectation to settle for anything less. It is no wonder then that Kevin chose The College Of The Holy Cross in Worcester, and Krissy, St. Michaels College in Winooski, VT. They did well at their respective schools and upon graduation set off on their careers without returning to Sparta. They're successfully launched. God Bless Them.

OK, one last story about the kids and I'll let you turn the page. When Kevin was about ten years old we were on a rafting trip down the Colorado River. Our guide rafted up to a little cove under an overhanging cliff and told us that some folks would jump off that cliff into the water below to where we were. I said, "Wanna give it a try Kev?" I was surprised he said yes, so up we climbed. About 10 feet up I said "OK Kevo, Let's jump from here." But he kept on climbing. About 15 feet I was getting anxious. "Kevo, how about now?" But he kept on climbing. Now we were about 25 feet above the roiling river and I tried to reason with my son. "Kev," I know you are very brave, we can jump from here and we can tell everybody about it when we get home." But he kept on climbing. Finally we came to the top of the cliff. It was about 40 feet above the raft that now looked about as big as a toy boat with toy people looking up at us. I tried one more time; "Kevo, it is OK to change your mind"—and then off the little idiot jumped. Oh damn, I thought, what the hell do I gotta do now, let him know his father is scared shitless? So I held my nose, looked down at what I swore were eagles soaring below me, and leaped feet first into space. I survived; Kev was already back on the raft as I paddled up. "That was fun, wasn't it Kev," I exclaimed as I plopped gratefully into the raft.

Want to do it again?" When my ten year old daredevil shook his head no I succumbed to an outburst of heartfelt honesty. "I don't want to do it again either, Kev."

Krissy, not to be outdone, also did her share of busting my chops. St. Michael's College in Vermont was partially paid for by the student loan we took out when Kris was a freshman or freshperson, or whatever. Brenda and I paid almost $250 a month to that loan for the four years she was in school plus an additional ten years after she had graduated. I didn't figure the exact cost of her education because it was irrelevant, but over fourteen years it came to a lot of money. But I did know when the final payment was due. Usually the final payment on a loan varies some from the set monthly amount due to interest or whatever. I called the Vermont bank to ask for the total of the final payment. I was politely informed that they could not divulge this information because the loan was taken out in Krissy's name. Accordingly, I called Kris to have her get the correct amount for me. She called me back; "I took care of it Pop", she said." The final payment was $72.60 so I paid it. We did it, didn't we Pop? You and me together, we took care of the cost of my education!" At $72.60 we did it??? Krissy has always had a terrific sense of humor. And she was quick. I can still remember how Kevin used to complain, "She always gets me so good!"

OK, one last story about the kids. When they got older and out on their own, Kevin and Kris always kept in close touch with each other. The fights and the petty jealousies were long gone; as brother and sister their relationship is as good as anyone could want it to be. It is comforting to know that they remember us once in a while, too. They gave us a wonderful vacation at an expensive guest house in Newport, Rhode Island for our thirtieth anniversary. They always to manage to make us feel appreciated. Like the time they hooked us up with a balloon ride in Colorado.

There we were, Brenda and I, floating silently in the air high above the ski slopes with nothing between us and the terra firma two thousand feet below but the wicker basket we were standing in. The air was crisp and the views spectacular and we felt as free as the birds with whom we shared the space. Landing was an adventure, we nestled sideways on some unsuspecting stranger's roof before rising to try again. Finally we did manage to land and the balloon chasers, the guys in the pickup truck who followed our flight, held the basket as we jumped out for the traditional champagne toast. This toast, incidentally, originated in the early days of ballooning in France. The balloon pilot of those days carried a bottle of champagne to share with any farmer who may have taken umbrage to a balloon landing unannounced in his pasture and scaring his cows. Brenda and I were a bit non-nonplussed to note that our balloon was being packed up by the chasers for shipment to Denver. Imagine how we felt when we were informed that the balloon had a hole in it and was being sent for repairs!

A few months later that I came across a news article saying that more people were expected to grow to be 100 years old than ever before. I e-mailed the article to the kids and said that they better be ready to take care of us in our dotage—and that we should be around for a long time. Krissy, who I already told you was quick, e-mailed her brother saying, "Next time we get a balloon with a bigger hole!"

Tugboat Career

Turecamo Towing Company, *Frances Turecamo,* Ship Work, Scows and Scrappies, Oil Barges, Changing Enviornment

TUGBOAT WORK

Turecamo Towing Company

The Turecamo Coastal and Harbor Towing Company had an interesting history. Years ago Bart Turecamo arrived on these shores from his native Italy and settled in Brooklyn, N.Y. Barney, as he came to be called, worked hard and established, as I understand the story, a company that specialized in paving the many new roads that were being built all around the city at the time. As part of his operation Barney purchased two tugboats that he used to tow the sand and traprock he needed for his roadwork. He had two sons, Vincent and Bart. When he retired he left the construction company to his son Vincent, and the tugboat operation to Bart. Bart always loved his boats; and through good management he established the company that I was proud to be a part of for twenty years of my life.

Frances Turecamo

I started with Turecamo as Mate aboard the tug *Frances Turecamo* and I first sailed captain aboard her in 1974. She was a smaller boat as sizes go, primarily designed for service in the barge canal systems of New York. The canal trade had mostly dried up by then, having lost its economic edge to the New York Thruway system. But she did the work I enjoyed. We shifted scows in the various creeks, delivered oil barges to smaller out of the way locations, and generally made ourselves useful towing sand and trap rock from the quarries upstate. For one full year we towed a barge loaded with powdered cement from a cement plant near Albany down the Hudson River and around the Battery, out the East River and Long Island Sound to Providence, Rhode Island. The trip took 26 hours one way to Providence and about 16 hours return. The trip overland takes about five hours. At first blush it seems to make no sense until you realize the barge we towed carried the equivalent of 105 truckloads of cement. The 26 hour trip meant little when compared to the number of trucks, drivers, and fuel that would be required to transport the same load. Water traffic is slow, but the volume carried makes it profitable. Over the years I sailed with many different crews. The crew I was with for the four years I spent on the *Frances* was the best of them all.

I was mate aboard this boat when I became engaged to Brenda. One day she surprised me in New Haven by traveling up there in a rain storm to meet me and getting lost around the docks in the process. She finally managed to find a boatman on the New Haven waterfront who picked her up in the rain and drove her to my tug. She arrived, wet and bedraggled, in the middle of the night and scared the hell out of me as she found her way into my room while I slept. Boatmen have a sort of earthy way about them as exemplified by the reaction of Charlie Olsen, the Captain, who, after hearing of her harrowing adventure the next morning, told her with unbridled admiration, "You have some pair of balls."

I've always tried to have Brenda meet my crew mates so my work wouldn't seem so mysterious when I left her each week. It was mysterious enough as it was. She was riding with me one trip when I was steering a light (empty) oil barge through a narrow bridge. I was approaching the bridge rather off center to allow for the current and natural slide of the barge and, at least to Brenda, the ever-narrowing opening was looming close. Unable to stand it any longer she turned and said to me, "You do know what you're doing. Don't you?" (Yes, I did, and no, we didn't hit the bridge.) Over the years Brenda got to know our crew fairly well. Patty, the cook and Bobby, the engineer took us out to a special restaurant in Brooklyn when we got engaged. Pat was exceptionally a lot of fun. He ran a business selling "Swag" (items that had mysteriously fallen off a truck) from his basement in Brooklyn on his week off. Brenda augmented her ensemble frequently when she "went shopping by Patty." Patty's constant squabbles with his wife Rose always amused us. One time he left for a week on the boat with the car keys in his pocket. The spares he had hidden away at home and he never told Rose the hiding place. When Patty got home seven days later Rose told him about the parking tickets that resulted from not heeding the alternate side of the street parking rules. Pat just couldn't understand why Rose didn't just push the car from one side of the street to the other every other day.

Whenever I mentioned that I worked on tugs I would invariably be asked if I worked on sea-going tugs, or else, did I pull the big ships in. Before I begin at my starting point about ship work let me quickly answer the first question first. The answer is yes. In that many of my voyages took me through the Caribbean, the Great Lakes, the Panama Canal, the Gulf of Mexico, the Gulf of Maine, the Bahamas, Puerto Rico, and various coastal ports between Florida and Nova Scotia, I guess it would be valid to say that I served aboard sea-going tugs. But there is a caveat. I do not personally define the boats that I sailed on as "sea-going tugs." They were big enough of course, and a lot of nautical miles passed under their keels, but I reserve my concept of true sea-going tugs to those specialized vessels that are owned and operated by companies like the Smit tugboats of the Netherlands. They are truly sea-going. Much bigger and stronger than the combination harbor/

ocean boats of the New York companies, these boats specialize in ocean towing and sea rescue services. Some voyages last for months as they tow giant oil rigs and ocean platforms thousands of miles to locations around the world. The design and construction of these boats is better suited for ocean conditions than the combination harbor/ocean tugs that I sailed on. Their towing equipment, winches, cables, shackles, and the like, is much heftier and geared for super heavy tows in all weathers. Their crews are specially trained in sea-going towing and salvage operations as opposed to our crews who doubled as offshore sailors and harbor pilots. So, yes, I do make a distinction between the boats I ventured out on, and the true sea-going tugs that specialize in ocean operations. But it has always been hard for me to make that distinction to a casual questioner.

Ship Work

Ship work was a very big part of the work I did on boats. People always asked how a tiny tug could push those enormous vessels into their berths. I answer that it really is a question of leverage. Did you ever come to a dock at a lake somewhere and find your boat floating a few feet too far off to jump into safely? Do you remember just grabbing the rope and pulling with a steady pull until your boat slid back toward you? If your boat was of any size there was no way you could lift that weight out of the water. But you could pull it through the water with relative ease. The identical concept applies to a tug and a ship. A tug pushing (or pulling) on a particular pivoting point will eventually move the ship through the water.

A ship needs tugs (they used to, anyway, but I'll come to that later) for two reasons. A ship steers when the flow of water is deflected by the position of the rudder. The location of the vessel's rudder is astern of the propeller and it is the propeller wash that exerts the force on the rudder that steers the ship. Obviously then, a ship can only be steered when water is flowing to the rudder. If there is no water moving, there is no turning no matter what position the rudder is in. The propeller always causes the vessel to move either forward or astern. The problem arises when you want to redirect the ship's heading but keep it in more or less in the same place. Let me give you two examples of the use of a tug. Think about a line from the tug going up to somewhere near the bow of the ship. Think about that tug now going full astern and acting as a forward brake up near the bow as the ship maneuvers ahead with the rudder hard over. Can you picture the stern of the ship turning as the ship pivots with the action of the tow rope pulling on the bow? Sometime the ship is required to dock in close quarters. A tug pushing on one bow and another pushing on the opposite quarter will spin the ship with no forward motion at all and enable the pilot to line up the vessel to enter a narrow slip or turn the ship in a narrow channel. At the risk of sounding dopey I'll say that a ship can't (at least in my time) maneuver sideways. Once a vessel is located at its proper berth the pilot usually will employ one or two tugs to push the vessel sideways and hold it to the pier until the vessel is secured.

The tug captain must be skillful enough to quickly maneuver his tug into any position against the ship that pilot requires. Today's tug has big rubber fenders. The old shabby braided rope, "Whiskers", have long passed into tug boat lore and I sailed on those old tugs too. But the object was not to use these fenders as bumpers to slam into a ships' side with impunity. A good tug boat captain was expected to be able to maneuver quickly and, for the most part, gently around a ship. Tugs all handled differently. Over the years I probably have steered maybe

70 different tugs at one time or another. One such tug, the *Dalzellido,* had even replaced the tradtional ships' wheel with a doorknob that I used to steer the boat! Single screw tugs maneuvered differently than twin screw boats. Some boats had what were known as "Kort Nozzles" with smaller rudders installed forward of the props so the tug would be steered when going astern. Some had greater rudder power than others and would maneuver more quickly. Some engine controls reacted slower or quicker that some others. Some tugs had variable pitch wheels but most didn't.

Variable pitch wheels were kind of interesting. It was kind of a pain to steer a tug with a variable pitch because in effect you really doubled the throttles you had to control. There was a control for engine speed and another for controlling the pitch of the propeller. The idea was to match up the speed of the propeller with the optimum propeller pitch—I'll tell you about "Pitch" in a minute—for achieving the most efficiency. Just imagine for a moment that a boat's propeller is encased in a block of cheese. The propeller will move forward through the cheese for each revolution it makes. A flat propeller—with no pitch—will only spin in place. A propeller with greater pitch will move correspondingly further through the cheese. (A fan with flat blades will blow less air than fan blades with pitch.) Anyway, the idea was to use one set of throttles to control the propeller speed—there was no reverse on a variable pitch engine—with the throttles controlling the pitch of the blades of the wheel. Using both hands to control the throttles left no hands left over to turn the steering wheel. You just had to be quick and coordinated to operate a boat like this successfully, but when you got good at it you had exceptional control of how the boat moved through the water. I spent a little over a year steering the *Kathleen*

Turecamo. There were very few in the pilot house who wanted to get involved with variable pitch wheels.

Each boat claimed its own characteristics. Over the years the adjustment time I needed to get comfortable with a boat was reduced. I like to think I learned to be pretty competent, and perhaps even good, at handling any boat. Ship handling techniques varied widely according to local practices. European tugs usually maneuver ships by using stern lines and pulling the ship in whatever direction it wanted to go. In New York, unless we were pulling a ship away from pier sideways, the use of a stern line was rare. Most pilots preferred the tug to be tied up alongside the vessel.

When a ship enters port a tug would come alongside while the ship was still underway and (without slamming into it) lay alongside the vessel. The deckhand would throw up a heaving line. The heaving line is a small half inch line with a weighted ball at the end called a "Monkey fist." Attached to the heaving line is the 8 inch diameter ship line. Once the ship line is secured the tug is towed alongside until the docking pilot requires its assistance. Then I would do what I liked to do best: Push against the ship or pull back on the ship line or let go and scurry around the ship pushing or pulling as necessary to land the ship safely in its berth. Ship's orders to the tug are transmitted by the docking pilot over the radio. The days are long gone when ship's steam whistles were answered in kind by the small peep whistles of the tug. There was always a certain romance attached to those sounds for me and sometimes I would wax nostalgic and answer commands by responding with my boat's peep whistle just for fun. One always had to be aware of what the boat could do, or what it could not do, safely. It is not ego speaking to say that most tug captains who were involved in doing a lot of ship work, including me, developed a good rapport with the docking pilots in the harbor. We formed a team that worked well together.

Sadly much of the ship work is being phased out. Larger vessels, especially the new giant cruise ships, are designed in such a way that prevents the tug from positioning itself alongside at a location where it can be most effective. And many of these new ships are of such a size that a tug would be overmatched. The bows and stern of these new behemoths are constructed with such a flare to the bow that a tug attempting to land alongside would cave in its wheelhouse before the side of tug landed alongside the ship. The pushing and pulling the tug used to do is being replaced now by bow and stern thrusters mounted in the ships hull. These thrusters allow the newer ships to do what the older ones couldn't: propel themselves sideways. By the time anyone reads this there will be new tug designs and new methods of ship work, and perhaps a new kind of boatman, but I'm writing how it was during my time (1965-1992).

Before leaving ship work I'd like to report a story I think is special. I would take Kevin or Krissy with me aboard the tug from time to time for a day or two. Kris was with me as we sailed a ship out of Staten Island. At the time she may have been in the fifth or sixth grade. The pilot was back aboard and the ship was underway out of the harbor. It was time for the tug to break loose and go back to the dock so I let Kris hold the wheel. "Turn it easy to the left Kris," I said. "Now put it midships with the indicator right in the middle." I handled the engine controls and the tug came away from the side of the ship smoothly. The more the space widened between the tug and ship the more Krissy's eyes widened also. One of the greatest moments of being her father came when we got home and Krissy was all excited and told Brenda, "Momma! I did a SHIP JOB!"

Scows and Scrappies

Many tugs did specialized work. Smaller, older tugs generally became relegated to the creeks and inlets that housed the many scrap iron yards (and the famous "junk yard dogs") that dotted the port. These were the boats that towed the scrap metal from the junk yards to ships that would carry it somewhere for recycling in foreign ports. The barges were referred to as "Scrappies" and were generally in pretty poor condition themselves. Many years of grounding on rocks in narrow channels, or of having heavy engine blocks dropped on their decks from magnetic cranes, or being banged around by bucket loaders, did little to insure the seaworthiness of these beat-up scows. I remember struggling with frozen lines and jammed shards of scrap metal when I first came to the boats from Puerto Rico during the winter of 1967. My partner saved my hands and frozen fingers by offering me his gloves and I've never forgotten him. He became a captain himself later on. Sadly Don was lost one night years later out in Long Island Sound. The bow of the "Scrappie" he was towing just collapsed. The scow filled with water and sank quickly dragging the tug and all hands down with it. I've always remembered him and his kindness from the time he helped the "Green Deckhand," me.

Other tugs earned their pay by towing rock from quarries up the Hudson River, some by towing sand from Long Island, some were shifting boats for the various non-descript vessels around the port, and some were engaged primarily in off-shore towing to ports along the Atlantic Coast. I was always bemused by the question, what did you tow? My answer always was, "anything that was floating and that had no motor or means of propulsion over the water had to be moved from A to B by a tug." It was as simple, and yet as complicated as that. The boatman had to deal with many types of water craft, many types of sea conditions, all kinds of weather, and understand tides and currents. Over the years the boatman who steered tugboats amassed a generous fund of local knowledge. We got to know the navigation channels, where the deep water was or where the eddys were, and the location of hundreds of docks and berths. We knew how best to "make-up" to various barges for better handling, how to tow multiple units, and to know how and when to tow alongside, tow astern, or push ahead.

I remember watching Eddie Oliver, our elderly captain, steering barges through those tricky currents that gave the name, "Hell Gate", to that particular section of the East River at its intersection with the Harlem River. The currents and eddys formed in "The Gate" are tricky to navigate because the current from each river flows in opposite directions. "Eddie," I said, "How do you line up these tows to come through here?" He kind of laughed and said that he couldn't answer that question. It was different every time, with every stage of tide, or with every barge. "You just get to feel it," he told me. "It only comes with experience." Years later I would answer that question to a younger fellow in the same way.

Oil Barges

We towed a lot of oil barges. I'll tell you about that now. Two factors were responsible for the volume of oil transport work that we did in New York. The large super tankers entering the port of New York sometimes were too deep to navigate the shallower channels to the docks. These ships would anchor in the deep-water anchorages and tugs would bring empty oil barges alongside to be loaded from the ship. When enough cargo was off loaded, the ship would then be light enough to safely transit the channel to a berth at one of the many oil terminals. Secondly there were, of course, many smaller terminals that didn't have the storage capacity to receive the full tanker load. Tugs would be chartered to transport barge sized loads to these locations wherever they were needed. Trips from New York harbor to Albany and points on the Hudson River were common as were trips to various locations throughout Long Island Sound like New Haven, Port Jefferson, or New London. We towed oil barges Down East to Providence, through the Cape Cod Canal to Boston, or to points even further east. As a tug boat captain I learned the location of many dozens of these terminals. It was important to know how the docks were designed, how deep the water was, and how the currant ran, and the location of the hose connections that would couple with the hoses of the various sized barges we that brought to them.

Changing Environment

When I began steering, the common capacity of a stock built oil barge was approximately 20,000 bbls. Tugs were usually in the 1500 to 2500 horsepower range. Twenty years later barges would run to 250,000 bbls. and would be handled by 8000 to 10,000 H.P. tugs. The work was the same but it was different, too. Heavy towing wires replaced the rope hawsers I used to use. Electric winches would replace capstans to pull up and tighten the barge to the tow. Articulated or integrated units became common when the tug would be securely attached with cables into a notch at the stern of a barge to form one unit even when towing at sea. I adapted to these changes as they came but, honestly, there came a time late in my career when I often wondered if it was I who was steering the tow or if it was the tow steering me. The tugs and tows are even bigger today. I'd be lieing if I said I liked, or gladly adapted, the new reality of boating. It is serious business now, the days when most of my friends were semi-pirates like Big Raul with his eye patch, or "Typical Tropical Tramps" like Lowell and Harry, or eccentrics like my friend the pilot "Bugsy" Moran, and so many others, have all passed into tugboat lore of time gone by. Some of the fun has, too. It has been twenty years since I last steered tugboat. I had good times during my boating life and I wouldn't change a thing, but now, like everything else, it has changed. I'm sure it's not what it was, and I don't feel any pressing need to return to it. Later, in some nostalgic time, I'll reminisce and raise a glass to Auld Lang Syne.

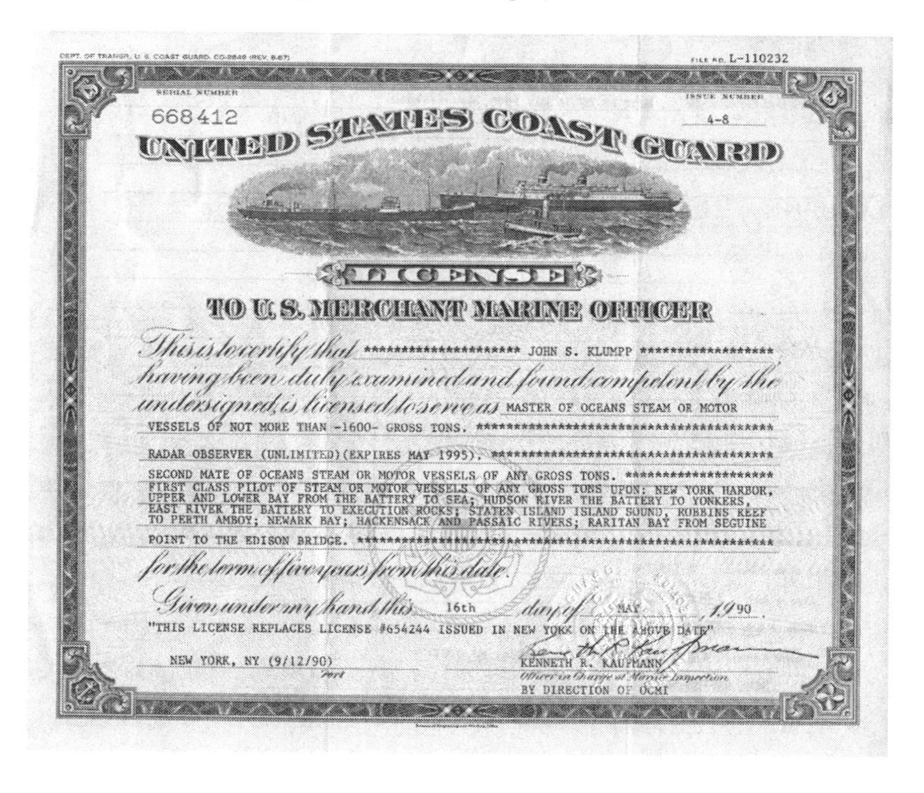

DEPT. OF TRANSP., U. S. COAST GUARD, CG-2848 (REV. 8-87)

FILE NO. L-110232

SERIAL NUMBER 668412

ISSUE NUMBER 4-8

UNITED STATES COAST GUARD

LICENSE

TO U.S. MERCHANT MARINE OFFICER

This is to certify that ********************** JOHN S. KLUMPP ******************
having been duly examined and found competent by the undersigned, is licensed to serve as MASTER OF OCEANS STEAM OR MOTOR VESSELS OF NOT MORE THAN -1600- GROSS TONS. **

RADAR OBSERVER (UNLIMITED)(EXPIRES MAY 1995). **************************************

SECOND MATE OF OCEANS STEAM OR MOTOR VESSELS OF ANY GROSS TONS. ********************
FIRST CLASS PILOT OF STEAM OR MOTOR VESSELS OF ANY GROSS TONS UPON; NEW YORK HARBOR, UPPER AND LOWER BAY FROM THE BATTERY TO SEA; HUDSON RIVER THE BATTERY TO YONKERS, EAST RIVER THE BATTERY TO EXECUTION ROCKS; STATEN ISLAND ISLAND SOUND, ROBBINS REEF TO PERTH AMBOY; NEWARK BAY; HACKENSACK AND PASSAIC RIVERS; RARITAN BAY FROM SEGUINE POINT TO THE EDISON BRIDGE. ***

for the term of five years from this date.

Given under my hand this 16th *day of* MAY, 1990.

"THIS LICENSE REPLACES LICENSE #654244 ISSUED IN NEW YORK ON THE ABOVE DATE"

NEW YORK, NY (9/12/90)
Port

KENNETH R. KAUFMANN
Officer in Charge of Marine Inspection
BY DIRECTION OF OCMI

The Eighties

The Reagan Years, The Strike, The Chemical Company

Mc Ivor at Rumms

THE EIGHTIES

I think I'll refer to the section on the Eighties as "The Doldrums." The doldrums refer to those lower latitudes near the equator where the wind doesn't blow with any particular direction or force. During the days of the majestic clipper ships and the "Ancient Mariner," sailing vessels could become becalmed in the doldrums and drift for days, or even weeks, whistling for a favorable wind to propel them up to the "Roaring Forties." That's where their sails would fill and they could speed their way with "a bone in their teeth" over the foam. In a way the Eighties were a slow point for me. I had settled into the routine of the young suburban husband. The boats, while still fun, were simply the job I went to. The bills were getting paid, we modified our house to our preferences, and the children were growing at their own pace. I guess you could say that things were rather ordinary in the Klumpp's life. Not bad, times were good actually, but they were ordinary. An "ordinary" life can also be a good life. They are not mutually exclusive. Besides, during this time we did some rather un-ordinary things, but first I'm going to tell you about the "Reagan Years" from his election to the Presidency in 1980 to the end of his second term in 1988.

The Reagan Years

I want to stress this again: when I write of political matters it is my own interpretation of them. Many people will agree, but many people will reserve the right to disagree with my opinion of the stewardship of Ronald Wilson Reagan. I won't fight them. As they say, everyone is entitled to their own opinion but they are not entitled to their own facts. Right now, twenty-five years after his presidency, Reagan's popularity and place in history is pretty high. However, I think he was a net negative for American Democracy. I wonder if my judgment will prove me correct in the long term.

Reagan was enormously popular upon taking office. The American psyche was at a nadir with 16% interest rates suffocating the country, gasoline and housing problems, and an international hostage crises that had been embarrassing the country for over a year. Carter was an ineffective president and his inability to free the U.S. State Dept. hostages that were being held by the government of Iran for 444 days showed him to be a weak and possibly incompetent one as well. When Reagan took over, the hostages were released and morning was declared in America. Reagan, with his cheerful demeanor, ebullient patriotism, and shameless support of military power incorporated with the will to exercise it, restored the confidence of the nation suffering from the malaise of the Carter years. But there was more to it than met the eye. Reagan, I think, was a charming pitchman for the Machiavellian manipulations of certain men behind the curtain. It was during his tenure that a group of disenchanted liberals coalesced into the cabal that became known as Neocons, the same group whose faulty thinking caused such damage to the country later during President Bush's administration. Reagan was called the "Great Communicator." His critics accused him of not being a very deep thinker. I agree with those critics. In my opinion he was a good man of sincere beliefs but the legacy he left for the nation troubles me. The legacy that tells us that government cannot cure our problems because the government *is* the problem. This misguided notion emanated from the minds of conservatives that wanted government (as I understand it, the government should mean us) out of their way in order to to effect policy for corporate gain rather than the concept of the common good.

Reagan came into office with three goals. He wanted to reduce government spending, reduce tax rates, and finally to reduce government regulation of business. The concept of reducing government spending did not apply to the defense industry. Reagan's team took aim at entitlements like Social Security, Medicare, unemployment and welfare programs. It was during his term that catch phrases like "Welfare Queens" (un-wed mothers) came into vogue. Terms like "Class Warfare" sprang up, not from those at the bottom, but from the wealthy at the top who feared that government taxation and demands of the underclass would impede their lifestyle. Reagan is on record as wondering whether ketchup could be considered a vegetable when computing and reducing the cost of lunch programs for poor schools.

The truth is Reagan was a lot more pragmatic than his handlers. While he did support the idea that Social Security should be voluntary, and he was against socialized Medicare programs or publicly funded healthcare, he did leave most social programs alone and truly was not the ogre some liberal thinkers accused him of being. (And he had to work with a Democratic Congress.) At the end of his two terms Reagan claimed that one of his greatest disappointments was not being able to bring spending under control. One of the main reasons was the increased spending for defense. He fought the "Evil Empire" of communism throughout his term and finally helped bring Russia's military to its economic knees. However, it was at great cost to our own economy also. Reagan inherited a $700 billion national debt and left more than a trillion dollar debt in its place. Internationally Reagan believed strongly in the reduction of nuclear weapons and he had some success with disarmament treaties with our arch-rival Russia. Domestically he fought hard for a presidential line-item veto for non-defense spending but was unable to get it. I questioned his priorities for cutting social programs and the mean spiritedness of a blind conservative policy but he was not all wrong; much of government spending was, and still is, wasteful and out of control. Both parties are responsible. I am, by nature, a liberal. And it is difficult to defend some of the excesses of liberal policy because some of the wasteful practices of government can be attributed to them. But in reality, both parties are culpable. Defense spending is still sacrosanct largely because all states somehow have garnered a piece of the action thanks to their representatives "bringing home the bacon." Battle lines have been drawn for years: Republicans favor tax cuts and the elimination of social programs that they consider abets the propagation of a lazy class of undeserving citizens. The Democrats favor retaining social programs and finding cuts in what they consider unnecessary corporate tax loopholes and wasteful spending by the defense industry. I favor the Democrats—you are free to take your pick. It's a free country.

There was a predominant conservative thought during the Reagan years that the best way to control government spending was to "Starve the beast" by sharply reducing taxes. I suspect this plan was postulated by those simply concerned with keeping more of their money rather than running a more efficient government. Either way the concept would have been a hard sell to the average Joe. Enter the Laffer Curve. In a nutshell, this Laffer Curve was economic hocus-pocus that introduced the idea that less taxes would result in more investment, which would result in more employment, which would result in more wage earners, which would result in the collection of more taxes, and we would all go to Heaven some day.

Unfortunately Reagan bought into this nonsense hook, line, and sinker. Reagan was a tax-cutter emotionally and ideologically. He reduced the tax rate from 70% to less that 30% for higher incomes. During his tenure this produced a short range benefit. What is less noticed was that Reagan was later forced to sign ten major tax increases to try to make up for this initial reduction because the deficit and national debt ballooned by almost one trillion dollars. By 1988 he had taken back almost half of the 1981 tax cut. Republican David Stockman, director of management and budget under President Reagan, blamed the "ideological tax-cutters" of the Reagan administration for the 20% increase of the national debt during the 1980s.

I think history has debunked this trickle-down theory of economic nonsense by now; all one has to do is take note of the corporate outsourcing of jobs to undeveloped countries. Reagan's policy always favored business and the wealthiest at the expense of the lower and middle classes. The fact that income adjusted for inflation over the last twenty five years shows a net loss for the middle and lower class wage earners is indisputable.

If you want to discuss the result of Reagan's economic policy you have to inspect the third leg of his agenda: government regulation of industry. Reagan implemented policies of supply-side economics and advocated a *laissez-faire* policy toward industry. He deregulated industries such as transportation, oil, and banking, with the result that corporate giants rose in this new game of monopoly. I am not a socialist although the knee-jerk conservatives may accuse me of being a rabid one. I believe that government has a legitimate role in protecting citizens from the potential excesses of corporate giants. The regulation of the food and drug industry, emission controls, child labor laws, and a minimum wage law are all within the purview of government. These beliefs were antithetical to the philosophy of those of the Reagan administration. He believed, with the input of his handlers, that free-markets would govern themselves. It was the rise of this concept which brings me to believe that the Reagan administration set in motion practices that are deleterious to our society as a whole.

The Reagan policies and attitudes have resulted in an almost unworkable imbalance in the distribution of wealth in our country. Unregulated and unbridled adherence to a capitalist religion has resulted in 2% of our people now controlling over 50% of the wealth of our country. The result is that wealth is now in a position to—and often does—control the political system to benefit the few.

Patriotism that bordered on Jingoism abounded during the Reagan years and continues in the neo-conservative mind set we see twenty-five years later. Mindless garnering of wealth, wars of choice and opportunity, class warfare, and the loss of the sense of common welfare and shared sacrifice are, in my opinion, the true legacies of the administration of Ronald Wilson Reagan. Generally speaking, the white collar and business class loved him and did very well during Reagan's administration. Working stiffs, blue collar and union workers, and the economically disadvantaged fell behind and became angry and frustrated. In a country that incorporates as its motto *E Pluribus Unum*, it appears that many of the many were left out of this lofty ideal. That is not democracy, it is oligarchy . . . look it up.

The Strike

I am no stranger to strikes and picket lines. After graduating from the Maritime College in 1961 I went down to Washington Street in lower Manhattan and joined the Master, Mates, and Pilots Union,

Local #5. I paid my initiation, and my dues, and put my hand up and swore to uphold the by-laws, etc. When I put my arm down they fitted me with a placard that read, "No Contract, No Sail." I was on strike before I ever worked on a ship! I remember my first assignment for picket duty. The voice came over the phone to my home in the Bronx; "Youse been assigned to the Erie Basin in Brooklyn tomorrow at midnight . . . . no, we don't give no names over the phone, just be there." I met a fellow picketer at the site and he informed me I could use the screw driver he had laid out on the front seat of his car. Then he showed me the knife he would use if they came after him again on the picket line. He said that his last time on a picket line "they" broke his leg. Believe it. I am not making this up. It was an exhilarating introduction to the waterfront for a callow 21 year old. To make a long story short: nothing happened as I whiled away eight nervous hours standing under a naked street light flickering above my head. I was really glad to see a cop patrolling the area every hour or so.

The tugboat union had an interesting history. Originally founded as a division of the Longshoreman's Union in New York, it eventually broke from the longshoremen when the latter group was being investigated for corruption on the waterfront. It joined up then with the National Maritime Union and was called, simply, United Maritime Division Local #333. When the NMU was going belly-up in the Eighties the boatmen re-affiliated with the Longshoremen (ILA) but there was no real sense of brotherhood anymore. During the devastating strike that broke the power of the tugboat union the longshoremen did not honor the picket lines. Perhaps they couldn't. It was a bad time for labor.

Oh yes, we had our share of strikes. We called it "Walking the bricks" about once every three years. They became so regular that we even looked forward to the extra time off! Anyway that's where I developed my affinity for "The Men Around the Barrel." They were the guys on the picket lines, or the fellows clad white in aprons and plaid woolen shirts that waited in the pre-dawn for deliveries of the days catch at the fish market, or the iron workers who shaped up for work at their site while waiting for the doughnut and coffee truck to arrive. That coffee truck staved off many an early morning chill. I never considered myself a corporate suit and tie man. I was more comfortable philosophizing (bull-shitting), or bitching, or solving local and world problems with the fellows standing around the barrel warming their hands or their backsides as the dry wooden dunnage burned away inside the empty fifty gallon drum.

The late Eighties brought a perfect storm down on the heads of New York tugboat workers. The Republican philosophy was never pro-labor to begin with, and when Reagan summarily fired the entire crop of the nation's air traffic controllers the GOP had found its hero. Reagan, correctly in my opinion, advised them that they would all be fired if the strike went on. The union stupidly challenged the administration. They struck, possibly thinking that they were indispensable to the operation of the airline industry, and were promptly all fired. While this strike had no direct bearing on the tug boats of New York it did not go unnoticed by the corporate powers who were itching to put the unions back in their place. They now had a friend in high places.

The second ill-wind to blow across the harbor was the fact that most of the old guard was gone and the scions of these founding fathers couldn't wait to show the old men how to run things better. The old guard that founded the industry fought the union for years, but in reality there was a grudging respect for each other and a pride in their history, their boats, and in their family owned industry. The old guard was passing away in the Eighties and were being replaced by their children who lacked the same attachment. Work was obviously getting more impersonal, more competitive, and more devoted to the bottom line as never before. More work was being done by fewer people. When I joined the Local 333 in 1967 there were 8000 registered members. At the time of the strike we were down to little more than 2000. Boats and barges were bigger. Crews were smaller.

The domestic flag shipping industry failed due to the effects of foreign competition. The same thing was happening to the New York boatmen in microcosm. The new guard had no real relation with the boatmen who helped build the industry of their fathers. They saw instead the union scale being paid and knew that if they could break the union's power they could hire personnel from the depressed areas of the southern states like Florida or Texas. It was about profits. Southern imports would work for less than half of what New York companies were paying, so the plot was hatched. Unfortunately the local union leadership never understood the changing economic dynamics. After one of the union meetings I personally asked Al Cornetti, the union president, what would we do when scabs arrived to break the union if we went on strike. His answer was right out of the 1930's. Fight them on the docks with baseball bats was what he said. I knew then that we were in trouble because those days were gone with the wind. So there you have it. The Perfect Storm arrived when four fronts collided: 1. An anti-union administration, 2. The old guard was dying out, 3. The rise of the young corporate Turks, and 4. An out-dated union leadership with its head up its ass. Here's how it went down.

At contract time the companies demanded, among other things, that we take a 60% cut in pay. In addition we would no longer have overtime, holiday pay, or paid vacations. The pension plan was to be terminated, captains would be considered management and no longer be allowed to be in the union. In 1988 the union, unwisely in my estimation, went on strike only to have our jobs replaced by crews of southern scabs who had already been hired and were lurking at a nearby Holiday Inn. Union pickets were enjoined from picketing anywhere in proximity to the boats while the scabs were brought down to the docks in armored vans protected by a security company aptly called "Knuckles Security." I believe that the cops, Coast Guard, and politicians were in collusion with this deal and we were screwed. It was over a year before the Labor Board found the balls to issue an order for us to go back to work. Their decision was laughable. We were to report to work until a contract was settled or an *impasse* declared. After a year on strike what the hell did they think an *impasse* was? The company predictably declared an impasse after two weeks. We were advised by the union and labor board not to give up our jobs again but to remain at work under the company rules while an unfair labor suit would be filed against them. I was allowed to return as captain but it was understood that I would be considered a management employee.

The companies tried to run us locals off the boats by insisting we now work a month on with two weeks off. My pay was reduced, but not nearly as much as the unlicensed personnel of the boat. Brenda got a job to help out, and I remember our young children crying, "Who will baby sit us now?" Before the strike a deckhand on the tug made $70 per day not counting any overtime. During the strike one little scab runt with a tattoo on his lip was swaggering around saying, "Ah don' need no damn union! Ah got me a good job now!" He was getting paid $35 a day with no overtime, and putting in double the hours of the union deckhand he replaced. In Florida—a right to work state—he was pulling down the lordly sum of $18 a day. The Asshole. Pardon my bitterness, but even today I detest those scabs and don't have much use for those Okiefanokie swamp dwellers I met from Florida. But at least, after a year I was back on the boats.

The court case ran on for more than two years with no decision coming from the federal judge. (What a surprise!) Anyway a settlement was finally reached when the union wound up signing for the identical demands that were offered four years earlier. The only difference was that the Labor Board insisted we receive back pay compensation. I figured I was owed in the neighborhood of $60,000 and I got paid off with the princely sum of $2,000.

Then there was the little matter of our pension plan. In those days there was a law called the Arisa Law which stipulated the minimum funding of pension plans. Due to the good economic times our pension plan had about twice the $40 million required by Arisa. The companies terminated the plan, set up a required equity fund for the boatmen as had been contracted, and I believe the over funded money of our plan reverted to the owners because they claimed our pension was non-contributory. These contributions, were negotiated in lieu of pay raises, so whose money was it really? Did they think we were stupid? It was not about right or wrong anymore; it was about what was legal. The golden rule applied. Whoever has the gold can make the rule. After twenty years in the union I was paid off with an equity of $600 a month.

All the boatmen took a screwing like that but, in reality, there was nothing we could do about it. The times had changed, the perfect storm hit, and that was it. Those who were old enough, retired. Those who were young left the industry, and those, like me at age 50 really had no place to go. But the old times were gone. I didn't like working for the new bosses. I didn't like working with the dumb-ass imports, and I didn't like working with some of my own union men who turned scab and helped break the union.

I know that you who read this today may find my position naive or quixotic or hopeless. I wasn't dumb or blind-sided by the events. I was fully aware that the strike would be lost and I understood the pragmatic approach by some of those who crossed the line. But my sense of morality was outraged. I knew better, but that's the way my chromosomes work. I guess that's why I favor more liberal causes than my more pragmatic conservative friends. But as I said, I wasn't happy on the tugs anymore. I needed to do something else. And in 1992 the opportunity arose and I jumped at it. Before I tell you about that, I have to devote a few more pages explaining how I and my family survived the year of the strike. It wasn't easy, but life was never guaranteed to be always fun. You have to deal with the cards that are dealt.

The Chemical Company

Sometimes you just do what you gotta do. I was on strike. We had to pay bills. I had to get a job. A friend who was in charge of quality control for a company called Reheis Chemical Company brought me in to work in the plant. The Reheis Company made the active ingredients that were used in making antacids and antiperspirants. They sold these ingredients to companies that marketed products like Tums, Rolaids, or Arrid Extra Dry. My first few weeks on the floor (meaning a general factory worker with no specific title) saw me operating fork lifts and filling chemical drums. The drums weighed 500 lbs when properly filled. The foreman of my shift was pleased to learn that I could figure out that if two full drums were placed on a scale the total weight would be 1000 lbs. Apparently some of the workers had trouble with that kind of sophisticated math. I didn't have the heart to tell him I also knew how to solve the problems of spherical trigonometry. All he needed to know was that I could add 500 to 500 and get the proper answer.

After a three week trial period I was allowed to join the union and work regular shifts that included overtime. I was assigned to the "Gel Room," an interesting little room where I stood, shovel in hand, under a chute from which plopped a white paste that had to be shoveled into containers. 130 lbs per container. Folks at the plant were amazed that I learned this job in two short days and was now working unchaperoned! Well, maybe it was more complicated than I thought. The fellow I trained after me had a little trouble. As you can imagine, working in a chemical company requires a lot of sterile equipment. We were required to wear white gowns, nets on our heads, and surgical masks for certain functions. The Gel Room was a clean place. I can't imagine how a customer would have felt if he received a container that contained the shovel that the new guy lost one afternoon! The new fellow informed me that he left his shovel in an empty container while it was under the chute. Now the containers were all filled up and and he didn't know which container contained the shovel. We had to dig through containers of white glop until we found it. As I said, you can't make this up. Later I was again promoted—this time to the "Reaction Room."

I stayed in the Reaction Room almost a year. The Reaction Room contained four vats, pots we called them. I worked two and my partner the other two. The pots had walls about five feet high and a diameter of about eight feet. Starting with a clean vat, we would add the required amount of water and the prescribed amounts of chlorides. I can't remember if we heated the vats or they heated themselves during the reaction created by adding powdered aluminum. That was my job; I would roll a 500 lb. drum of powdered aluminum alongside the vat and, using a large scoop, proceed to scoop out the powder and pour it into the pot. The addition of this aluminum would trigger a chemical reaction that would eventually create aluminum hydrochloride—the active ingredient I told you about. I made two pots per twelve hour shift. I shoveled, with my trusty scoop, 1000 pounds of powder every day into those pots. Aluminum powder was in my hair, my nostrils, the back of my throat and down the back of my neck. My shoulders ached from scooping, and my back ached from bending face down into the drums. We scooped at a certain rate—too much aluminum would choke the reaction and too little would cause the reaction to stop and ruin the batch. The reaction in the pots was like watching a pot boil except the gas given off by the bubbles was hydrogen that had the potential of blowing up. It was sucked out by vents above the pots and the Reaction Room was a separate concrete structure attached to the outside walls of the plant. Bad enough you might say, but it wasn't the work that bothered me as much as the hours.

Rotating shifts are an invention of the devil. One week the eight to four, the following week four to twelve, and the following week twelve to eight. The plant worked round the clock; that I understood. But I never understood why workers just couldn't be assigned to a regular shift of days, evenings, or nights. Rotating the shifts means the worker never really gets to acclimate his body or circadian rhythm to a set pattern. It can't be healthy. And to make the cheese more binding, we at the chemical company were mandated to work overtime almost every day. The required O.T. was assigned in four hour increments—either the four hours before the shift or the four hours after it ended. The schedule was God damn inhuman. And after every shift I would pull into the Shell Station on Route 10 and nap for twenty minutes so I wouldn't fall asleep at the wheel on the way home. I'd come home after a forty minute commute, filthy with aluminum, take a shower and go to bed. We survived; the bills got paid, and we had food on the table. Life didn't seem to be as carefree. At fifty years of age I had developed a maturity and a sense of responsibility. I also learned to be especially indebted to my wife Brenda who never in her life voiced a word that wasn't positive, and who also pitched in by going to work (in addition to caring for the family) to help out during financially difficult times. We did it together. Many times I remember she would drive down to that Shell Station with our neighbor Sandy, the Man (there was also Sandy, the Dog) to drive me the rest of the way home so I could sleep. To anyone who reads this sometime in the future, know this; my wife Brenda is special.

Writing this chapter on the eighties may read like life was a downer, but it wasn't really. It was real. It was life. It was why children should respect their elders who have been there and done that. But we had fun, too. My next chapter will tell you about the favorite activity of the Klumpp family. Through the years we always found the time or the money to go skiing.

Fifty Years of Skiing

Early Techniques, The Tripod, Steamboat Springs, Racing, Ski Instructing

FIFTY YEARS OF SKIING

Early Techniques

For starters I'll tell you about cable bindings. If you started skiing in 1962 like I did, the cable bindings attached your boots to the ski. It was primitive, and just a little further advanced from tieing your feet to the ski with leather straps. Here's how they worked. The toe plate was a simple half inch grooved plate that the toe of the boot pressed up against. Forward of the toe plate was a hook that held the cable that you passed around the heel of your boot. You pushed down a lever forward of the toe plate which tightened the cable around the back of your heel. You'll see them now only in antique stores or mounted on walls of restaurants located at the foot of the ski slopes of today. Why am I telling you this? I guess I want you to know that I started sliding down slippery slopes at the very dawning of popular skiing in the U.S. Sure, folks had skied for centuries but it wasn't until the early sixties that the sport began to take a hold on the general population of sport enthusiasts in the States. Entrepreneurs carved out slopes on pristine mountains, built lodges at the base, and then hired instructors from Austria, France, or Switzerland to create ski schools to teach Americans the sport without killing themselves. The apres—ski scene was always accompanied by instructors with names like Emo, Hans, and Franzie, who played Tyrolean music and yodeled for us.

There is a lot that I want to tell you about skiing. If you are reading this, and you are not a skier, why, that's just too bad. The techniques we employed may mean nothing to you but I'm going to write about them anyway. Early skiing, if you don't go as far back as carrying a long wooden staff to pivot around, involved what we called "snow-plowing" and stem turns. In that era of cable bindings, your boot was only loosely hooked to the ski. The heel moved up and down, and any up-weighting movement would not be transferred to the ski. Later when step-in bindings were introduced, the whole boot would be attached to the ski. One was then taught how to hop the tails of the ski off the snow and, with a kind of twisting from the hip, one would redirect the tips down the hill to create the beginning of a new turn. (If you did it right!) These step-in bindings came into vogue in the early 70's and were accompanied by the advent of metal skis. While I'm at it I might as well as tell you now that the recommended length of a ski was measured by extending your arm straight up over your head. The proper ski would reach your wrist. Today, in 2011, my skis reach my chin. The other change around this time was the replacement of the low cut double-laced leather boots with boots with soft inner liners and hard plastic shells with clips that fit them snugly to the feet. Getting in and out of these boots, and on and off the skis, was a terrific advancement. So, for years we attempted to "Ski Like Stein." We tried to keep our boots locked close together in a narrow stance and angulate our bodies into that famous "Comma" shape as we made swooping turns down and across the fall line. The natural route a ball will take as it rolls down the mountain is the "Fall Line." It took me years to approach that style, and later, many years to shed myself of that muscle memory when a new technique rose to take its place.

The early 1990's saw a dramatic change in the dynamics of a ski. A ski is a complex tool, made from layers of wood and various metals designed to withstand various pressures and buffering materials designed to dampen chatter at high speeds. My first pair of skis cost $19. Today my skis are of the latest technology and cost $1000 with bindings. A ski endures terrible stress as it adjusts to the turning and torquing effect it must absorb as one changes direction at various speeds and steepness. It was this torquing effect that stymied designers for years. Everyone knew a ski would bend—skis were already produced with the idea of being "soft" or "stiff" depending on the type of skiing involved. A "forgiving" ski would have a softer shovel (front) and tend to enter turns more easily but chatter at high speeds or on steeps. A "stiff" tail (back) ski would take more edging to turn but would track better at higher speeds. All this was already known and incorporated in the creation of a ski. But it was the breakthrough in torquing that radically changed the mechanics of skiing. (Think of holding a ski on both ends and then twisting it like you would wring out a wash rag—that's torque.) This happened during the late 80's early 90's. Once a ski was made that wouldn't break under those conditions the shape of the ski could be altered radically. The shovel and the tail were now made much wider than the waist of the ski. Simply enough, they were called "shaped skis." A turn was no longer required to be initiated by hopping and redirecting the tail. A turn now could be manufactured by the simple act of increasing the angle the edge of the ski had with the snow. The wider shovel would bite into the snow creating more torque on that end and the ski would follow that pressure around into the turn. A turn could be initiated by the simple act of turning the ski on edge and letting it do the work.

The Tripod

I have always considered that my attraction to skiing was based on a tripod of enjoyment. The legs of the tripod were not necessarily equal, but all three were important. Athleticism was one of the legs, and probably the least important. You don't have to be a super jock to enjoy skiing. Trails were groomed for beginners, intermediates, and those more advanced. You could find a slope that fit your talent and judge your progress as you learned. The trick was to enjoy the sport at whatever level you were comfortable.

I ski like crap in powder. We hardly ever see much of it in the East, and certainly not in any measurable depths—except for the time Brenda and I and some friends decided to go to Chamonix and try out the Alps. It snowed on that trip. It really snowed. Forty inches of the white fluffy stuff fell in two days, and a few avalanches in the area caught our attention. We had planned to join a tour and tackle a ski trip over the Alps from Chamonix, France, to Courmeyer, Italy. The guides promised us a stop along the way for an authentic Italian lunch of various pastas and grappa. The lunch was as advertised, but I'm here to tell you about the powder so here goes:

My first mistake was paying for the trip with my credit card upon which was displayed the logo of the Professional Ski Instructors of America, a group to which I belonged at the time. "Oh ho," said the guide as he processed my card, "Who is the instructor in the group?" "Shit," I thought, "I'm in trouble." How much trouble I was to soon learn. We skied out of the lodge directly into the deep powder and I promptly plopped right on my face. It was like landing on a soft pillow, but it was a very undignified pose that I posed with my rear end sticking out of the snow. I plopped about every twenty yards. I couldn't get the hang of it. I was wearing out fast trying to push myself out of the snow. We were skiing with our friend Fr. Dan Murphy, a priest, who skied up to help me extricate myself from the damn powder. I was cursing up a storm—remember I am a seaman by trade—and Dan jocularly said he never heard me talk like that. That's when I told the priest to go and perform an anatomically impossible feat on himself. I shouldn't have said it, but Dan laughed and then told me, "O boy, now you better pray!" It got worse: The guide, watching me exhaust myself, eventually suggested that I join the lower level group of skiers. It embarrassed the hell out of me, but that was nothing compared to when he told me later that a group of women were calling it a day and I might consider heading down the mountain with them. When I got back to the hotel I scissored the crap out of that credit card and burned it in an ash tray. It is kind of a funny (but true) story, and I eventually profited by my humiliation. I developed an empathy for struggling skiers. I was athletic enough, but on that day, my athleticism had nothing to do with my ability to enjoy skiing. Because on that day I certainly did not.

The second leg of the tripod is what I call the aesthetics of the sport. Quite simply, the views witnessed from the mountaintop feed my soul. And the feeling I get of being one with nature—even when buffeted by high winds, zero temperatures, stinging sleet, and frost bite—gives me a feeling that I'm glad to be alive. I've learned to love the feeling of exhilaration while swooping down the slopes, land-bound and yet free as a bird. I love to feel the wintery wind stinging my face and making my eyes tear. Only a free spirit can know this. I often stand in wonder on a mountain top and gaze upon fifty mile views capped by an azure blue dome above me. That's when I feel humbled and grateful to be in God's cathedral—and I tell him so. I can go on like this forever so I'll just try to draw you a postcard with words. Close your eyes. Picture royal blue cloudless skies, snow-dusted pine trees and stands of white barked Poplars. Picture a lone porcupine silently nestled among the trees, and then notice the shadows making spidery designs on virgin snow. Picture the appearance of a lone skier who, when he sees you, jauntily waves in your direction and emits a joyous yodel as he glides by and disappears around the next bend. I didn't make that up. I witnessed it while skiing with my friend, Mary Cunningham, at Stratton Mountain many years ago. I've never forgotten.

As usual, my story comes with a story. I was skiing with Mike Maguire. We were instructors at Shawnee Mountain together. While gazing out from the top of the chair lift I mentioned to Mike that, because I was employed by the Dept. of Corrections at the time, I spent too much time in the jail and not enough time on the slopes enjoying fresh air, the blue sky, and the beautiful scenery. Mike replied, "I know just how you feel, buddy." And then we both laughed—Mike was an elevator repair man!

The third leg of my tripod is as important as the others. Sociability. On the chair lift it doesn't matter who you know. When riding a chair lift, passengers share a common interest and common stories and you don't have to ski well. Nobody cares—provided the skiers code of conduct is adhered to. Princes and Paupers (a metaphor because paupers can't afford a lift ticket) can be comfortable with each other on the mountain. Unhappily though, I have to say that that was how it was; folks generally are changing now. Maybe there is too much money around; the $7 lift tickets now set you back $92. Some lodges now boast of exclusive clubs complete with martini bars and climate-controlled cigar and brandy rooms. Some even boast of valet service to carry the skis and heat the boots of plutocrats intent upon maximizing a sybarite existence. Many folks can't afford to ski anymore and that's a pity.

The post-ski phenomena that is the happy ending to a long day is called "Apres-Ski." French I guess, and it means the party you share at the end of a day on the slopes. In the early days when we all could party hearty, we would gather around the bar at the base lodge and celebrate with brandys or beers and forget to go home until well after dark. Jimmy's old house is falling down now and the crowd has scattered. Brenda, me, and Ray Smith, who is almost 80 and still looking sartorial splendorous in his sporty Brooks Brothers attire, are the only ones from the old crowd who still make it to the slopes. Nowadays a good hot soup at home and a roaring fire does us a world of good. But then, as I write this, I confess to the age of 71 years young. Some claim that is the new 51. Perhaps. Maybe some Ben-Gay for the tired muscles that we never used to have helps, but the warmth and friendship shared by old friends who still care enough to challenge the mountain is enough to reinforce the old feeling of *Gemultlekeit* that makes the long trip to the mountains worthwhile.

And, as usual, I have another another story to relate before I turn the page. I went skiing with Roy Thoresen a few years ago. Roy owns a house at Stratton Mountain in Vermont. Roy likes to ski and he also likes to cook. In real life he is a chef—and a good one. At the end of the day we went home to his house and sat down to a dinner he prepared of ostrich steaks. We had vegetables too, of course, but I was so shocked by the prospect of eating ostrich that I'll be damned if I remember what the vegetables were. And then in the morning guess what? Ostrich and Eggs! Life is good. Skiing is good. Skiing is social. End of story.

Steamboat Springs, Colorado

The town of Steamboat Springs hasn't changed much to this day. The mountain has. Hundreds of new ski runs have been hewn out of the evergreen and aspen groves that covered the hillsides. High speed chairs and gondola lifts are the norm, replacing the rickety wooden two seat chairs we used to ride. It is hard to imagine the growth that has transpired on the mountain since the early days of the 1970's. But Steamboat and the Yampa Valley remain pretty much now the way they always have been. It was then, and still is now, a working ranch town in the beautiful Yampa River Valley. The cows and corrals are still there but the recreation industry dominates the economy. Skiing had always been popular in Steamboat. Howelsen Hill is located right in town and was the site of early ski jumping activities. Just across the way looms the three peaks that have been developed as the Steamboat Ski Area. One peak, Storm Peak, would be renamed Mount Werner, after Buddy Werner who was a three time Olympian and a native of the town. Buddy died in 1956 when caught by an avalanche while making a movie in Saint Moritz, Switzerland. Today "Buddy's Run" from the top remains one of the favorite slopes for skiers at Steamboat.

Brenda and I liked the area right away. The pioneering atmosphere was enhanced by friendly lift attendants who wore cowboy hats and bandanas. The snow was not at all like back East where we had gotten used to scraping our skis over exposed rocks or icy patches. At Steamboat we found Skier Heaven: wide slopes for cruising, friendly forgiving snow, and enough "Sunshine On Our Shoulders" to supply enough vitamin D for a year. Suffice it to say that I fell in love with Colorado, and Steamboat in particular, and I bought a condominium on the mountain after that first trip. I paid $32,000 for it which will shock you, I know, with prices as they are today. But I was working on the tugs at the time and figured I could work a schedule of two weeks on and two weeks off and be able to travel one round trip each month to my mountain home. The best laid plans of mice and men oft times go awry. I never made it to a permanent residence in the Rockies. Brenda and I were married that fall and my life took a different turn. We still own that condo in Steamboat, majestic views and all. That's where the kids learned to ski.

Steamboat is known as a great place for children's programs and we can attest to that. We signed Kev and Kris into the Kiddie Corral where they would have an hour of ski lessons in the morning and again in the afternoon. In the meantime there was nap time, play time in the jungle gym, and lunch time for socializing over peanut butter and jelly sandwiches. That allowed Brenda and me to hit the slopes and do our thing on the black diamonds. Ski slopes, by the way, are rated as to degree of difficulty and the level of skiers prowess to navigate them. Trails marked with Green Circles are for novices, Blue Squares for intermediate skiers, and Black Diamonds for those more advanced. There are some that are labeled Double-Diamond for experts only (and one Triple-Diamond that I know of), but we stay away from them. As the day advanced, Brenda and I began to feel a little guilty about leaving the kids for so long. We knocked off about two P.M. and went to retrieve our offspring. We knew they would be clamoring for us by now. Guess what. Not so. They were having the time of their lives without the doting parents, and emphatically told us not to come back until pick-up time! That was shock number one.

Shock number two occurred the following day when BK and I were high on the mountain and all of a sudden a row of little munchkins paraded into view. They were cute little tykes with hats and goggles askew and both hands on their knees sweeping toward us single file. And then we saw him in the middle of the line of little daredevils. "Kev!" we shouted. "What are you doing? How did you get up here?" Kev told us Ranger Bob took them up the gondola and no, they weren't scared because they sang "Old MacDonald Had a Farm" all the way up. (Ranger Bob will go to Heaven some day.) And here came Ranger Bob! The big, tall, lanky guy gathered the munchkins up, counted heads, gave a little pep talk, and off they went around a corner and out of view. Kev never even waved good-bye!

Krissy, a year younger, wasn't ready for that group and her lessons were confined to the lower mountain. Not to worry though. She caught up. Remember that Triple-Diamond slope I told you that I knew of? It is located in Sugarbush Ski Area in Vermont. Years later, when Kris was in college, my girl and I challenged that slope together and lived to tell the tale. The sign says to consider skiing the route in threes. One could then stay behind to help the injured skier and the third would be available to ski down for assistance. And we did it. Krissy and her Pop.

Racing

We spent a week in Steamboat every year that we could afford to go. Sometimes the finances weren't there, but mostly we managed that trip out West. We got to know our way around the mountain and picked a few favorite slopes of our own. Brenda hurt her knee on one of our favorites and had to be taken down the hill in a toboggan—a ride scarier than doing it on skis. She got mad at me because I told her to shrug it off and ski slowly down on her own but she would have none of it. They took her to the hospital and the next time I saw her she already had her leg wrapped up and was directing me how to push the wheel chair. I guess she was hurt more than I thought. But BK has moxie (look the word up). She took up ski racing in Steamboat.

Billy Kidd is the ski representative for the Steamboat Corporation. He was also the first U.S. skier to win an Olympic medal in Slalom. He meets folks at noon each day on the mountain and skies with everyone for an hour. He gives cute lessons like skiing "with your hand in your pockets" is the surest way to blow a chance at a medal and also is the surest way to the emergency room. It is really true. Body language tells a lot. A novice or nervous skier tends to keep his arms and elbows close to the body in some sort of protective position, but you just can't ski like that. It's a difficult habit to break. Billy took Brenda aside one day and asked her if she ever raced. He told her that she was ready for the next step that would graduate her from a recreational skier to a more dynamic advanced one. If I had told her that she would have told me she wasn't interested, but when Billy told her she believed him and my BK took a giant leap forward.

Most ski ares host the NASTAR program. NASTAR is the acronym for the National Standard Amateur Race. It is a slalom course. You ski between the gates placed along the route. The course is skied daily by a Resident Pro who has a registered handicap with an Olympic skier. He sets the handicap time for the course. No one beats the Olympic time of course, but the object is to record a time within a certain range of the handicap based on age and gender. They are fun but challenging courses and even novice skiers get their blood pumping in the starting gate before kicking through the timing wand and going for the Gold. My Brenda developed the "Eye of the Tiger." She became a racer and likes to sport the medals she's earned on her jacket for all to see. We all raced. One wonderful day at Steamboat the whole Klumpp family medaled on the same course.

As usual, I'll end this segment with another story. I raced a lot. Always got a Silver, which wasn't awful, except my time always fell so tantalizing close to Gold that I chased the elusive dream at slopes all over the country. I'm talking about less than two-tenths of a second off. It became a family joke. The kids, who by now both had won Golds, would enjoy breaking their Pop's chops. One time I was planning to buy a car and wondered aloud what color would be nice. My loveable Krissy with the sharp wit said to buy a Gold. She opined that it would be the only way I would ever get that color! BK used gold plate flatware for the fancy table settings for guests and the kids invariably would insure that my place was indicated by the pedestrian silver knife, fork, and spoon. And then one day I broke the barrier. The only problem was that day was April 1st and you know what day that is. Besides that, my irrepressible daughter mentioned that, because it was late in the season, they were probably giving out medals just to get rid of them, Not true!! Just to prove it was not a fluke I went on to win more of them. I won Golds at Steamboat, Aspen Mountain (called Ajax), Windham, and Stratton Mountains. For a long time after that I had the kids address my e mail to "Johnny Gold." I don't race anymore, and Brenda doesn't, either. But it is nice to look back at that time and remember when we had the "Eye of The Tiger."

Ski Instructing

You may have noticed that I've referred to certain ski techniques or equipment in a more critical or analytical way than you would have expected. You also might have surmised that my knowledge of the nuances of the sport indicates a greater than just casual involvement. You would be right. I have been a certified member of the Professional Ski Instructors of America Association for the last fifteen years. It started out quite by accident. Kevin and Kris were members of the Pope John

High School Ski Team. Ken Liebler, their coach, was a ski instructor at Shawnee Mountain in the Poconos. We got to be friendly and he asked me if I had ever given a thought to instructing. I hadn't, but when Ken explained the discounts granted instructors for equipment and lift tickets I realized I could save a lot of money on my many trips to the slopes. The biggest advantage would be realized later when I found a new cadre of friends who shared my interest in the sport.

The way you get to be a ski instructor is by taking the instructor training clinic at your local mountain. If you can ski decently enough you get certified to teach the entry level novices the art of putting their boots on the right feet, how to carry their skis without tripping over them, and how to step into their skis with the pointy end facing forward. Don't laugh—I have encountered these problems with beginners more than once in my career! A beginning teacher is relegated to teaching the lower level skiers how to slide down a slight hill without panicking. They teach speed control with the infamous "Snow Plow" (now called the "Wedge") technique and finally how to stop. It is amazing to see what a break through this is for a newbie when they realize that they can actually control their descent on these long sticks and to stop before hitting the wall of the lodge. Technically this is an application of the concept of Dynamic Balance—understanding the forces at work called proprioceptive awareness (a fancy word to describe the body's sense that enable one to maintain balance while moving). When I was teaching at this level I thought teaching was a snap. I thought that as long as I could ski better than a beginner I was good enough to teach. I was wrong.

Ski instructors today teach what is called the "American Teaching System." The early ski resorts usually imported European instructors to run their ski schools. Depending upon where the instructors came from, a student might learn the French style of skiing, or the Austrian, or even the Swiss style. When I learned to ski at Stratton Mountain in Vermont in 1962 I learned in the Austrian Style of hopping the tails and wedeling down the hill in a succession of tightly linked turns. Time and technology have made "wedeling" obsolete. As skiing became more popular in the U.S. it became apparent that a standardized method of skiing would be preferable to the hodge-podge approach that was in use. Students then could be able to travel to or ski at different areas and still learn from the same standard manual of instruction. An organization called the "Professional Ski Instructors of America" embarked on a study of the various techniques being taught and adopted some of the better programs while discarding some of the weaker ones.

The American Teaching System was born. The teaching model included three considerations for controlling a ski and collectively applying them to the overall concept of balance for effective skiing. Hence the acronym BERP. Balance was maintained by the proper application of Edging, Rotation, and Pressure. Edging is the ability to tilt the ski on its side to increase the angle of the edge of the ski with the snow. Rotation is the turning the direction of a flat ski on a horizontal plane by rotating femurs within the ball joint of the hips and ankles. Pressure is the result of the speed of the ski holding an edge in the snow. Pressure is controlled by the knee action like shock absorbers and varies from leg to leg as adjustments are made. Sounds simple, no? Well, no. The trick is to develop mechanics to enhance these concepts. I'll try to simplify it for you so you won't think that I am some out of control ski nut.

A beginner skier will tend to ski on a flat ski and predominately utilize the practice of rotation to redirect the ski. There is very little edging involved and very little pressure control because the skis remain mostly flat on the snow. As the learners advance to the Intermediate level they begin to edge their skis to create sharper, more controlled turns. (By the way: How many ski instructors are used to change a light bulb? Ans: five. One to unscrew the bulb and four others to watch the turns.) Improving skiers learn to control their speed by creating turns of varying shapes across the Fall Line. They begin to experiment with edge angles which results in a beginning awareness of pressure changes on the ski. Advanced skiers are more dynamic. They edge their skis earlier in the turn and edge at a higher angle. They learn to control various turn shapes by effective rotation of their legs and use their knees to manage the pressure that builds with the higher edge angles in the snow. As I said, it all sounds so simple. But it takes years to truly master the techniques required to ski well. Just the thrill of sliding down a mountain with the wind in my face is enough fun for me no matter how I'm skiing. I once knew an instructor who lost one of his legs, I never did ask how. He was an excellent skier on his one leg and I asked him what made him take up the sport. His answer was interesting. He told me that he really didn't consider himself handicapped. While wearing his prosthesis he was able to do anything anyone else could do—except for one thing. He couldn't run or move fast on his own. He wanted to feel the wind on his face and the wind blowing through his hair. He could do that while skiing on one leg without the prosthesis. He could go as fast as he liked . . . and from watching him ski I saw he did it better than most of us.

Joining the PSIA opened up a whole new appreciation of the sport for me. I enjoyed the clinics when we practiced with senior instructors. I enjoyed the challenge of trying to create that perfect turn. I enjoyed the hours I've spent on the slopes in fair weather or foul trying to teach others what had been taught to me by skiers levels above me.

I enjoyed the camaraderie we instructors shared. We were never too busy to indulge our passion for the sport and would talk about it or demonstrate some finer points at the drop of a hat. We cared about the sport. We wanted to share it. I wanted to become a Level Two certified instructor, capable of teaching intermediate and some early advanced lessons, but I was afraid of the difficulty of the exam and the possibility that I couldn't pass it.

As I write this I'm thinking about Barb Marshall, one of the smallest yet most dynamic and talented skiers I've known. When I was having trouble passing a teaching segment on my Level Two certification I contacted Barb for help. She was an examiner, a certified level of competence that I will never achieve, and she willingly helped me to learn what I needed to know. (One of her criticisms was that I tended to make my lessons more complicated than they needed to be.) Barb spent three days with me on the snow at Killington Ski Area and then e mailed me additional information that she thought would be helpful to study before finally taking the exam. She was typical of the instructors I got to know. Every instructor and examiner I met encouraged me to continue my quest. I practiced for four years unlearning the old habits and learning the new standards developed by the association before I was good enough to pass the exam. And when I finally did make that Level Two (a modest goal, but a big one for me) all those great skiers who helped me along were as happy as I was. I'm thinking of Bob Shostek, then President of PSIA-E, who laughingly told everybody that he didn't have to answer my damn e mailed questions anymore. Or Pete Robertson, the ski school director at Bromley Mountain, who once old me not to give up because he knew of a guy who didn't pass the exam until he was sixty-eight. I beat him by four years!!

One final note. The exam takes four days to complete. Two days of having three different examiners grading you on skiing ability followed by two days of three different examiners grading you on teaching ability. It is a stressful experience. On my final day of exams I encountered other instructors from my mountain who were taking various workshop exercises of their own. They had finished for the day, but they waited with me in the lodge for the exam results to be tabulated. Then they cheered when it was announced that I passed. I received the coveted Level Two pin and I let the prettiest girl pin it on my chest. All the blood, sweat, tears, and years, were worth it. I don't teach anymore, but the pin is still on my jacket.

PROFESSIONAL SKI INSTRUCTORS OF AMERICA

EASTERN DIVISION

By authority of the Board of Directors and upon the recommendation of the Education Steering Committee hereby confers upon

John Klumpp

the certification of

Master Teacher

With all rights, honors, and privileges appertaining thereto.

PRESIDENT — On April 2, 2005 DATE — CERTIFICATION CHAIRPERSON

One Thousand Miles

The walk day one, The wellness center, The walk day two

ONE THOUSAND MILES

Kate was my God-daughter, the daughter of my cousin Delia and her husband, Tony. I come from a rather small family but I was honored when Dee asked me if I would accept that appointment to insure that Kate would grow, as the say, in wisdom, age, and grace. I didn't have much to do; Dee and Tony took care of that very well, and we watched Kate grow into a woman we could all be proud of. When Kate was a little girl, I would send birthday cards and small presents. As she grew older I resorted to the Communion and Confirmation cards with the "boost" inside in the form of a check. Predictably, more and more time would elapse, and the distance between us would grow. Kate went away to Boston College, later graduated from law school, and eventually married and had a son of her own. Little by little as the years passed I lost touch with her, and my communication with Dee and Tony became the once a year Christmas card.

And then I heard that Kate had been diagnosed with breast cancer. What could I do? I didn't have it in me just to show up in Massachusetts after 15 years and say "Hello, I heard you have breast cancer." I have this definite character flaw, and I always handle stressful situations poorly. I'm ashamed to say I messed up on this one, also. I didn't know what to do, so I did nothing. And we lost Kate when she was only thirty-two years old. She died at her parents' home in North Andover, Massachusetts leaving behind her husband, her family, and her two year old son to grieve for a life taken so early. And I stayed in Jersey.

A few years later my Aunt Dot wanted to visit the family in New England. At almost ninety years of age, Aunt Dot had never ridden in an airplane and she didn't want to start. I volunteered to drive her to her visit. I met Dee and Tony while up there, and we had a long talk. We shared a lot of stories about Kate, and I had the chance to say how sorry I was. I was relieved that they understood, but I knew I was still wrong—I should have been there with them at that terrible time. It was, as Tony told me, the hardest and most painful experience one could imagine. When I returned home I met my neighbor Linda, and the rest of my story follows.

Linda was soliciting donations for her up-coming walk for breast cancer research. I asked her about it, and found out that the Avon Corporation was sponsoring a twenty-six mile marathon walk through New York City that Fall. I could join that walk if I could raise the required amount of $1600 in time. A light went off in my head. I would do it for Kate! I called Dee and Tony that evening and asked if I could dedicate a walk to her memory. Of course they agreed, and my association with the Avon Foundation was born. I volunteered a day a week stuffing envelopes and making phone calls at their walk headquarters and I still managed to raise the $1600. Linda and I would do the walk together and I decided to keep a journal of the walk that I would share with my sponsors. Now I'll share one of them with you:

Come, join me now for a walk through the streets of New York. We will walk thirteen miles Saturday, and thirteen more on Sunday. We'll sleep overnight in tents but I guarantee you will not get tired.

The Walk Day One

This is where we "Walk the Walk." So sit back now, and take an armchair tour with me through the Big Apple (which, to those of you who may be shamefully uninformed, is what New York is colloquially called) Hang on! Here we go!!

BK, my long-suffering spouse, and I rose at 0400 hours and, as the car was already packed, just grabbed our coffees and headed to the South Street Seaport. Brenda drove, explaining that I could rest a little longer in the car so as to be ready for the walk. She's considerate like that. That's one reason I've loved her all these years. But rest? No way. I was pumped, man. I was raren' to strut my stuff. We arrived at the Seaport on time at 0530. I dropped my duffel bag into a waiting truck and was given a bag of breakfast consisting of a muffin, orange juice, banana, and some other goodies. BK also managed to purloin a bag of breakfast, also. I didn't ask how. But it was still dark, walkers and well wishers were milling around, and the early morning air was filled with the palpable aura of impending adventure mixed with the unmistakable odor of fish that was emanating from the Famous Fulton Fish Market located next door. The sky began to brighten and, looking over the silhouette of the Brooklyn Bridge, we watched as the gold and reddish hues of clouds overhead heralded the arrival of the sun.

We're off! 2500 walkers shuffled in groups or pairs across Wall Street, the earliest northern boundary of old New Amsterdam. We walked by the location of George Washington's first inaugural, and the location of the famous stock exchange lying dormant in the early morning hours. We turned uptown when we reached Broadway. North we shuffled, our strides a bit longer now, to Fulton Street and to the Trinity Church Cemetery where Alexander Hamilton and Robert Fulton have been sleeping all these years, and then on down to the site of the World Trade Center where spirits of today's heroes and just plain decent people may be sleeping still. Nobody said much around here. The walk was quiet.

North was our direction, and would be, for the entire route of our thirteen mile trek along the west side of Manhattan all the way up to the Henry Hudson Bridge to the Bronx. The waterfront of the west side of Manhattan is now wonderfully developed. Where there were once dilapidated piers there are now brick and concrete walkways, bicycle and skating paths, and parks boasting of various activities such as driving ranges, musical amphitheaters and just plain old sitting and watching the world go by places. Our route was supported by fully stocked rest stops every four miles, and pit stops every 2 miles in between. Why so many pit stops? Think of the Imodium commercial. "Gotta go, Gotta go, Gotta go!" Porta Johns were always available; there were plenty of them and they were clean as could be. No problem there. But I have a story for you.

Porta John lines were invariably long and I was patiently awaiting my turn for a number One. I had almost reached the Porta-John door when a frail looking elderly lady in sneakers inserted herself right into the line alongside mine. "I hope you won't mind, dear," she said to the startled girl next to me. "I walk slower than I used to, but I still pee fast!" I laughed so hard that I almost had an accident right there on the line.

Our first pit stop came at 21st Street. We paused here for a brief while we filled our water bottles and ate some oranges and bananas. We watched the walkers file out still steppen' strong and enjoying the coolness of what portended to be a warm and slightly muggy day.

Now a word about my walking buddies. Linda is my neighbor who lives only a few houses away from me in Sparta. She encouraged me to do this walk. Linda is a veteran of two previous hikes of 60 miles each. She walked three consecutive days, twenty miles each day, in order to accomplish this daunting task. She is a caring and dedicated woman who took time to assemble about 50 cancer awareness ribbons and pins that she distributed to walkers and spectators alike. Linda could walk the shoes off me but adapted her pace to mine and walked with me pretty much the whole day. Janet was, like me, a newcomer to the event. She works with Linda; and trained by pushing her double-seated baby stroller up to 6 miles every day. Those two kids must have been out for more air than a 747! We also inherited a stranger. Nikki was found with teary eyes near the beginning of the walk. Her husband, Scott, had come with her to participate in the walk but he was assigned to security and wouldn't be walking with her. Alone, and never having been in New York before, Nikki wasn't relishing the lonely trek at all. Linda adopted her. Guess what? Nikki proved to be a dynamo! Not too big, but strong. A mountain biker and marathon runner, she wasted no time in putting Ole Goldenglutes in his place! It was Nikki who referred to me as the *weakest link*!! She was a major-league disrespector, and I enjoyed the witty repartee that we engaged in throughout the weekend. By the way, Little Nikki turned out to be a cop in Connecticut. That teary eyed girl we adopted wasn't helpless at all!

We passed the Intrepid Aircraft Carrier Museum at 40th Street and finally crossed under the west side highway to emerge on Riverside Drive somewhere in the 80's. Riverside Drive, for my money, is one of the most elegant streets in New York. The old architecture brings ones fancy back to the days of Clarence Day and "Life With Father." The residential apartment buildings along this street are so much more ornate and sturdy than the metal and glass cages that have sprouted along the East Side. There is money here but it's not ostentatious; it's old money, and people living here are New York people. I like Riverside Drive for another reason also: Riverside Park. The park lines the west side of the drive for its entire route and shields local folks from the sound and commotion of the over-used West Side Highway. It a quiet street, with plenty of room to walk, and it has benches to sit on while whiling away the hours under shady sycamore trees. (Whose leaf, by the way, is the symbol of the NYC Dept. of Parks).

We encountered a group of supporters waving placards and ribbons as we passed the Soldiers and Sailors Monument on 89th street. I was happy to see them, and I waved back like the happy wanderer. Right along this time we encountered another group of happy trekkers; four ladies from Connecticut, and we established a friendly rivalry as to which of our groups walked faster (they did). But for a while we strutted side by side and sang songs from any old musicals we could remember. The walk really wasn't work; it was fun. People we encountered were fun. Sharing the experience was fun.

Riverside Church came next. It is a really beautiful Gothic cathedral, and I have a story about it. The story is not directly related to this walk but it's fun to relate anyway. Long ago, even before I became the Johnny Goldenglutes of song and legend, my curiosity took me to investigate this stately edifice. If you ever see it, you will notice a beautiful bell tower, and inside, an elevator to take you almost to the top. I went up. And I then climbed an iron staircase to the location of the bells. The Carillon, if you want to be fancy. All of a sudden a bell tinkled. Then another, then a few bells began to sway. The medium sized ones first, and then to my horror, the big-ass jumbos started rockin' back and forth! BOOM CLANG CLANG BOOM! I was Quasimodo in the middle of an afternoon bell concert! No one told me! My feet dashed to the iron stairwell and, with my eyes wild and my hands over my ears, I rushed out and away from that medieval clamor! I survived and made it across the street to the plaza outside Grant's Tomb. For years that monument to General Grant had been in disrepair, but it's fixed up nicely now. I sat there on a comfortable bench and listened to the remainder of the bell concert. When it was over I continued my walk home.

Our lunch stop along the river was in a nice park at 138th street. It was probably mile 8 in our walk and I was ready to graze a little. Chicken Wrap sandwiches, salad, and various cookies and brownies, made up the lunch du jour. It tasted good. The Snapple was great, the cola was great, taking off my shoes and socks and stretching out in the grass was great, too. I thought, "I'm enjoying this!" But, like all good things that must come to an end, lunch break ended and the walking shoes (sneakers) went back on the feet. I rolled over on all fours, lifted my butt to the sky and struggled to rise (I think that's when the *weakest link* came into use). I rose, painfully but manfully, to the vertical and the trek northward resumed.

There is a park under the George Washington Bridge where my father swam in the Hudson River as a boy. He told me the story of the Little Red Lighthouse. It is still there, but no longer in use because the supporting abutments of the George Washington Bridge adequately define the spit of land that the lighthouse used to guard. It was slated for demolition years ago after the bridge was completed in 1937. Hundreds of letters asking to save the lighthouse were sent by the children of Harlem to the authorities. They donated pennies from their piggy-banks and finally the authorities were swayed; the children of Harlem had saved their Little Red Lighthouse with its adjoining park and famous swimming hole. You can still find the story of the Little Red Lighthouse in libraries in the children's section.

There is one more adventure that I almost forgot. The walk from the park back up to the Henry Hudson Parkway is steep. To me it looked like Everest without ice. The girls naturally climbed up with no problem. So much for the "Weaker Sex!" I puffed and panted. My feet were telling me in no uncertain terms that they were very, very, unhappy. And the asthmatic dragon that was puffing through my tortured lungs was gasping in solid agreement with my rebelling bod. *Weakest Link.* The appellation tormented me. It drove me on higher and higher. Finally, with the aid of Nikki who was pushing my butt, and Linda, who was pulling my arm, I made it to the top! Nikki and I walked to Dyckman Street and descended to the waiting buses. We did the 13 miles. The time was 2 PM and we were heading to the wellness center on Randall's Island.

The Wellness Center

Goldenglutes was tuckered out. If I had any intention of continuing on to the full 26 miles that day I was disabused of that notion midway up the last hill to the Henry Hudson Parkway. That was at about mile 12 or so. As I said before, the girls did it well. The Glutes did it, period. But we all did it!! Success!!

Linda and Janet still had some gas left in their tank. They chose to forge on over the bridge to the Bronx. Both girls expressed a desire to at least cross two more bridges that would take them through the Bronx and back into Manhattan. Nikki could have accompanied them, but she planned to run a marathon the following week and didn't want to overdo her training. So we separated for a while. Linda and Janet pressed on while Nikki and I boarded the bus that was chartered to take us to Randall's Island where we would pick up our tents and spend the night.

What can I tell you about those bus seats? Only that I thought I was sitting on a cloud in Heaven! I had been vertical and on my feet since 0530. That was 8 and ½ hours ago! The ride to the wellness center took about 20 minutes. Upon reaching our destination we were required to check in with the walk registrars. I can honestly say that this event was very professionally run. This check in was their control that all walkers would be accounted for and no one would be left on the street. (As an aside, I may say here that the walk was well patrolled by volunteers. The rest stops were adequate, and if any walker tired, or was in distress, they were tended to. Vans were available to carry them to the next rest stop or to the wellness center itself)

I located my duffel bag and my tent location, F 60. I was a bit disappointed that my tent hadn't been assembled for me. I was "Goldenglutes!" Didn't they realize that? It wasn't too difficult to assemble—especially after I employed two pretty young volunteers to set it up for me. After all, I'm from the Bronx, what the hell do I know from tents? After setting up and unpacking, I surveyed my surroundings. I found everything orderly, and there was a genuine spirit of fun and adventure in the air. Hadn't we all shared the same walking experience? I found the massage tent, the conference and breast cancer info tent, the podiatry people, and chiropractors and first aid people also. Later that evening Linda availed herself of their proffered services as she got her blistered feet tended to by caring volunteers. I asked her if the blisters hurt and she replied that, yes, they were pretty bad. But then she smiled up at me and said, "but blisters don't need chemo, do they." Linda, my caring neighbor, had said it all. She had captured the essence of the walk.

I found the Yoga tent and thought I'd give it a try. So, for an hour I stretched and grunted to the strains of some mysterious alien music under the baleful gaze of an instructor intent upon forcing my aching body into positions it was never forced into before. I survived. At the closing ceremony the following day I encountered a woman who came up to me and said, "I saw you doing yoga." I could only grunt some unintelligible reply.

Next came the showers that were a welcome and important part of the day. Trailers were set up there, the kind you see hauled by the big semis, and were, in reality, big portable shower rooms. And they were super clean. I don't know how they were hooked up, but I welcomed the cascade of steamy hot water that warmed my tired muscles. It was really enjoyable and I felt frisky enough for a little fun. I was surprised to see a lady had wandered into they men's shower truck by mistake. She was entering the next stall. I waited for a little while then started singing in a loud voice, "Getting to know you, getting to know all about you!" And that's about as far as I got. The lost lady screamed and took off from the shower truck like she had just been shot from a canon. I wonder if I should have waited just a little longer before bursting into song. At least until she got wet . . . . The shower felt good and I felt squeaky clean as I trouped back to my tent to dress for dinner.

The girls and I were all back together again. Linda and Janet did manage the two bridges for a total of 17 1/2 miles that day. Congratulations!! So now we secured a place at the food tent and headed for the serving line. There was no line! Dinner was served from 5 o'clock until 8 o'clock so people could spread out and dine when they wanted to. Beef, chicken, string beans, baked beans, carrots, roll and salad was the epicurean reward for those who braved the rigors of the days walk. It was good, too. We dined outdoors under another tent and there was a picnic air about the whole experience. I was lied to though. A scoundrel, who shall be nameless, but you know who you are Linda, promised me my fill of Mrs. Walker's cheesecake if I finished the walk. Sort of like the donkey and the carrot ploy. Well, cheesecake there wasn't. I settled for pedestrian pound cake; but the hot coffee that washed it down hit the spot. A band was playing somewhere, but ole Glutes had had enough. I found my tent, introduced myself to my tent mate (an airline pilot for Jet Blue,) and assumed the horizontal for a refreshing sleep.

At my age the meaning of an all-nighter means not having to get up to pee. Well, it wasn't an all-nighter. With my trusty flashlight I plodded to the Porta John in the dark a few times (Musta been the chilly night air.) I tucked the flashlight under my chin and then let fly in what I hoped would be the right direction in the dark.

The Second Day

We rose refreshed and found that the same trailers that held the showers the night before now had outdoor banks of sinks attached. We lined up to throw water on our face and brush our teeth and get ready for the day. Would you believe I got in line behind a guy who spent 10 minutes working on his comb-over! I couldn't believe it! It could only happen to me. Why he was fretting over a few strands of unruly hair when he was going to walk another 13 miles mystified me. For me, "Johnny Bald," that posed no problem. A few swipes and I was on my way to the breakfast area.

Eggs Florentine! Canadian bacon! Oatmeal! Fresh fruit and coffee. Nuff said. I was ready, the girls were ready, the tents were packed, and we were on our way. One last thing. We had a great send-off by a crew of volunteers doing sort of a can-can with pom-poms as we left the wellness center to cross the Harlem River Footbridge to the East Side. Can I repeat it too often? It was fun!!

We crossed the footbridge over the Harlem River to the East Side Drive just above Ninety-Sixth Street. We climbed to the Promenade that covers the Drive and enjoyed an early morning stroll past Gracie Mansion, the official residence of the mayor of New York. People were out early to share the early morning air and the beautiful view of the narrowest part of the East River. This is the "Hell Gate" area. It was named by the early Dutch navigators who braved the treacherous currents formed by the ebb and flow of the tide between the Long Island Sound and the Upper Bay of New York Harbor.

At around Eighty-Sixth Street we turned on to York Ave and continued our trip down the east side of Manhattan. We strolled past the U.N. building and on down to our first rest stop on Twenty-First Street at Peter Cooper Village. One third of the day's trek was down. I was going to make it!! Leaving Peter Cooper village we walked to the area that I consider to be the most interesting of the walk. The Lower East Side. Lower Manhattan has a little topographic lump the sticks out here east toward the river, and since there are no numbers lower than 1, the additional avenues that run north and south along this quasi-peninsula are called avenues A, B, C, and D. Hence the nickname "Alphabet City" below Fourteenth street. New York City is made up of different neighborhoods. Each adds their unique flavor to the make up of the whole. Each neighborhood has it's own distinctive name: "Little Italy" on Mulberry Street, "Chinatown" on Mott Street, "Tribeca", the triangle below Canal Street, and "Greenwich Village", to name a few. We were now walking down Avenue A between Fourteenth Street and Houston Street which is properly called "Howston". Don't let me hear you say it any other way! During the late 1800's this particular area was known as Kleindeutchland. Little Germany.

There is a history here that is tragically interesting. Allow me to digress a little here to share it with you. In the late 1800's and early 1900's this neighborhood was the hub of German immigration in New

York. If a population study of this type had been made, *Kleindeutchland*, as it was called, would have been the 5th largest city in Germany at that time. Over a million German-speaking immigrants inhabited the area on the east side below Fourteenth Street. The religious and social hub was St. Marks Evangelical Lutheran Church (we walked within 2 blocks of it). One Spring morning in 1904 the church sponsored a steamboat outing to a picnic site on Long Island. The steamboat was called the *General Slocum*. 1300 German immigrants boarded the ship that morning, mostly women and children because the men were working, and set out for their annual event. The *General Slocum* caught fire shortly after leaving the dock at East Third Street and flames spread rapidly throughout the ship. The old wood, the paint, and the varnish, burned well and the ship turned into an inferno within minutes. The *Slocum* inadvertantly fanned the flames as it continued to steam full ahead over the same East River site that we were walking past. The captain had intended to ground the ship on North Brother island on the other side of Hell Gate. Whole families leaped from the burning pyre and drowned in the treacherous currents of the Gate. Those trapped inside were immolated. 1034 picnic goers perished on that fateful day. Fathers returning from work found the neighborhood decimated. One extended family lost 29 members; the pastor of St. Marks lost his wife and daughter. Half the choir was gone, and many fathers lost wives and all their children. The soul of little Germany was gone. Within 5 years the German immigrants were mostly gone also, having moved to other places to escape the tragic sadness of the event. They couldn't stand the empty school desks, the empty stores, the empty church. This old neighborhood that we walked through Sunday morning had literally, 100 years ago, died of a broken heart.

The neighborhood has changed now; it's vibrant. We dodged the street vendors selling their fruits and vegetables. We stopped at a rest stop on Broome Street and watched a Tai Chi class going through their routines. But I like history, and for just a while, as I was passing through there, I touched the past.

I'm sorry if I saddened you. But we have to learn to cry if we want to enjoy being able to laugh. And now I want to laugh. We were on HOWSTON Street and I could see the famous Katz's Deli across the street. It's been there a million years and still sports that famous sign probably left over from World War 2 (or 1?) that says, "SEND A SALAMI TO YOUR BOY IN THE ARMY!" Some things never change. I wanted a juicy pastrami on rye with mustard, horseradish, and a pickle, so badly I could taste it; but I couldn't stop. Reluctantly I continued with Nikki toward another famous New York street called Delancy Street.

Now we were in the famous Jewish Lower East Side: Orchard Street, Essex Street, Rivington Street, some of the most ethnically famous streets in the city. This is the birthplace of "Old Banjo Eyes" Eddie Cantor, and George Burns who was born Nathan Birnbaum, and the famous Marx Brothers, who were born as the Marx Brothers, the famous boys of Minnie Marx. Go rent a movie. See Amy Irving in *Crossing Delancy* and remember that we walked right by Guss's Pickle Store featured in that movie. We happy walkers were seeing New York up close and personal. We walked down the infamous Bowery that was immortalized in song, to Chinatown. The intersection of Bowery and Canal is also a famous area for diamond buying. Thirty-Seven years ago I bought my long-suffering BK her engagement ring there and I've never regretted it: neither the ring, nor my life with BK. Thirty-Seven years, and this neighborhood hasn't changed. Left turn here on Canal and we walked across the Manhattan Bridge, which seemed like uphill all the way, and alighted in that "borough of churches," called Brooklyn.

Remember that I told you about neighborhood names? Well, we happy trekkers (now at mile 8) had lunch in a beautiful park in a rather old and seedy area called "DUMBO". That's right, most of you have never heard of "Down Under The Manhattan Bridge Overpass". A developer has recently purchased much of this area and plans some chic boutiques and upscale housing to replace the dilapidated warehouses left over from the now defunct Brooklyn Navy Yard where the famous battleship *Missouri* was launched. It's a great idea; the area is ripe for gentrification and, with its proximity to downtown New York, I think that it's a can't-miss concept. Too bad the Glutes is too poor to invest!! The Dumbo idea is not so Dumbo.

In the shadow of the Brooklyn Bridge we ate lunch, took a welcome rest, and socialized. I met Frank the day before at the end of the walk. I found him again today at lunch still going strong. He deserves mention. Frank is middle aged, and has two daughters. Breast cancer has never invaded his family, and I wondered why he was making all this effort at his age. What he told me puts him in the Goldenglutes Hall Of Fame. Frank said, simply, that he was walking for his daughters. Breast cancer is prevalent enough, he said, that there was always a possibility one of his girls would be victimized by it. He was walking to raise money for research because he loved his family. He wanted to do all in his power to give them the best chance possible chance for survival. It was his way of protecting them, and by extension, the extended family we all share.

After our lunch our walker group hooked up again. For much of that morning Nikki stayed together. We let Linda and Janet keep a more comfortable pace on their own because they were a bit faster than we were. The *Weakest Link* was sputtering now. I was really stiff after stopping for lunch. For about five blocks or so I was stepping gingerly like the oo oo bird. But training tells, and when the kinks wore off, Goldenglutes was smilen' and strutten' with the group again! No first aid attention for me!!

We walked through a beautiful neighborhood called Brooklyn Heights. The quaint tree lined streets with row houses neatly manicured gave walkers like me a better impression of Brooklyn than I had before. I remember more people were on the streets greeting us as we passed. Bowls of candy were offered, and lots of "nice going" from well-wishers kept me pumped. I guess we did about 4 miles until our last stop before the Brooklyn Bridge and home. But I was trailing again. Linda stayed with me and we reached the last stop around 2 PM. I asked Linda to chill here a while; we were pretty much in the middle of the pack, and I wanted to rest 10 minutes so I would finish strong, and not look like something the cat dragged over the finish line.

THE FINISH LINE AHEAD!! We rejoined everyone again at South Street and were milling around, happy and proud of our accomplishment. Nikki asked, "Did you do the finish line yet?" I didn't know there was an official end to the trek but Linda and I found it. A kind of victory gauntlet about 50 yards long awaited us. I happily braved the cheering throng; I high-fived and low-fived the well wishers. I hooted and laughed and accepted the hugs of strangers who apparently didn't mind my sweaty appearance. We did it!! Not just Goldenglutes, but all the walkers there, and all the sponsors like you who supported us. WE ALL DID IT TOGETHER!!

Now sing along with me;

"Down in front of Casey's old brown wooden stoop
we boys and girls together formed a merry group
That's where Jackie Casey and little Jimmy Crowe
And Jakey Krauss the baker who always had the "Dough"
And pretty Nellie Shannon, with a dude as light as a cork,
First picked up the waltz-step,
On the Sidewalks of New York.

Things have changed since those days,
Some are up there in "G"
Others, they are wanderers, but they all feel just like me.
They'd give up all they've got, if they could but once more walk
With their best girl, and have a twirl,
On the Sidewalks of New York

East Side, West Side, all around the town
Tots sing, "Ring around Rosie", "London Bridge is falling down"
Boys and girls together
Nikki, Janet, Linda, and me, as light as a cork
Tripped the light fantastic
On the sidewalks of New York

"The Sidewalks of New York". 1894

So there it is; you've walked the walk. Linda and I proceeded to walk this marathon every year for eight consecutive years. We picked up a core crew of stalwarts who joined our venture for walk #2 and we all stayed together for every one after that. Linda, Marivelle, Thom, Nikki, and John became known as the "Team Goldenglutes." I became infamous as Johnny Goldenglutes who, at every walk sported the pink T-shirt that proclaimed, "Tough Guys Wear pink!" Ladies loved to pose for pictures with "The Glutes" and one even ventured to say that my participation gave them more support than their bras.

Each year we picked up additional walkers for our team. All were fun. All contributed stories that I included my journals. Who could forget Melissa and Nancy, aka "Double-Trouble," the girls who panty-raided me and Thom in our tent at 2 AM? Or Carole, who was so unused to Porta-Potties that she managed to place her Gucci purse in the men's urinal every time she visited one and then proceeded to tell us how they thought of everything—even to supplying an attached bucket inside the Porta-John so she wouldn't have to put her bag on a dirty floor! Brett walked with us wearing leg braces after his automobile accident while his parents,Nikki and Scott, pushed a wheel chair in case Brett needed a rest. Probably, over the years, seventeen additional walkers became goldenglutes and glutelettes by joining one or more of our walks. That included my son, Kevin, and my daughter, Krissy. All told, Team Goldenglutes raised well over $300,000 for our adopted cause.

My Summer training walks would total about 100 miles. The walk would add another 26, so I could boast of an annual walk of 125 miles. Eight walks of 125 miles each totals one thousand miles walked for breast cancer. I'm sure Kate knows this and is pleased with her God-father who never really forgot her after all.

The Bush Years and 9/11

Iraq and Bush One, Intermission, 9/11, The Afghanistan Reprisal, The Second Iraq War, Domestic Policies

Kevin and Katie at the White House

THE BUSH YEARS

Iraq and Bush One

Hang on. This is going to be a rough ride. The Bush years, father and son, will be defined by history in light of the U.S. involvement in the Middle East during their terms. Today we can call it Bush 1 and Bush 2. The country was tangled in wars with Iraq during both of their administrations and the nation was seriously divided over whether they were justified. Many Americans, displaying flags of patriotism on their lapels, stood four-square behind the policies of the government. It also seemed that just as many were uncomfortable with a perceived penchant for the administration's use of the hard power at their disposal. Not surprisingly, most of the differences evolved around party lines, and unfortunately, but predictably, degenerated into the demagoguery and name calling that squeezed out any real chance of mutual meeting of the minds. I have had difficulty composing my thoughts regarding this difficult time. I have opinions, serious opinions, regarding the stewardship of our country during the years of the two Bush administrations. There will be much written and much debated about this time in our history, and hopefully future critiques will prove to be less biased than the one I plan to share with you at this time. Events are too new, feelings are too raw, and the future too uncertain to write totally objectively of them now. One thing is certain: both administrations can be defined by wars of choice in the Middle East, attempted nation building, and the rise of stateless terrorists.

George Herbert Walker Bush succeeded Ronald Wilson Reagan as the 41st President of the United States. During his administration the country of Kuwait was attacked by Iraq over a dispute regarding oil. Iraq claimed Kuwait was illegally tapping into Iraqi oil by drilling wells diagonally from Kuwait to oil reserves under Iraqi land. Bush, despite our ambassador notifying Iraq that we had no interest in inter-Arab affairs, led the charge for United Nations sanctions and the establishment of a 32 nation force to oust the Iraqi army from the occupied territory of Kuwait. The resulting war was tragic-comic. Saddam Hussein, the Iraqi dictator, predicted the "The Mother of all Battles" and watched the decimation of his army in just 100 hours. The victory was hailed by all save a few ideologues who had assumed that Hussein would have been removed and a government friendly toward U.S. interests would emerge from the wreckage. That idea would again surface eight years later with the election of George W. Bush, the 43rd president.

I thought Bush the elder a decent fellow. He had spent eight years as Vice-President, and had also served as director of the CIA and ambassador to the U.N. His credentials were impeccable. The fact that he enlisted in the Navy immediately after Pearl Harbor, and served the entire war as a naval aviator who survived being shot down over the ocean, went a long way in describing both his courage and patriotism. Aside from the Gulf War, however, Bush's tenure was unremarkable. He drew the ire of Conservative Republicans when he raised taxes after promising not to do so. "Read my lips," he had said, "No new taxes." After the Gulf War his approval ratings sank and he began to be perceived as a president with no serious plans for the future. He admitted that he wasn't much "on that vision thing" and, with no idea of what he really wanted to accomplish as President, it was no mystery why the public voted him out after one term.

Intermission

Bill Clinton succeeded him as president. He was called "Slick Willie" by some, and he had some trouble keeping his pants zippered in the Oval Office, but you won't hear much of him from me. He is a hiccup in the narrative that will define our involvement in Middle Eastern affairs. The real story continues with the election of "Dubya", the nickname given by the press to Bush the Younger whose middle initial was "W." No one considered Bush the Younger to be much of an intellectual, and most understood the real seat of power would rest with the man who had nominated himself to be Vice-President. No one objected to the excessive vacations that Bush the Younger took at his beloved ranch in Crawford, Texas. He was coasting along just fine. Vice-President Dick Cheney had things under control in his absence, holding, among other things, secret meetings with oil executives and foraging for information on Iraq. The cataclysmic events of September 11 popped the cork on all that.

9/11

On the morning of September 11, 2001 Muslim hijackers commandeered four jet liners while in the air and shattered the perception of American invulnerability forever. I was sleeping late that day; perhaps I had been working late the night before, I'm not sure now. Brenda's phone call awakened me around 0900. She told me to put on the TV because a plane had crashed into the World Trade Center and it was all over the news channels. I remember thinking it was some sort of small plane accident and I thought briefly about the bomber that flew in the fog and hit the seventy-ninth floor of the

Empire State building during the war years. In that case it was too bad for the bomber, and in this case I assumed it would be too bad for the small plane also. I went back to bed. The urgent jingling of the phone roused me again. "A second plane just crashed into the second tower!" That got me up, quick. I don't know what it is, but people just don't seem to want to be alone during moments of high drama. I was no different. I quickly dressed and drove to the local breakfast spot to share the news. I was befuddled upon entering the store. The TV was on, the news was being blared throughout he world, and the local denizens were ignoring it like they always did. The TV was just simply background noise as the locals went about drinking their coffee at the lunch counter and chatting about local events of interest to them. It is hard to believe in this day and age that some folks just don't seem to be aware that there is a larger world where people live and die and things happen outside the confines of their town.

It was a spectacular event. The television news stations covered it all live. I watched the smoke and flames billowing from the upper floors of the towers and I was astounded as I watched them come down about a half hour apart. They just telescoped in on themselves. They just crumbled straight down as if a giant hand pushed on them from the top and crushed them like you would a milk container. Smoke filled the scene, there were photos of people frantically running from the billowing grey cloud that rose from the debris to cover lower Manhattan with its deadly ash. It had to be roughly akin to the scene at Pearl Harbor—scary, bewildering and exciting. Later, as the events could be assimilated, the reality and magnitude of the cataclysm took hold. The human factor was finally absorbed into our consciousness and we were appalled by the scope of the tragedy. Cameras caught desperate people leaping hand in hand to their death from 100 stories up rather than being burned in their office. Perhaps the most poignant statement of the day occurred when a witness described seeing bodies falling from the sky. Another witness stopped the show. "I saw them LAND!" We heard of 350 brave firemen and 60 police and Port Authority officers who dashed into those towers never to emerge. We saw Fr. Mychal Judge, a Catholic chaplain to the Fire Department, die, crushed by falling debris as he ministered last rights to a fireman at the scene . . . . and it didn't matter a damn to anyone ever again if Fr. Judge was gay. The human toll was horrific. Some entire companies were wiped out as their offices turned to rubble. Some city neighborhoods were decimated as the toll of human life rose. Our parish pastor and friend, Fr. Dan Murphy, lost his brother Ed when the offices of Cantor Fitzgerald were demolished. And then the personal news filtered in. Cell phones recorded messages of love and good-byes bravely spoken to wives, husbands, and children, as trapped citizens met their fate, and their broken-hearted families were left behind. 3000 innocent human beings died that morning of September 11, 2001 in that dastardly attack of terrorism.

We had to sort it out and get our arms around the magnitude of the event. The Mayor of New York, Rudy Giuliani and President Bush, neither of whom I really cared for, were magnificent as they rallied the stunned populace. I have to give them their due. Their popularity world—wide swelled as they portrayed the face of a Nation bloodied but unbowed and determined that it should never happen again. At a time when there was no need for nuance, at a time of black and white, of us against them, President Bush was the man for the job. His simple explanation of "They hate us for our freedoms" seemed to resonate well. Of course it was simplistic and wrong, but at the time was sufficient to unite an angry populace against a heretofore largely unrecognized enemy. We learned of the stateless but powerful group of

Islamic terrorist extremists that was masterminded by a wealthy six foot Arab reportedly on dialysis named Osama Bin Laden.

The Afghanistan Reprisal

The 9/11 terrorists trained in various places—including a flying school based in Florida—but the central nerve of al-Queda was their recruiting and training camps located in the wilds of Afghanistan. The United States unleashed their vengeance on those camps immediately. The Taliban—a militant governing group that rose in Afghanistan following the ouster of the Soviet Union from that country—had offered safe haven to Osama Bin Laden and his terrorist organization. The plan was to roust the Taliban and destroy al-Queda headquarters and the several training camps that were known to be located in the Hindu Kush Mountains in the ungoverned areas between Afghanistan and Pakistan. The country and the world was behind our efforts on this front. With the assistance of the local war-lords our special forces quickly rousted the Taliban but the mission was not completely successful. The porous borders were not adequately sealed, and Bin Laden and much of the Taliban force escaped through desolate mountain passes and found refuge in Pakistan. Inexplicably at this point the Bush Administration abruptly lost interest in the affair and proceeded to invade a different country, one that had no connection at all with the events of 9/11, and despite being ruled by an acknowledged dictator, was not at war with us. Iraq was in Bush's sights.

The Second Iraq War

I do not intend to editorialize or otherwise embellish this account of the Iraq War. A simple reconstruction of the facts would appear that I am doing otherwise. The facts are damning of themselves, and it is what it is. There are plenty of books written about this conflict. It's a free country; you can study them and form an opinion of your own. I have.

The Bush Administration's justification for the invasion of Iraq was based on a series of lies. The claims that Saddam Hussein had been having active communication with al-Queda, and that Iraq was trying to obtain yellowcake uranium from Africa to manufacture nuclear weapons were proven false. These claims paled compared with the Big Lie that Saddam Hussein possessed weapons of mass destruction and was preparing to use them. We were told that we could not afford to wait for "the mushroom cloud" over our country if he wasn't stopped. U.N. Inspectors found no evidence of any such weapons and neither did anyone else. The big lie was exposed. Finally, the Bush Administration had no choice but to resort to that last resort of scoundrels, Patriotism. We were told we were invading Iraq to give them their "freedom."

It didn't take long; the U.S. and our British allies overran the Iraqi forces, overthrew Saddam, and set up a provisional civilian administration to run the new Iraq. The new administration installed by the United States proved woefully inept, and when the army of Saddam was disbanded, the stage was set for the civil war that followed among the Shiite and Sunni sects for control of the country. Iraq fought, bled, and died over inconclusive battles, and the United States, trying to keep the lid on this tinderbox, sacrificed the lives of over 4000 servicemen and women and brought home over 20,000 injured or maimed. Tens of thousands of Iraqis died and there were over 2 million refugees straining the resources of neighboring countries. The United States was embarrassed with the disclosure of multiple prison offenses and the use of internationally recognized torture tactics. The active occupation of Iraq lasted seven years and cost our country over 2 trillion dollars. The Iraq we left behind is now under a relatively unstable elected government, it is still torn by sectarian factions, and still suffering from a wrecked economy that can't even supply enough electricity to keep the lights on.

Secretary of Defense Rumsfeld was asked by the press why the administration invaded Iraq rather concentrating on the terrorists in Afghanistan. His answer was astounding. He said we invaded Iraq because it was do-able. What he didn't say, but what I believe, was that the plot to overthrow Saddam Hussein was hatched as far back as the Reagan administration. The young neo-cons of the Reagan years were a group of former Liberal "intellectuals" who grew alarmed at the apparent appeasement policies of our government and turned internationally conservative. They espoused a policy of American Exceptionalism and believed that it was the right—and even the duty—of the U.S. to exercise whatever force was necessary in order to establish a "Pax Americana." And that included establishing hegemony over the geo-political events of the Middle East. The lynchpin of that policy was the obviously the control of Iraq. And the fact that twenty-five percent of the known oil reserves of the Middle-East were located under the sands of that country didn't hurt, either.

President George H.W. Bush didn't completely buy into the idea and left Saddam Hussein standing. The neo-cons were forced to hunker down and endure eight years of Clinton before they could turn the simple perceptions of Bush 2 to their advantage. But even George W.

Bush had doubts until he was told by his director of the CIA that it would be a "Slam Dunk" that Iraq had weapons of destruction. What I believe he meant, and no one in the press picked it up, was that it would be a "Slam Dunk" that the public would accept the "Big Lie." And for a while they did.

Domestic Policies

The stewardship of George W. Bush brought us to the brink of economic disaster. He inherited a budget surplus and left with a deficit of over a trillion dollars. Tax cuts on upper class incomes coupled with his wars of choice insured we would not take in enough money to meet obligations. Foreign borrowing propped up our economy. Free trade enthusiasts ignored the resulting loss of domestic jobs and the labor force suffered. Cities died, and states struggled to maintain unemployment obligations. Finally a banking crisis brought on by the collapsing housing market brought our country to its knees. The banks and investment houses begged for financial bailouts from the government before the economy fell off the cliff. Bush approved the bailouts and left office with a 19% approval rating . . . . the lowest approval rating of any President in our history.

In my opinion, George W. Bush was in way over his head. Apparently he was well received while Governor of Texas, but he was in no way qualified, either by inclination or intellect, to be President of the United States. He was a decent man but a limited one. Probably he would be a pleasure to enjoy a beer or a round of golf with. However, I, and many others, believe that he was totally devoid of any intellectual curiosity—a damning fault for one entrusted to make enlightened decisions. His simplistic analysis of complicated issues coupled with his folksy, bordering on inarticulate, manner of speaking made him the perfect instrument to promulgate the devious machinations of the cabal that I believe planned his election. I believe that he, like President Reagan before him, was callously used by that group of former liberals-turned-neo-cons whose wrong-headed policies did great harm to the economy, honor, and prestige of this country.

I have written admittedly harsh words. I warned you they would be. But for now I stand by my bias. You don't have to accept mine. History and the many books that will be written will eventually create the definitive reality of this era.

Major Kevin returns from Afghanistan

Dept. of Corrections

The Barge, The Beginning, The Work, The Escape,
The Lesson, The End

DEPARTMENT OF CORRECTIONS

My career took a unique turn in 1992. Not that spending half of my life floating on the water wasn't unique, but this was different. I went to jail. On second thought perhaps it wasn't so different after all. Dr. Samuel Johnson, the famous British essayist of the 1700's, once remarked that going to sea on ships was like going to jail—the only difference being one has a chance to be drowned. Well, I didn't drown. But I did spend the next ten years of my life in jail. Don't be nervous, and don't jump to conclusions. Let me tell you about it.

New York City was facing a crisis. The year was 1992 and there were too many inmates for the beds available in the prison system. The city clearly needed another correctional facility but was hampered by the local population who promptly told the Mayor "NIMBY." (Not in my back yard) A stop-gap solution was implemented with the rental of two accommodation barges from the Bibby Corporation in England. These barges were originally designed to house offshore oil workers, but they had been refitted to house British troops when Argentina contested ownership of the Falkland Islands in the South Atlantic close to the Argentine mainland. New York converted these barges into floating jails to hold about 150 inmates each and placed them on the East and North (Hudson) Rivers at lower Manhattan. The idea of a permanent floating prison was formed at that time and plans were made to construct a prison barge that would be moored on the Bronx side of the East River across from the correctional facilities at Rikers Island. The barge, the *Vernon C. Bain*, was named after a respected warden who died in a tragic car accident. It was completed at a cost of $161 million and delivered to the city in 1992. I'll tell you about the barge in a minute, but first I'd like to set your mind at rest about what I was doing there. The U.S. Coast Guard regulates the safety requirements of vessels in the harbor and the *Vernon C. Bain* fell under those regulations. The Coast Guard mandated that, because the barge was a maritime facility, a minimum of three licensed maritime officers were to be included with the staffing of the barge. I was hired as one of the licensed captains who would represent the Coast Guard on the barge. No, I wasn't an inmate, and no, I wasn't really sent to jail. But I was hired as a civilian employee of the New York City Dept. of Corrections.

The Barge

At a length of 600 feet, which translates to two football fields end to end, and a height above the water of about 50 feet, the *Vernon C. Bain* was a big boxy barge. I didn't know what to expect when I first boarded her and was a bit surprised that most of the inmates were to be housed dormitory fashion with 50 assigned to a dorm. I had expected cells, probably because that's what I saw on TV. It is true that the barge did contain 100 cells, but the dormitories defined the jail. The prison barge was geared to accept 700 inmates to be housed in the sixteen dormitories. Did I mention the barge was big? It was. I was amazed to find it contained a full sized gym with basketball courts and risers from which to watch the game. Weight rooms and outdoor rec on the roof rounded out the fitness facilities. There was a complete library and three chapels for worship on the lower deck. The main deck boasted of a modern medical facility complete with X-Ray machines and a dental office and lab. It might shock you to learn that a nail technician was on the scene on a routine basis to cut the inmates' toenails. No shit. The dining room on the next deck was for the uniformed staff and maintenance workers and the fully equipped kitchen boasted of three separate refrigerators. One for kosher, one for Halal, and one for general use. Of course it was fully air-conditioned and climate controlled as well. Inmates were fed in their dorms and their medications were delivered there also. It was a different world for me and I didn't quite know what to make of it all for a long time. I learned a lot of useful information and some just plain unimportant stuff like holding a match to bullet proof glass and counting the number of reflections you see. The number of flames indicate the number of glass panes that you are looking through.

The Beginning

I don't want to jump too far ahead of myself so I better tell you how all this started. I was unhappy on the boats but I felt trapped because of the perceived lack of opportunities available to a fifty-two year old with only tugboat experience on his resume. My opportunity rose unexpectedly when I met Jack Brady, a friend from the Maritime College days. Jack was already employed by the Corrections Dept. as a licensed captain aboard a retired ferryboat that was being utilized at the time. From him I learned of the plan to bring up the new barge so I put my application in for consideration when it should arrive. I'm sure Jack helped my application along, but tragically my friend was killed in a car crash before the barge arrived. I was sure that my application was probably placed on the back burner and was surprised when, months later, I was requested to come down to the Correction Dept. offices to complete papers for employment. This was a monumental move for me and I confess to being a bit intimidated by the austere setting of the ancient office building in lower Manhattan and the uniformed staff walking about. But there was no turning back.

After completing the paperwork and meeting the other captains, we were all whisked away in a Corrections van complete with barred windows. What was going on! Damn! I was being hijacked! Jesus, what a time to be seen by anyone I knew as we sped through Manhattan and on up to the Bronx. We were discharged onto a waiting police boat that promptly whisked us off to Long Island Sound where the new barge patiently awaited our arrival. It happened that fast. We stayed on the barge that night and I had to borrow a portable phone to tell Brenda where I was. She asked if I got the job. I replied that I thought so, but I wasn't sure. All I knew was that I was stranded on a big barge for the night without a change of clothes or a toothbrush and I was due to report to my tug for crew change in the morning. I told Brenda to make up an excuse to the company for me and I would try to figure out what was going on. I received the surprise of my life the following morning when the barge was being towed to its permanent berth. My boat, the *Michael Turecamo* was doing the towing! Stanley, the captain on the opposite week, looked up and saw me looking down at him from above. I was his relief, and all he could say was "What the hell are you doing up there?" I told Stanley, "I guess I just quit." That was it; the end of a thirty year tugboat career and the beginning of a ten year career with the Dept. of Corrections of the City of New York.

It was interesting and really a little bit of fun as the new crew assembled in the unique Maritime Facility. The barge lay empty for a few months and we took the time to learn the various electrical and fire fighting systems and the relationship between the uniformed staff of "New York's Boldest" and the civilian employees of the department. Here is a little tidbit of information for those of you readers who noticed my reference to "New York's Boldest." It is a fitting appellation for those who work cheek by jowl with some of the most violent offenders who are removed from society. I was surprised to learn that CO's (don't call them jail guards) went about their duties in the jail unarmed. It made sense to me only when I was reminded how much more dangerous a jail could be if a correction officer's weapon found its way into the hands of an offender desperate enough to use it. So, yes, the corrections officers are the boldest of the city employees. And just so you know, the police are "New York's Finest", the firemen "New York's Bravest", and sanitation workers, "New York's Strongest." I, and the other licensed personnel, didn't have a title at all. In retrospect we made that mistake early on when we reported to work in non-descriptive clothing. It would have been better had we insisted on a uniform. A uniform would have prevented the impression of some jail officials that we were hired as workers for the maintenance staff. At times the situation proved awkward as we tried to assert our authority for the inspection of what we considered to be a vessel and we ran afoul of a Warden who considered it, first and foremost, a jail. We all generally got along harmoniously except on some occasions when our interests diverged. We, for example, would be more concerned with the repair of a damaged fire sprinkler nozzle than with the repair of a broken lock on a cell door or a project to remove the glass facings from the wall clocks that were scattered about the prison. We would lose those battles; there was, after all, a far less chance of a fire breaking out than a chance of an inmate using a broken shard of glass on someone to settle an old score. Fortunately we had the authority of the Coast Guard to back us up. In practice, though, our authority was limited by pragmatism. The last thing the U.S. Coast Guard needed was to enter into a pissing match with the mayor of the City of New York if they tried to close a jail full of miscreants that folks didn't want out on the street. However we did serve a function and we kept busy monitoring events in our strange new world.

The Work

Most of our efforts concerned the maintenance and operation of an ultra-sophisticated fire detection system that was too sophisticated for its own good. The barge contained four distinct fire reporting zones, each with fans and ventilation systems that were regulated by a network of fire dampers located within the piping grid. It was a confusing hodge-podge of electrical equipment and mechanical apparatus. And something always went wrong. False alarms would sound, dampers would not operate, fan belts would break. The system required a huge amount of maintenance that simply overwhelmed us at times. It was because of the needs of this system that the job of the Marine Captains shifted from the realm of supervisor to that of maintenance. Over time we assumed more responsibility for the system and worked hand in hand with maintenance to keep it functioning. For my part, I was just as happy coming to work with a particular project in mind rather than simply observing and reporting on conditions. I guess the staff recognized me also because twice I was awarded the civilian employee of the month and got a plaque attesting to that fact. My picture was taken with the Warden, and posted on the bulletin board. Wow!! How far could I be from the tugboats?

I circulated throughout the dorms while tracking down ventilation or temperature alarms reported by that overly sensitive system we wrestled with daily. On my patrols I was frequently surrounded by those guests of the City. I never experienced any discomfort working in the belly of that beast. Any communication I needed to have with the inmates was always civil, and at times even jocular, as they got to know who I was or what I was doing in their space. The only trouble I had was remembering to lock the doors. Getting into the jail space was easy enough when you had a key. For me, the thing to remember, was once inside, to turn and lock myself in or an inmate might simply walk out through the door I just left open. That would be a bad thing . . . . It was harder to remember than you would think. We are all used to using a key to enter our home or locking it when we leave. But how about while we intend to remain inside? Most of us are not in the habit of immediately inserting our key into the backside of the door to lock ourselves in. Most inmates are institutionalized anyway. They will approach a door or sliding bar barrier and patiently wait for a CO with a key. It is a good thing, too. One time there was a computer glitch and all the jail doors remained unlocked for I won't tell you how long, but there was no issue that had to be addressed because no inmate even bothered to try the door on his own.

The Escape

I did manage to watch one attempted escape. It wasn't successful so I'm able to relate that I could find humor even in a jail. As I mentioned before there was an outdoor recreation area on the roof of the prison. Inmates would be assigned outdoor rec on an hourly basis, dorm by dorm, throughout the day; basketball and make-up soccer games were popular. The area was encompassed by a chain link fence perhaps thirty feet high which was topped off with razor wire in case someone got the idea to vacate the premises. One day, one did. I was in the control room when alarms sounded all over the barge signaling there was an escape in progress. Anyway, I made it up to the rec area—careful not to get in the way of the CO's—and there he was, our disgruntled guest climbing up the links of the fence in his bid for freedom. His soft sneakers had no problem slipping through the links to gain a foothold for his climb. The problem was the heavy steel tipped boots worn by the COs couldn't fit into the links so they couldn't climb after the escapee. What to do? I couldn't believe my eyes. Here we were in the twenty-first century attempting to thwart a jail break by the ingenious method of throwing basketballs at the guy's ass to knock him off the fence. This you can't make up. Futility personified; I had to laugh at the ridiculous situation we were in. The human spider man made it up and over the razor wire and took a Brodie into the East River fifty feet below. (remind me to tell you who Brodie was.) The guys leap for freedom lasted only those fifty vertical feet. The police launch that was dispatched from Rikers Island across the river was there to pick him up when he surfaced, dazed and bleeding, and promptly deposited our wanderer back where he belonged.

Now for Mr. Brodie. Steve Brodie claimed to have jumped off the Brooklyn Bridge in 1896 and survived with only a slight pain in his side. He later opened a bar called the Bowery Tavern and regaled his patrons with the story of his famous exploit. The *N.Y. Times* wrote that he did leap from the bridge feet first to win a $200 bet. Later his claim was disputed as rumors spread that a dummy was cast off the bridge and Brodie emerged all wet after having jumped off a nearby row boat. The truth is elusive, but it is a fact that from then on, taking a spectacular fall would be known as "Taking a Brodie."

The Lesson

There is a recreational pier located at he foot of Tiffany Street in the South Bronx. Neighbors from the area would gather at the pier during the summer to fish, party, or just get together for a summer evening schmooze in Spanish. The crew of the *Vernon C. Bain* would occasionally hold parties on the pier in the evening after the change of tours. I was always invited. One evening I found myself in a rather pensive mood as I leaned against the railing looking over the swirling eddies of the East River. The lights of Rikers Island loomed in the distance and I was dwelling on the twist and turns of fate that brought me to my present situation. Who would ever figure that I would be working on a prison barge? One of the Correction Officers stepped away from the raucous gaggle of revelers and leaned on the rail alongside of me. We both silently gazed over at Rikers for a while and then we started to talk. We had a quiet conversation. We shared our past and how we arrived at where we were. We chatted easily and grew comfortable with each other's company. The party that blared behind us was all but obliterated from our consciences as we both stood sharing each other's space. We were of different genders, from different races and cultures, and with an appreciable gap in age, but we found the common ground of values and hopes shared. I was a white guy from a fairly affluent suburb and a bit socially isolated by a life lived on water. I had never worked with women before, never associated with any minority groups, or never shared experiences with people who were not pretty much like me. The night on the pier was a growing moment. In the darkness of the evening above the roiling river I learned that we are all truly a piece in the great mosaic of shared humanity. That is the lesson I've taken from my time with Corrections. A lesson that I couldn't have bought at any price, but one that was inadvertently taught to me for free. It was a good party.

The End

It had to happen. The Coast Guard, after years of monitoring the prison barge, finally accepted the reality that it was, de facto, a jail and not a boat. They ceased interest in its operation and cut off our reason for being employed there. We were to be eliminated by attrition and were officially placed under the auspices of the Supervisor of Maintenance. I was just as happy with this arrangement and settled in until retirement time. I was approaching age 62 and had accumulated the required 10 years of service necessary to retire with 17% of my pay and medical benefits paid from the city benefits program. It was a fair deal. I was ready to retire so, at age 62 in July 2002, I submitted my papers to the Correction Department's retirement offices on the 14th floor of 17 Battery Place in Manhattan and went home.

It was a quirk of fate. I got my first job out of college when I was hired by the Gulf Oil Corporation. Gulf Oil at that time occupied those very same offices on the 14th floor at 17 Battery Place in Manhattan. You could say I rode the elevator up to the 14th floor in 1961 and then rode it down forty one years later. 17 Battery Place, one of the oldest buildings adjacent to the picturesque Battery Park at the tip of Manhattan Island . . . . the Alpha and Omega of my working career.

Epilogue

the firefighter STEPHEN SILLER
TUNNEL to TOWERS RUN / WALK
FINISH
Widmer
84
11521

EPILOGUE

Well, I finished the book. I never intended it to be more than a memento for the kids but somehow it grew into a life of its own. I'm glad; I had fun writing it. But more water has flowed under my keel since those days of Corrections. I'm on the wrong side of seventy and my wonderful life-long sidekick BK is now a genuine senior citizen herself. My Z4 Babe, who enjoys tooling around each summer with her sports car, now qualifies for Social Security and Medicare. Just like me. And we are proud grandparents to boot. Kevin and Kris, the kids who made our life worthwhile, are parents with families of their own. Brenda and I have been married 37 years and we still live in our "cute little starter home." But the world spins and life goes on.

There are so many things that Brenda and I have shared. So many adventures, and so many good times that far outweigh the bad. I couldn't put it all down in the book, but for the kids' sakes I'm going to write down a few more adventures. I hope that one day those kids will say, "Wow! Grammy and Pop sure were something!" I could tell them how we mushed our team of nine huskies for miles through the Colorado mountains, or rode in a basket under a hot air balloon 2000 feet in the air. I could tell them how we hiked into the Grand Canyon or hiked the Matterhorn in Switzerland. I could tell them we've seen Niagara Falls, the Golden Gate, the Golden Horn, and the castles on the Rhine. I could tell them about ballroom dancing and barbershop singing competitions. I could tell them how we gambled in Las Vegas and panned for gold in Alaska (and came up with a few chips worth about $12). Brenda sky-dived from a plane at 10,000 feet in New Jersey and I ran out of air while SCUBA diving in the Caribbean. And yes, I could describe to them the sparkling blue ice glaciers of Alaska, the Fjords in Norway, the awesome vista from Pikes Peak, the Black Sea, the Black Forest, the narrow Bosphorous, and the seals nesting at Fisherman's Wharf. I listened to the chimes of Big Ben and I heard the call to prayer from the minarets of the mosques of Istanbul . . . . it has been quite a ride.

A few years ago at Krissy's wedding, I wished the kids a full life. I told them they must cry before they could appreciate laughter, know fear before being truly brave, and sometimes they needed to feel sadness so that happiness can take its place. Life is a long learning process; some things we learn earlier than others. Sometimes it takes a long time to learn who we are—and who we are isn't always the person that we let others see. I've let you see a lot of me in this book. I need a chance to unveil a little more, a little more of a lesson that has taken me a lifetime to begin to understand.

The most important lesson I have struggled with during my lifetime is Empathy. Love, OK. Sympathy, OK. Even anger, OK. All emotions make us who we are. But Empathy is the emotion that makes us who we want to be. It was hard for me to learn. Hard to give it more than lip service, but, at advancing age, I know now that there were many times I should have tried to walk in another's moccasins. Many times I have hurt someone by word or deed who deserved better from me. Many times I was too self-centered to realize that it wasn't always about me. I struggle with it even now. Many things I would change if I could, but I don't expect those three spirits of Dickens to visit me anytime soon. But I'm trying to learn. Trying to be better. That's all I can do. I'm an ordinary guy.

One last thing: during my retirement I usually supplemented my income with part-time security work. It was the last day of my assignment at Verizon headquarters when one of the women in the office came to say good bye. "See you when we get home," she said. I looked perplexed. She laughed and said "Not that home! I mean the heavenly home. That's the one we are all going to eventually." I thought about that and figured she was right.

See you when we get home.

John Klumpp,

Sparta, New Jersey,

April 2011

Acknowledgments

This book would not have been possible without the forebearance of my wife, Brenda, who endured countless solitary hours while I sequestered myself in my "Man Cave" trying to bring order to the jumble of words floating around my head.

A special thanks is due to my dear friend Donna Richards of the Sussex County Community College who struggled mightily to edit my rather casual approach to spelling and punctuation. It was she who convinced me that people may actually be interested in my story. And to Assistant Professor Gary Mielo who gave me the nerve to publish it. Thanks, also, to Chris De Milia and my neighbor Gerry Donnelly who provided valuable technical support.

And, finally, to my family, and all the friends and foes, remembered or forgotten, who touched my life over the years. They never knew they would be in my story, but my life would have been empty without them. Thanks everyone, just for being you.